The Celling of America

An Inside Look at the U.S. Prison Industry

Edited by
Daniel Burton-Rose

With

Dan Pens and Paul Wright

A *Prison Legal News* book

Common Courage Press

MONROE. MAINE

First edition, third printing

Common Courage Press
Box 702
Monroe, Maine 04951
Phone: (207) 525-0900   Fax: (207) 525-3068

Library of Congress Cataloging-in-Publication Data
The celling of America: an inside look at the U.S. prison industry /
edited by Daniel Burton-Rose with Dan Pens and Paul Wright. -- 1st ed.
p.   cm.
"A Prison legal news book."
Includes index
ISBN 1-56751-140-6. -- ISBN 1-56751-141-4 (alk. paper)
1. Prisons -- Government policy -- United States. 2. Criminal justice,
Administration of--United States. 3. Prisoners--United States--Social Conditions. 4.
Prisoners--Legal status, laws, etc.--United States. 5. Convict labor--United States. 6.
Prisons in mass media--United States. 7. Prison administration--United States.
I. Burton-Rose, Daniel. II. Pens, Dan. III. Wright, Paul, 1965-

HV9469.C46 1997   97-45071
365'.973--dc21   CIP

"Just Say No?" by Philip McLaughlin, originally appeared in *North Coast Express*, September 1994.

"Demanding Death" by Mumia Abu-Jamal originally appeared in *Endeavor*. Reprinted
by permission of the author.

"Letter From Exile" by Ray Luc Levasseur originally appeared in *The Madison Edge*.
Reprinted by permission of the author.

"Not All Prisoner Lawsuits 'Frivolous'" by Jon O. Newman originally appeared in *The
Corrections Professional*. Reprinted by permission of the author.

"America's Private Gulag" by Ken Silverstein originally appeared in *CounterPunch*.
Reprinted by permission of the author.

"The 'Honorable Men' Defense" appears courtesy of the author. Copyright © Mumia Abu-
Jamal, 1996.

"Changing the Evil That Ills This Society" by Mussa and Ed Kinane originally appeared
in *Peace Newsletter*. Reprinted by permission of the authors.

Contents

Part III
The Downward Spiral
Prisons Do Their Damnedest to Increase the Misery

Part IV
Workin' for the Man
Prison Labor in the U.S.A.

Part V
Money and Warm Bodies
The Prison-Industrial Complex in the United States

Part VI
Crimes of the Keepers
Racism, Corruption and Brutality

Part VII
Permanent Lockdown
Control Unit Prisons and the
Proliferation of the Isolation Model

Part VIII
Prisoner Struggles and Rebellions

Acknowledgements

We are grateful to the contributors whose work appears in the book as well as to all those whose articles have appeared in the pages of *Prison Legal News* over the years. The editors of *PLN* also extend our appreciation and thanks to those volunteers and supporters whose efforts have helped *PLN* become what it is today. These supporters include Sandy Judd, Fred Markham, Allan Parmelee, Dan Axtell, Ed Mead (*PLN's* co-founder), Matt Esget, Heather Yancey Pens, Scott Dionne, Dan Tenenbaum, Cathy Wiley, Jim McMahon, Janie Pulsifer, Michael Misrok, Cindi Susat, Rollin (*PLN's* publisher) and Zuraya Wright, Julya Hampton and the Washington state ACLU, Rhonda Brownstein and the Southern Poverty Law Center, the Solidago Foundation, the Center on Crime, Communities and Culture of the Open Society Institute, Mike Kipling, Mickey Gendler, Frank Cuthbertson, Joseph Bringman, Robert Kaplan, Curtis Taylor, Ellen Spertus, the Arm the Spirit and Solidarieta Proletaria collectives, Walter Tillow and the folks at Prompt Printing, George Hoyt and all of *PLN's* loyal subscribers, without whose support over the years we wouldn't have been able to do it.

The editors would also like to thank Julianne Burton-Carvajal, the Good Folks of Alpine Ave., Josh MacPhee and Peter Rose.

Introduction

William Greider

The bookshelves are abundantly stocked with scholarly studies of the United States' criminal justice system, but there are few, if any, like the book you are about to read. It was mainly written by criminals. Two of the co-editors (Dan Pens and Paul Wright) are in prison for felonious crimes and so are most of the contributing authors. Robbery, murder, sex offenses, violent political attacks and other offenses. In the mainstream currents of American politics, this automatically disqualifies them as commentators. In the real world, their essays are sharply informative because they are grounded in reality, the clarifying experience of dwelling within the penal system. We should listen to them. We will learn from what they see and know. We may begin to think more clearly about all that must be changed.

The burden of their message is that the United States has descended into a cruel era of social vengeance, as though the problems of crime and social deterioration will be solved by ratcheting up the level of torment imposed on the imprisoned and by elaborating even more irrational terms for deciding on their punishment. The nation builds prisons instead of schools. A new industrial sector has arisen around the penal system. Companies move in to capture the profit opportunities present in this new commodity—the millions of people who are imprisoned.

This approach may temporarily mollify public fears of crime and satisfy desires for retribution, but it does not of course solve the crime problem. Indeed, the political crusade to "toughen up" the criminal justice system may be understood as a great evasion—a retreat from the deeper and more difficult questions of social and economic relationships. In a sense, the binge of prison construction amounts to giving up on the possibility of building a more equitable society.

Another consequence that law-and-order advocates do not yet grasp is that they have also retreated from the idea of equality before the law. This book contains numerous shocking examples. The corruption of law is promoting a kind of hopeless cynicism among many citizens who lack the means to defend themselves with expensive lawyers or other perfectly legal methods for manipulating the system. In the long run, I think this corrupting impact on the public values of fairness and decency will prove even worse for America than the damage done to individuals.

One remarkable quality of this book is that, while the collective indictment delivered by these inmate commentators is harsh and devastating, their tone and style is relatively restrained. One would expect otherwise, I think, especially given the facts they are presenting and their own confinement. Yet, for the most part, this is a work of observing and reporting with clear-eyed analysis. There are occasional bursts of heartfelt pain and rebellion, but generally the writers seem to have concluded that the facts themselves are strong enough.

Anyway, if one can read these accounts without becoming deeply troubled about the state of the criminal justice system, then no amount of personal exhortation would likely persuade. I take the dispassionate tone of these prisoners as a kind of implicit compliment to the rest of us, the readers on the outside. It seems to assume—generously—that there are still many Americans who are prepared to listen to facts and to respond to the indictment. I think these authors are right about that. Cynics would say they are hopelessly naive.

The understated tone is consistent with the source of the material. These chapters are collected from a unique publication, *Prison Legal News*, edited by Paul Wright and Dan Pens, both of whom are prisoners in the Washington state prison system. Founded in 1990, *PLN* has managed to connect up with a wide network of correspondents in state and federal prisons. Some simply report the news from their corners of the penal system. Others offer deeper analysis of the prison industry as a business sector or detail the latest outrageous abuses from within.

As a regular reader of *PLN* I am struck by the fact that every issue delivers real news, informs me of something I missed in the regular press or, more likely, something that was ignored by other media. When you think about the mass of information that inundates us from so many sources, it is amazing that a small, under-financed publication written and produced by prisoners can still regularly scoop the big media.

These voices, though despised and ignored, deserve to be heard in the larger political debate. One will not agree with every observation and conclusion, but this book delivers a strong sense of what is being left out. Indeed, I think it is probably true that Americans will not begin to restore humane values to their criminal justice system until they grasp that they must listen to these voices too.

William Greider is the National Editor of *Rolling Stone* magazine and the author of several books, most recently *One World, Ready or Not: The Manic Logic of Global Capitalism* (1997) and *Who Will Tell the People: The Betrayal of American Democracy* (1992), both with Simon and Schuster.

Part 1
THE NEW POLITICS OF CRIME

Crime as a political issue was first exploited to good effect by Richard Nixon who used it as a "wedge issue" in the 1968 Presidential elections. John Erlichman wrote that in 1969 when the Nixon administration looked out from the White House and saw 300,000 anti–war demonstrators they felt like the Revolution was imminent. The state responded with a deeper investment in domestic counter-insurgency operations. Using "crime" as its excuse, the Nixon administration stepped up repression (even while being investigated for crimes of their own). Nixon's success at the polls helped to propel the crime issue as a political propaganda tool in every campaign since.

With the fall of the iron curtain and Soviet collapse, the effectiveness of communism as the designated bogeyman began to decline. That's when "Crime" stepped to the forefront. Since the ruling class media and state bureaucracy had once been able to convince the restless masses that communism was a threat to working people, why not now convince them that their interests are threatened by *poor people*? On its face it seems like a ludicrous proposition.

The Congressional Budget Office disclosed in 1992 that a staggering 77 percent of the before tax income growth of U.S. families between 1977-89 went to the top one percent. In the years 1977-92, after-tax income of the bottom 80 percent of the population (adjusted for inflation) fell 2.2 percent, while after-tax income of the top 1/5th, rose 28.1 percent, and the after-tax income of the top 1 percent soared 102.2 percent! How is it possible then, to convince the restless masses that the new bogeyman on the block is the *"poor"*?

Crime!

Put the fear of crime into them. Splash crime on the front page of every newspaper. Make it the lead in every news broadcast. Make sure that most of the images of "criminals" are minorities, and you propel the myth faster, riding the undercurrent of racism that has always run strong in America. Portray poor people as filthy, drunken, violent brutes on television shows like *Cops,* and the restless masses are more inclined to view the poor with fear and revulsion. Feed the masses an unrelenting diet of crime, crime, crime, and they'll soon ingest the new bogeyman.

The propaganda machine of the American corporate class has become more sophisticated since it took on the task of creating the commie bogeyman ninety years ago. It took nearly fifty years to make anti-communism the national religion. It has taken less than two decades to instill an irrational fear of "Crime" into the American masses. And now poor people, women and children, immigrants (making a return appearance from earlier periods when they were also demonized and scapegoated) and prisoners are the targets of anger and frustration.

Prisoners make an especially easy target for attracting the fear and loathing of the American public. Prisoners have no economic or political power whatsoever. There is little social stigma to stand in the way of openly reviling prisoners. They make the perfect scapegoat. As such, the new politics of post-Soviet bogeymanism have struck prisoners particularly hard.

CITIZEN ANTI-CRIME INITIATIVES?

How the Gun Lobby Bankrolls the War on Crime

Paul Wright, May 1996

Recent years have seen a plethora of so called anti-crime initiatives placed on various state ballots. These initiatives purport to be efforts by state citizens who are fed up with crime and ready to do something about it. While this sounds good, it simply isn't true. These initiatives are no more populist, grassroots efforts than election campaigns by Phil Gramm and Newt Gingrich are supported by small citizen donors.

In 1993 the first "Three Strikes" initiative made it onto the ballot in Washington state. It was voted into law by 76 percent of the people who voted. Since then seventeen states have passed similar laws. Not to be outdone, California passed a three strikes law and a three strikes initiative. Supporters of these laws loudly proclaim that they are "the will of the people" and that "the electorate has spoken." But this ignores the fact that in American politics the first election that must be won, before a single vote is cast by the electorate, is the race for money. This is a story of three initiatives in Washington state: one failed and two didn't. The only differences between them were money and how they won that first race by getting the gun lobby to bankroll them.

When many states, especially in the West, were founded, their laws and constitutions included provisions for citizens to put measures on the ballot to be voted on directly. This was seen as a populist measure by which the people themselves could enact laws that politicians, all too often corrupt and in the thrall of rail and cattle barons, would not pass themselves. In order to qualify for the ballot initiative, gatherers have to draft a law, put it in petition form and then gather a certain number of signatures from enrolled voters. The number of signatures is usually based on a percentage of the number of people who voted in the last gubernatorial election. The petitions are then presented to the Secretary of State for verification of the signatures whereupon the initiative is certified for inclusion on the ballot.

The idea of voter initiatives is a good one. Washington voters have passed initiatives eliminating a state sales tax on groceries, codifying women's right to an abortion, and limiting how politicians raise money for their election campaigns. All of these were laws unlikely to be passed by legislators, especially the last one. But recently so-called citizen initiatives have turned into big money campaigns where special interest groups literally buy their way onto the ballot. In cases where other big money interests are opposed there are ads and countervailing viewpoints are presented in the media. But with so-called "anti-crime" initiatives, which target poor people and people of color, there is no counterpoint or opposition. It's like shooting ducks in a barrel with a shotgun.

Faced with increased efforts to restrict gun ownership, the gun lobby, most notably the National Rifle Association (NRA), began funding these "anti-crime" initiatives through its Institute for Legislative Action. Many commentators were making a connection between the availability of guns, especially handguns, and an increasing homicide and gun-related violent crime rate as people were being shot with progressively more powerful handguns. To distract attention from the correlation between handgun availability and gun-related crime and deaths, the NRA responded with its "Guns Don't Kill People, People Kill People" slogan. It began a well-orchestrated propaganda campaign that the focus of legislators had to be not on restricting gun access, but on targeting the "criminals" who misused guns (in many respects this has been a thinly veiled racist campaign that aims to keep guns out of non-White hands). For the most part this campaign has been an enormous success. The media is flooded with accounts about crime which bash the poor, minorities, and prisoners. Gun control has been a non-issue except in the context of how many legislators lost their 1994 bid for re-election, because they voted for the so-called "assault weapons" ban in the 1994 Clinton crime bill.

Initiative 590: Three Strikes Yer Out

In 1992, John Carlson, a right wing radio commentator (the Rush Limbaugh of Seattle), Patricia Lantzy, Jeralita Costa and Ida Ballasiotes formed a group called Citizens for Justice (CFJ). Their first act was filing Initiative 590, which was a three strikes law that had failed to win passage in the legislature. Both Costa and Ballasiotes were crime victim advocates and they have since gone on to careers in the state legislature where they act as professional prisoner-bashers. The initiative sought to impose a life sentence on any person convicted for a third time of any one of three listed felonies.

All told the I-590 campaign raised $42,252 and spent $36,938 of it in a failed effort to get the initiative on the ballot. So who bankrolled them? The list is interesting. Pemco Insurance Company was the first donor who kicked in $10,000; Bruce McCaw, chairman of McCaw Cellular phones donated $3,000; and the Citizens Committee for the Right to Keep and Bear Arms donated $10,000. (It is ironic that the Committee to Keep and Bear Arms is donating to anti-crime issues since their chairman, Alan Gottlieb, is himself a convicted felon who under state and federal law would be ineligible to legally own firearms.) Other big money donors included the Washington Council of Police Officers for $1,000; William Boeing for $5,000; Richard Baldwin for $2,500; $5,000 from the NRA in Washington DC; and $1,000 from the Allison company. In fact, the bulk of the money donated was from rich individuals like Boeing and McCaw, Pemco and the gun lobby. The "individual citizens" who are supposed to be so concerned about crime donated a paltry $747. In short, citizens aren't willing to put their money where their mouths supposedly are.

When it became readily apparent to the initiative backers that they weren't going to get the signatures they needed to qualify for the ballot, they gave $5,000 to Northwest Alliance to pay signature gatherers for signatures. The $5,900 donation from the Washington D.C. NRA came on June 1, about a month before the initiative backers had to present 181,000 signatures to the Secretary of State in order to qualify for the state ballot. They used the money to send out a mass mailing of petitions but they still failed.

Initiative 593: The Return of Three Strikes

After the Washington state legislature failed to pass a three strikes law in its 1993 session and in the wake of the failure of I-590 the year before, its backers decided to try again. This time bankrolled by the gun lobby's blood money, they proved that all it takes to get on the ballot is having enough dough. By now Ballasiotes had been elected to the state legislature and she did not appear as one of the initiative's backers. David LaCourse, a purported businessman and "unpaid" volunteer for CFJ, emerged as a frontman for the group. Carlson—who also had a column in the *Seattle Times*—was heavily promoting I-593 on his radio show and in his column.

All told I-593 would raise and spend $210,616, with $14.67 left over once the campaign finished. In addition to donations the campaign would owe LaCourse, Carlson and Lantzy, the campaign treasurer, some $40,616.34 for money they loaned the campaign. These loans were paid back. The total amount of money donated by the NRA's Institute for Legislative Action was a whopping $91,146. The other big money donors were: $10,000 from Pemco Insurance Company; $8,000 from Services Group of America; $4,090 from William Boeing; $2,500 from Victoria Wise; $3,000 from the Citizen's Committee for the Right to Keep and Bear Arms. One would think that if people felt this strongly about this, or any other issue, they would not hesitate to donate their money to it. Instead, the ones who felt most strongly about this were the gun lobby, who kicked in almost half of the total raised.

Sherry Bockwinkel is the godmother of the paid ballot initiative. If you have the money and want to get something on the ballot in Washington state, you go to her. She has successfully represented: timber and developer interests in getting a "property rights" initiative on the ballot; an initiative financed by aluminum and agricultural industry which sought to ban gillnet fishing under the guise of protecting salmon; and an initiative that would allow unregulated casino gambling on Indian reservations. Bockwinkel summed up her political strategy in an interview this way: "One of the first things I ask when people come to me with an initiative is whether they can raise $250,000. The harsh reality is that's what it costs to run a state-wide campaign. You have to pay to play." Bockwinkel has made a very lucrative living off these initiatives. She heads two initiative business, Camera Ready and LIMIT, which do everything from print the petitions to pay people to get the signatures needed to put them on the ballot.

So if the citizenry doesn't feel strong enough about crime issues to donate their money to them then surely they believe in the cause enough to obtain the required 181,000 signatures from their fellow concerned citizens, right? Guess again. The single biggest expenditures for the campaign is to pay people to get signatures. Signature gatherers are paid between 50 cents to a dollar for each signature they get. The closer they are to the July 1st filing deadline, the more they get paid. I-593 campaign records show some signature gatherers getting paid $1,438: 13 different signature gatherers in Bellevue (a plush Seattle suburb) received $1,394; 82 other signature gatherers were paid a total of nearly $30,000; 30 signature gatherers got $10,800; James Lynch was paid $630 and Sherry Bockwinkel received some $16,000 for gathering signatures and another hefty $30,000 for "artwork." LaCourse was paid $5,000 for undisclosed services. The team spent $1,323 on their victory celebration party. The only other major expense listed on the disclosure forms are $30,000 to Ackerman/McQueen Advertising.

The spending paid off. I-593 made it onto the ballot this time and was passed into law by 76 percent of the people who voted. Its impact has been felt across the country as other states and the U.S. Congress hurried to pass their own versions of "Three Strikes You're Out" laws. That the entire crime and punishment debate was sharply shifted to the right. Any mention of gun control was simply not on the agenda. Instead the only topic was politicians and so called "victims' rights" groups trying to outdo each other in how draconian they could be in passing new criminal laws and tormenting prisoners.

In a fund raising letter that CFJ sent to supporters they said that "Three Strikes" was only the first step. Their program envisioned four stages to essentially change the face of the criminal justice system in Washington. The next step was an initiative to increase the penalties for gun-related crimes (remember, criminals misuse guns, gun availability has nothing to do with it); then one to revamp the juvenile criminal justice system; and lastly, one to make "life tough for prisoners."

Initiative 159: Hard Time for Armed Crime

Initiative 593 was an initiative where enough signatures qualified it for the ballot to be voted on directly by the voters. That type of initiative gives organizers from January 1 to July 1 to gather the necessary signatures. Initiatives to the legislature by contrast require the same number of signatures but give organizers until December 31. The initiative is then presented to the state legislature which must either pass the initiative as written or put it on the next ballot. The legislature can also write its own version of the law and let voters choose between the two.

In 1994 CFJ launched its I-159 campaign as an initiative to the legislature. Dubbed "Hard Time for Armed Crime," the initiative would substantially increase the penalty for crimes committed with firearms, create new crimes and also expand the state's death penalty to include car jacking, drive-by shootings and any deaths caused by someone trying to avoid a three strikes sentence. The initiative was transparently racist in its focus on the types of gun crime already punished by state law but largely committed by minority youth.

I-159 raised a total of $117,062. The money came from the usual suspects: The Committee for the Right to Keep and Bear Arms donated $5,000 and the NRA donated $10,000. Pemco gave $10,000; Services Group of America $4,000; Kathryn Johnston of Phoenix Partners, a Seattle brokerage house, $6,700. LaCourse would "loan" this campaign $41,650. Where LaCourse got the money to loan the campaign is not known. Under state law all people making donations to initiative campaigns must be disclosed to the state's Public Disclosure Commission. One way to get around this requirement would be to funnel the money through a front man who can then "loan" it to the campaign. Or promise to reimburse the person for any loans made during the campaign.

As of December 31, 1994 the campaign had spent $112,815. The bulk of this amount went to Washington Initiatives Now (WIN) for signature gathering. All told WIN got almost $50,000. An outfit named APC Inc. was paid $15,300 for "consulting" and a woman named Sonja McDonald received $5,312 for the same reason. Given the fact that the disclosure forms list the fees paid to WIN to be for "consulting," it is safe to assume that "consulting" means signature gathering. So all told some $70,000 of the $112,000 spent went to buy signatures. The rest of the money was spent on printing, postage and media costs.

Not surprisingly, the initiative got enough signatures, was sent to the legislature where it was voted into law with an overwhelming majority. A telling incident came when the Seattle Public Defender's office brought a Black man to testify before the legislature as someone who would be affected by this law. While awaiting his turn to testify one of the legislators, a Tacoma cop, summoned police to detain the man because he looked "suspicious." Apparently minorities don't come to testify about legislation all that often.

In both cases where initiatives passed, before the first ballot was cast the money race had already been run and won by CFJ. The role of the gun lobby in bankrolling these initiatives went largely unreported at the time. Most importantly, no one was asking "why is the NRA doing this?" After all, the NRA hadn't seen crime as a big priority in the past. But beginning around 1992-93 NRA ads began to boast of the role the group had played in passing this type of legislation in several states. As the NRA's role in stopping gun control legislation was being attributed to the rise of gun related crimes, the NRA struck back by actively promoting high profile campaigns like Initiative 593. With the passing of I-593 the NRA could say "we're in the forefront of the fight against crime" and "we're tough on people who misuse firearms." All too often, though, the political payoff for the NRA has been mixed. In the federal 1994 "crime bill" the so-called "assault weapons" ban was passed by Congress along with a federal three strikes law and many other repressive laws. Ironically, the only thing that came close to derailing the bill was the NRA's opposition to the included assault weapons ban. In most states the trend towards more draconian criminal laws is also being accompanied by increased restrictions on citizen's access to firearms, despite the NRA's opposition to the latter.

One interesting note is that Carlson "loaned" the I-593 campaign almost $2,000. LaCourse "loaned" it almost $20,900, and then more than $41,000 to the I-159 campaign. This generosity would imply he is a man of means. However, on May 25, 1995, Greater Seattle Printing sued LaCourse and his wife, as the officers of CFJ, for over $8,000 that CFJ and LaCourse owed and had not paid for printing done in the I-159 campaign. LaCourse sent out copies of the lawsuit as a fundraiser. Apparently the coffers of the gun lobby are running low. So if LaCourse has tens of thousands of dollars laying around to "loan" campaigns, why can't he pay his debts? What happened to the $117,000 the campaign took in? My suspicion is that the NRA gave LaCourse money but didn't do so openly, so they could avoid alienating gun owners who understood that the initiatives would criminalize a lot of ordinary gun owner behavior.

Buying the Ballot

Why is it necessary to pay signature gatherers to hustle the signatures necessary to get a measure on the ballot? One initiative organizer said the difference was that a volunteer would only stand in the rain gathering signatures for an hour, while a paid signature gatherer would stand in the rain for eight hours or more. A more mundane reality is that most people don't feel strongly enough about whatever issue involved to do anything about it, either by donating their money or by collecting signatures. So what started out as a populist idea has become a means by which big money corporate interests can put laws on the ballot and have them voted on.

On an even playing field this isn't necessarily a bad thing. A recent "property rights" initiative, which was an initiative to the legislature, was overwhelmingly passed by the state legislature. In a few weeks people opposed to it, including environmental groups, gathered enough signatures (yes, by paying for them) to get the measure on the ballot where voters rejected it. Opponents of other initiatives have run ads and media campaigns often resulting in the measure being defeated when voted on. The difference is that prisoners and the poor people likely to be criminal defendants have no lobby, no money, and consequently no voice. So when voters got to vote on these initiatives the only information they had were the shrill cries from Carlson and the rest of the corporate media. Since the three strikes law was passed in 1993 some 77 percent of the defendants convicted under it in King County (Seattle) are Black, despite the fact that Blacks make up only some five percent of the county population and about the same number of Whites are eligible for a three strikes sentence as Blacks.

A practical way to reserve the populist spirit of the initiative process would be to make paying signature gatherers illegal. In 1993 the Washington state legislature passed House Bill 1645, RCW 29.79.490 which made it a misdemeanor to pay signature gathers per signature, rather than on an hourly basis. The legislature claimed that paying people by the signature encouraged fraud. Bockwinkel filed suit in federal court challenging the constitutionality of the statute and Judge Barbara Rothstein held the law was unconstitutional and struck it down.

So why weren't there any more "anti-crime" initiatives from the CFJ in 1995? After all, they promised at least two more in their plan to revamp the state's criminal justice system. The answer may well lie in the fact that the NRA has fallen on tough times financially. The November 2, 1995, issue of *Rolling Stone* reported that the NRA had a cumulative operating deficit of more than $50 million. Most of the deficit is attributed to overspending by the Institute for Legislative Action, which has funded initiatives like I-593 and I-159, and declining membership revenues. The NRA's credit rating is the lowest possible given by Wall Street firms. In addition the NRA is being audited by the IRS. With no gun money the financial wind has been taken out of the CFJ's sails.

If the CFJ had, or does, carry through on its promised four initiatives it will essentially revamp the entire criminal justice system in Washington state—which will cost taxpayers tens of millions of dollars as the costs associated with these policies come due—for less than a million dollars spent on their part. So the gun lobby in Washington DC gets to dictate policy in Washington several thousand miles away. Washington may as well hang up a sign "criminal justice system for sale." Fortunately, it looks like the one major bidder is broke.

THREE STRIKES RACKS 'EM UP

Paul Wright, June-December 1994

In November of 1993 Washington voters passed Initiative 593 "Three Strikes You're Out" by a three to one margin. About 30 other states are considering some of the "Three Strikes" legislation, and it is the centerpiece of the 1994 federal "crime bill." The proponents of "Three Strikes" claim it will keep "career criminals" off the streets and in prison where they belong. Within what passes for mainstream American politics today no one is seriously opposing such measures. (On the other hand, groups which have some degree of knowledge about the criminal justice system—such as the American Corrections Association (ACA) and the Judicial Conference of the United States, which represents federal judges—have gone on record opposing the "Three Strikes" legislation.) The only dispute about "Three Strikes" in the national political field is how wide the net should be cast: all third time felons or just the "violent" ones? Life without parole or at least 25 years without parole? This is hardly a debate.

It seems that no one has pointed out that these laws have already been tried in the past. Until 1984 Washington had a "habitual offender" statute which mandated a life sentence for a defendant convicted of a felony for the third time. Most states have some version of this law on the books. The law's main purpose is to avoid trials whereby defendants will plea bargain to other charges in exchange for prosecutors agreeing not to "bitch" them.

Just who are these "career criminals" that are the focus of "three strikes" legislation? Fred Markham once told me that prisoners reminded him of the Wizard of Oz. The Wizard said he was not a bad man, just a bad wizard. Likewise, the vast majority of prisoners are not bad men, just bad criminals. Anyone who has done time in prison will tell you that they are not filled with rocket scientists. Most of the people in prison are not evil nor professional criminals:

they tend to be poor people with emotional, drug or alcohol problems, who are caught doing something stupid. The "professional career criminal" tends to be a media myth (unless of course we count savings and loan bankers, Fortune 500 companies, Oliver North and company and that lot).

In March, 1994, Samuel Page became the first person in the U.S. convicted and sentenced under a "Three Strikes" law. He plead guilty in Seattle. All told about 15 people in Washington state, mainly armed robbers and sex offenders, have been convicted of a qualifying third strike [that number now tops 83. -eds]. According to the latest report by the Washington Sentencing Guidelines Commission, in Fiscal year 1993 there were 204 defendants who would have qualified as "Three Strikes" defendants had the statute been in effect at the time (the law took effect December 2, 1993).

On April 15, 1994, Larry Fisher, 35, was convicted of his third strike in Snohomish county superior court in Washington. He is in prison and will stay there for the rest of his life. Fisher was convicted of putting his finger in his pocket, pretending it was a gun, and robbing a sandwich shop of $151 dollars. An hour later police arrested him at a bar a block away while he was drinking a beer. Fisher's two prior strikes involved stealing $360 from his grandfather in 1986 and robbing a pizza parlor of $100. All told the take from Fisher's criminal career totals $611 dollars; he has never physically harmed anyone.

How much will society pay to protect itself from this $611 loss? On average it costs $54,209 to build one prison bed space, and $20,000-$30,000 per year to house one prisoner (the costs are higher if financing and related costs of prison building are factored in). If Larry Fisher lives to be 70, the total cost to the state for his incarceration will be approximately $1 million dollars. Is society really getting its money's worth?

There are a lot of things wrong with these three strikes laws. Aside from the fact that their brunt will be borne almost entirely by poor people, there is the matter of proportionality. Everyone has heard the term "an eye for an eye." The original meaning of this was that punishment should be proportionate to the offense. Does stealing $611 dollars merit life in prison?

There are already numerous laws which mandate life without parole for certain first time or repeat offenses. The federal Armed

Career Criminal Act, passed in 1988, mandates 25 years without parole for a three-time felon found in possession (not using, mind you, just possession) of a firearm. Michigan mandates life without parole for possession of more than 650 grams of heroin or cocaine for a first time offender. The only other offense in Washington state which carries a life without parole penalty is aggravated murder.

Terrible as Social Policy and Worse as Law

When the laws make no difference in punishment between killing five people, having a gun, having 650 grams of an illegal drug or stealing $151 dollars, there is something wrong. Washington and California police have reported that since the "Three Strikes" laws went into effect suspects have become more violent in resisting arrest. A suspect, knowing that if convicted of petty theft will spend his life in prison has, quite literally, nothing to lose if he has to kill a few people to avoid arrest. Seattle Police Sgt. Eric Bardt was quoted as saying: "It now looks like some of these three strikes cases might try to get away or shoot their way out. Believe me, that's not lost on us. We're thinking about it." The result of this will likely be the continued broadening of the death penalty.

It is perverse logic where the proponents of these type of laws cite with approval the increasing numbers of people receiving such sentences—be it life without parole or the death penalty—claiming they are a deterrent. If such laws were effective the numbers of people being prosecuted under them would decline. Neither the mainstream media nor the politicians have any interest in using logic or common sense in formulating public policy. All these laws will achieve is an increasing number of poor people in prison, more violence and more state repression.

No laws will be passed making corruption by public officials or endangering public health by corporations a "strikes" offense. In 1989 the federal Sentencing Guidelines Commission was going to increase the penalties and punishment for corporations convicted of crimes, including making its executive criminally liable. Corporate America promptly lobbied the Commission and Congress and these amendments never materialized. Unfortunately, poor people affected by three strikes laws don't command a voice that Congress or the media will listen to. The rich get richer, the poor get prison.

Karl Marx wrote that history repeats itself, first as tragedy, then as farce. In 18th and 19th century England people were hanged for offenses like pick-pocketing and poaching. In this country many mandatory minimum sentences were repealed in the '60s and '70s as people realized they did not work and their only effect was to destroy what chances prisoners had to rebuild their lives. Unfortunately, this repetition of history will not be farcical for those swept up by baseball slogans masquerading as social policy.

These three strikes laws give the impression that most defendants had a chance the first few times around. In reality, by the time most defendants step into a courtroom for the first time they already have a couple of strikes against them: their class, alcohol and/or drug problems, illiteracy, joblessness, poverty, and often their race or a history of abuse. They've been striking out a long time before they got up to the plate.

Assuming a three strikes defendant has been to prison twice before he gets his third strike, it would seem that it's only fair to receive a decent chance to get out of the conditions that led to their imprisonment in the first place. Instead, most prisoners go back to the same neighborhoods, with the same poverty, joblessness, illiteracy and other problems from which they came—conditions they are even less able to cope with after the brutal and dehumanizing process inherent in the prison experience which they have undergone. Legislators and prison officials are endeavoring to "make prisons tougher" by eliminating what token vocational and rehabilitational programs now exist. Combined with idleness, overcrowding, endemic violence, a self-fulfilling prophecy is being created: more third strikers. It's hard to get any wood on the ball under these conditions.

Will things get any better? "Two Strikes" proposals in both Washington and Georgia passed into law. On September 1, 1994, the California legislature passed its "One Strike Rape Bill." As originally drafted by Republican state senator Marian Bergeson, the law required that nearly all sex offenders be sentenced to life in prison without the possibility of parole. Critics immediately attacked the law as so harsh that it might prompt rapists to kill their victims. The version finally approved—signed into law by Republican Governor Pete Wilson, who had made this law a major part of his re-election campaign—calls for a penalty of 25 years to life for sexual assaults involving torture, kidnapping or burglary with intent to commit rape. Lesser sex offenses would have sentences of fifteen years to life.

Under California's previous sentencing laws a single rape conviction involving a weapon netted an eight year sentence with the prisoner usually released after five years or less. The same offender sentenced under the one strike bill will spend nearly 13 years in prison and then be freed only by the decision of a parole board. Those sentenced to the maximum term of 25 years to life will not be eligible for parole for more than 21 years.

The California DOC has not yet determined what impact this new law will have on prison capacity. According to the *Corrections Yearbook*, as of August 1, 1994, the California Department of Corrections (CDC) was the most overcrowded prison system in the country, operating at 185.8 percent of its rated capacity. The "One Strike" bill is touted as being the harshest in the country. One prosecutor was quoted as saying its purpose was to make sex offenders "stop, leave the state, or be locked up." What effect this will actually have on crime rates remains to be seen. Likely, it will be little or none, or will actually make things worse.

Georgia's Democratic Governor Zell "Zig-Zag" Miller, up for re-election, signed that state's "Two Strikes" law into effect in April, 1994. It was also approved by voters on Nov. 8, 1994. According to some newspaper accounts, Miller actually signed the law into effect no less than seven separate times at different sites around the state while on the campaign trail. Among the law's provisions are sentences of life without parole for any person who already has one prior offense found guilty of specific crimes. The law also gives mandatory minimum sentences of ten years to first time offenders and treats juvenile offenders as adults. The Georgia legislature voted 166-7 in favor of the law. For the moment Georgia can lay claim to having the most punitive prior offender law on the books.

Given the national stampede towards draconian punishment, doesn't seem like it'll be long now before they dispense with the wimpy one strike stuff and just go for the death penalty.

FEAR AND LOATHING IN CALIFORNIA

Willie Wisely, December 1996

The three strikes sentencing law in California is a failure in all respects, according to criminal justice experts. They point out that three strikes is applied more often than not to people of color, that it hasn't reduced crime, that it's overwhelming the court system and bankrupting the state treasury. Supporters, consisting of conservatives, prosecutors, police, and other special interest groups, counter that the law is working; street crime is down, and more career criminals are behind bars with life terms. Wading into the sea of controversy surrounding the three strikes law, the California Supreme Court recently held that judges retain discretion to strike prior convictions so defendants with a third serious or violent felony will not automatically face 25 years to life in prison.

In *People v. Romero,* the state's high court, controlled by Republican appointees, ruled that the three strikes law did not preclude trial judges from striking allegations of prior convictions, even in the absence of a motion by the prosecutor requesting such action. Republican lawmakers were quick to denounce the decision, vowing to overturn it through legislation. "The justices showed they are more interested in protecting the turf of the bench than they are about protecting the safety of Californians," said Secretary of State Bill Jones, who backed the 1994 sentencing law as an assemblyperson.

Republican Governor Pete Wilson was similarly critical of the ruling, saying, "We cannot tolerate a situation which permits judges who are philosophically unsympathetic or politically disinclined to 'three strikes' to reduce strong sentences." Senate Minority Leader Rob Hurtt (R-Garden Grove), quickly authored a bill aimed at nullifying *Romero.* Regularly scheduled vacations for state legislators were delayed one week while both parties tried to resolve their differences over the bill. Senator Diane Watson (D-Los Angeles), was the only one to voice publicly what others would only say off the record. "Why not allow an opportunity for some time to go by and have the bill voted on in August? We stayed another week [already]. I don't see any need to rush this through. The public needs time to react."

Rob Stuzman, a spokesman for Hurtt, responded: "The downside to that is, every day that goes by is a day that criminals don't have to live under the tough sentencing guidelines of 'three strikes.'" The new bill would sharply limit judicial discretion in three strikes cases, allowing a judge to disregard previous convictions only if none of them were violent, the new offense was neither violent or serious, and the last previous conviction or release from prison was more than five years ago. Prosecutors would still have the power to drop prior convictions, but would have to explain such decisions on the record in open court. Other lawmakers expressed reservations about the bill.

The California Supreme Court made a careful, smart, measured decision and we ought not to make the court lackeys to hysteria," said Assemblyperson John Vasconcellos (D-San Jose). "It seems to me what they did was smart." Assemblyperson Barbara Lee (D-Oakland) said the decision "opens the door to begin addressing the real problems surrounding three strikes," which she said unfairly targets Blacks. Many Democrats said the Republicans needn't worry because most judges are conservative anyway. They pointed out that the Supreme Court merely allowed discretion in outrageous cases, such as the case where the prosecutor asked for a life sentence for the man who stole a slice of pizza.

"I do believe there is nothing in the decision that will have violent criminals wandering the street," said Assemblyperson John Burton (D-San Francisco). "They're judges—that's the name, judges. They're supposed to judge things." Burton said the next step for Republicans would be to "get rid of judges and have the district attorney prosecute a case and decide the sentence." Burton and Vasconcellos were joined by Lee, Assemblyperson Tom Bates (D-Berkeley), and Senator Nick Petris (D-Oakland), in saying the Supreme Court's decision was fair, particularly because most judges are former prosecutors who agree with the three strikes philosophy anyway. But is the law fair and effective?

In March 1995, Jerry Dewayne Williams of Los Angeles got 25 years to life for stealing a slice of pizza from a group of children on a pier. In March 1996, jurors acquitted Michael Newhouse, a homeless Los Angeles man, of charges of possessing a minute amount of cocaine. The case was prosecuted under the three strikes law. After the acquittal, the judge upbraided the prosecutor. "This case constituted a refusal by the district attorney to exercise the discretion that is vested in him by law and is part of his job," Superior Court Judge David Yaffe said. "If he refused to exercise that discretion... because he is afraid of the public reaction, then he's a craven coward who is afraid to do his sworn duty," the judge continued. "If he refused to exercise his discretion because he's trying to demonstrate that the 'three strikes' law does not work, then he is an arrogant bureaucrat who is trying to make fools of the 70 percent of Californians who voted for that law."

Los Angeles District Attorney Gil Garcetti, who was seeking re-election at the time, refused any comment. Although the prosecution refused to dismiss Williams' prior convictions, they did reduce charges against the grandson of one of Garcetti's campaign contributors, allowing the man to avoid a life sentence under the three strikes law.

A provision in the three strikes law prevents jurors from being informed that defendants face life sentences. If the defense tells the jury about the possible sentence, the prosecution can demand a mistrial. In San Jose, a jury convicted Anthony Garcia of shoplifting several pairs of pants from a department store. When jurors learned he faced 25 years to life some of them wrote angry letters to the judge stating that they felt "trapped" and "misled." Garcia was sentenced to 26 years to life. Some judges and prosecutors refuse to impose the harsh sentence in cases of petty crime.

In Monterey County, Joel Murillo faced a term of 35 years to life for stealing television sets. But, Judge Robert Moody exercised his discretion and disregarded a prior felony conviction, sentencing Murillo to an 18-year term. Moody, a career prosecutor before becoming a judge, is known as a tough, conservative sentencer.

David Bristow was a rising star in the San Bernardino County District Attorney's office. He switched sides and became a public defender, however, when he was fired for refusing to prosecute a Pomona man under the three strikes law for possession of .23 grams of cocaine. The man had prior convictions for robbery and burglary and would have been sentenced to 25 years to life on the possession charge. The ACLU gave Bristow its Conscience Award "because of his courage and conviction."

San Francisco District Attorney Terence Hallinan, a defense attorney before election to the top prosecutor's job, is frank about his dislike for the three strikes law: "I didn't want to become District Attorney to put everyone in prison for life no matter what they did." Since he took office last January, Hallinan established a panel of four prosecutors to review all potential three strikes cases. "We pretty much use 'three strikes' [only] for vicious people," Hallinan said. "I myself feel I am able to tell the difference between a bad person and someone who has just done the wrong thing. If you restructure 'three strikes' to reach violent or vicious people, you can make a real argument for it."

The cost of California's growing prison system in general—and the cost of housing tens of thousands of three strikes prisoners in particular—is bankrupting what was once the richest state in the country. To finance the biggest prison building program in the world, Governor Wilson has borrowed $7 billion from Wall Street investors. The interest payments on those loans cost state taxpayers several hundred million dollars a year and the increasing debt load may prompt financial institutions to lower California's bond rating, resulting in even higher interest rates on existing loans.

But Wilson, who is in his last year of office, is asking the legislature to approve a $1.8 billion bond measure to build six new prisons immediately. Wilson claims the overall cost to society is greater when a career criminal is loose rather than locked up for life: "The question isn't whether we can afford 'three strikes' and its accompanying need for prison construction. It's how we can afford to live without it."

As of August 11, 1996, the California Department of Corrections housed 141,925 prisoners. The state's prison population is projected to exceed 230,000 by 2001 and all available bed space will be filled by April of 1998 [230,000 was the original projection. The CDC then changed it to 210,000 in the spring of '95, and changed it again to 182,000 in the fall of '96. *-eds*]. James Gomez, director of the prison system, has said the only way to deal with overcrowding is either to stop accepting new prisoners or start letting prisoners out early. No one is likely to stem the flow of incoming prisoners and even if the legislature approved 20 new prisons none would be ready for operation until 2000.

In the meantime, the crime rate has been slowly declining over the past few years. With the aging of the Baby Boomers, people now between 38 and 50 years old, crime has declined. California Attorney General Dan Lungren was quick to attribute the lower crime rate to the "success" of three strikes. That's merely politics. Three strikes, like all other sentencing laws, is unlikely to ever have a measurable effect on the crime rate because only a small minority of those responsible for committing crimes are ever arrested, charged, tried, and sentenced to prison. And tough sentences serve only to get politicians elected, they are never a deterrent.

In a study authored by Vincent Schiraldi, Christopher Davis and Richard Estes of the Center on Juvenile and Criminal Justice in San Francisco, the racial disparity in three strikes sentencing is clear. Blacks are sent to prison under the law 13 times more often than Whites. Some 43 percent of prisoners with a three strikes sentence are Black, although only 7 percent of the total state population is Black and they represent one-fifth of all Californians arrested for felonies.

And, overall, 85 percent of persons receiving stiffer sentences under the three strikes law were convicted of a nonviolent offense according to Franklin Zimring, Director of the Earl Warren Legal Institute at the University of California at Berkeley. "We're worried about Willie Horton and we lock up the Three Stooges," Zimring said. Using three strikes to imprison people for minor offenses "is a perverse way to crack down on crime," he concluded.

Rather than focus on the roots of crime, politicians, the media and the public in California have scapegoated prisoners, a powerless group which lacks monied lobbyists and organized support. People in prison are not the cause of California's problems. But because lawmakers have shirked their obligation to serve the public's best interest in favor of appealing to the mob mentality, the problems will continue to worsen and the state's debt will continue to grow.

LETTER FROM EXILE

Ray Luc Levasseur, February 1993

Remember Eugene Debs? He was one of the first socialists I ever read, before I moved on to the hard-core. I used to quote him in letters—"where there is a lower class I am of it, where there is a criminal element, I am in it, while there is a soul in prison, I am not free." I don't know if he wrote this before or after his stint in Atlanta, but it always impressed me. Enough so I named a cat after him.

I don't think prisoners and their struggle need to be romanticized, but what phase have we entered when the liberals/Left—including that highly suspect group "progressives"—make no mention of prisons? They write enough about police and police repression (check that—not enough, but more than about prisons), and then let it die on the vine as if humanity ceases to exist after a booking.

I don't think this lack of consciousness problem is so much that predominantly White, middle class leftist/liberals have never experienced prison. It's more a case of their not being personally or politically threatened by it.

They go on and on about Big Brother, civil rights violations, suppression of dissent, and so on, but they all pass "go" and collect their $200. They can play monopoly like the rich folks—but without the "Get Out Of Jail Free" card. That wasn't the case in the past.

At the turn of the century through the '20s, radicals, Wobblies, immigrants, union organizers, felt the crunch. Communists and unionists in the '30s. Reds in the '50s. Enough radicals and militants in the '60s-'70s to make people think. Blacks—radical and otherwise—having long been held in the revolving door. And Latinos in the last few decades. Nowhere do you come up against the power of the law and naked force as blatantly as it's wielded in prisons. A virtual slavocracy as embodied in the Thirteenth Amendment to the Constitution. We have barely any rights the State is bound to respect.

If the Left did have any political consciousness about the issue— and some leftists do—they're not likely to act on it, because they lack the strength and resources to wage a vigorous struggle. In their publications, leftists often refer to the risk of imprisonment due to their activities, but I wonder how many would remain active if they seriously thought their actions carried the risk of imprisonment or bodily harm.

Prisoners often mirror-image what is happening in the street. With the exception of "criminal justice" issues, the general level of political consciousness among prisoners is low. They are ripe for new ideas and alternatives, but don't see any. This is understandable given that there is no organized movements presenting any offerings. This is a period of near-total abandonment of prisoners. Combine that with the conditions of survival, and it tends to breed an unhealthy cynicism.

Many Marion prisoners have been involved in individual and group acts of resistance over the years. For their efforts, they have been subjected to beatings, torture, transfers, isolation, more time—the whole nine yards. They see nothing positive coming out of it other than maintaining their integrity while staring down the worst abuses. They get no support outside and solidarity is lacking inside. Their hopes hinge on one more crack at the street. One more payday or payback, and hell hath no fury like an enraged ex-con.

For five years now, prisoners have been sentenced under the new rule of mandatory sentences with no parole. Young dudes are coming in with big time. You can't do time on the installment plan anymore—the sentences are too steep, with no parole release. You do more than a couple of bits and your whole life is gone. So, the prevailing attitude is next time why show any consideration to cops or witnesses since you're coming back for 20 to 30 after doing 10 to 15? The prevailing informational exchange is based on methods of criminal operation. So while a totally unsuspecting and scammed soul takes refuge in the fact that a million women and men are locked away, the next generation is slipping up to their back door, and ex-cons come out of their own frightful situation without a pot to piss in, and no prospects of getting one.

The reason there was such a high level of political consciousness among prisoners of an earlier era was because they reflected what was happening on the streets of the country at an earlier time, and to a lesser degree, internationally. Prison conditions are such that confrontations and rebellion will continue regardless of the existence of external movements. The lowest common denominator with us, without significant outside support, is how much suffering and bleeding we will endure before we are willing and able to sacrifice even more for a chance to turn the situation around. Or has the current situation become a permanent and expanding part of a larger nightmare we are all getting sucked into?

Part II
THE DISTORTED LENS

The Corporate Media Filter
of Crime and Justice

If the perception of reality is more important than reality itself, the next question is who is responsible for shaping and forming the perception of reality in the United States? That role falls largely to the corporate media, especially network television, the news weeklies and daily newspapers. With the mass media owned by a shrinking number of corporate conglomerates, the messages they convey are increasingly uniform, bland and supportive of the status quo. With regards to prisons and prisoners, this means shrill repetition of politicians' lies and prison officials' propaganda.

What little analysis has been done on "crime issues" has shown the massive increases in sheer volume of crime news reported by the mass media. The not so surprising result of this is that crime, and the fear thereof, is the number one concern of a majority of Americans even though the rates of most major crimes have been declining steadily since 1991. It's the same phenomena that a study of Gulf War coverage found: the more "news" you consume, the less you know.

One popular myth is that the mass media is "objective": impartial and balanced. All too often "objectivity" is nothing more than a code word for pro-government policy bias. In the overwhelming majority of articles about prisons, prison officials are the only sources deemed worthy of interview. As prominent media critic Edward S. Herman (writing with Gerry O'Sullivan) stated simply: "An unbiased press would treat biased sources with extreme caution." Ours doesn't, and this bias is especially clear with prison coverage. Prisoners' knowledge and experience is never taken into account. Prisoners are seen by the majority of people in the media, consciously or unconsciously, as mute, passive beasts, the serfs of yore, to be talked about, but never talked to. (*Prison Legal News* was created to give the imprisoned a voice with which we can speak truth to power.)

In essence, the corporate media is doing little more than parroting Department of Corrections/Bureau of Prisons press releases and presenting them as "news." The consumers of news, the American public, are left with a stilted and inaccurate picture of prison reality. Numerous prison-related issues which should concern the public, from the real reasons behind prison litigation, to "free world" jobs moving behind prison walls, or the existence of political prisoners in the United States and the enforcement of basic human rights inside U.S. borders, are not sufficiently covered and explored. The corporate media, by willfully ignoring the dimensions today's prison crisis has reached, is keeping the public disinformed, and in doing so subverting the public interest.

MEDIA BOWS TO POWER

Will Mumia's Voice be Silenced Forever?

Noelle Hanrahan, October 1997

The promise of death is not enough; the state of Pennsylvania wants to still Mumia Abu-Jamal's voice and enforce his silence. The Pennsylvania Department of Corrections has banned journalists access to the entire PA prison population, in what prisoners have labeled the "Mumia Rule."

A prolific writer and author of a searing compilation of essays, *Live From Death Row*, for 16 years Mumia has not only been fighting to stay alive, he has been waging a battle for the freedom to write and speak. In August of 1995 he came within 10 days of being executed by lethal injection.

The stark reality of a place where men and women wait for death is a secluded and secretive world. What happens behind these walls is restricted, censored, and suppressed. Over 3,000 men and women live under a death sentence in 38 American states. 40% of America's death row inhabitants are Black. Censorship can be lethal.

Just days before the Pennsylvania Department of Corrections ban on interviews went into effect, the Prison Radio Project/Quixote Center recorded the only essays by Mumia in over two and a half years. Armed with a digital audio tape machine and cameras, recording engineer Janice Leber and photographer Nolen Edmonston came away with thirteen recorded essays. Amidst a torrent of lockdowns, investigations, torture, and the banning of reporters, Mumia's voice will be heard. These recordings could prove to be the very last images and recordings of Mumia in prison.

Democracy Now!, Pacifica's cutting edge radio show hosted by Amy Goodman, premiered these essays. Although over one million people were able to hear Mumia's voice throughout the United

States, broadcasts across Pennsylvania were censored. WRTI, Temple University's radio station, and its affiliates pulled broadcasts of Mumia's essays and canceled all of Pacifica's programming just moments before the essays were to air.

As the United States gears up for assembly line executions, it must dehumanize its victims. A key component of this strategy is to make these men and women invisible. In an ominous trend, in December 1995, the California Department of Corrections—the largest prison system in the U.S.—eliminated all media access to prisoners. The public's right to know has been sacrificed to protect California's 3-billion-dollar-a-year, and ever expanding, prison industry.

It is our job as journalists to reach behind the iron curtain as it falls across the American landscape so we may hear prisoners' voices; voices of dissent and voices of those we condemn.

The State Correctional Institute (SCI-Greene), a new supermaximum security prison in Waynesburg, PA, is designed to eliminate human contact. Isolated in the farthest reaches of rural southwestern Pennsylvania, it is eight hours from the homes and families of eighty five percent of its captives. Men are held in solitary confinement, allowed out of their cells one hour a day, five days a week, to exercise in a small, barren wire cage.

Prisoners on death row are allowed just one, two-hour non-contact visit per week, and two strictly-timed ten-minute phone calls a month.

If prisoners are under investigation for a disciplinary infraction—such as "engaging in the profession of journalism"—all visits and phone calls are denied. A date with death in the form of a death warrant means complete isolation as well.

As they entered, Leber and Edmonston passed electrified gates topped with coiled layers of gleaming concertina razor wire. Once inside the ultra-modern control unit prison, the antiseptic sterility and bright white lights presage a regimen of psychological and physical torture.

At the guard station, Janice Leber had to disrobe, taking off her dress to pass through a metal detector. The visiting area for death row, just outside the "D" pod housing unit holding eight cells, is recessed deep in the complex. In the non-contact visiting cubicles, they are separated from Mumia by a thick wall of plexiglass.

Guards admonished Leber and Edmonston not to speak to Mumia

until "that woman"—as they referred to a prison administrator—was present. Negotiating with bored, yet nervous guards revolved around the guards' constant internal calculation: "Will granting this request cost me my job?" When the prison administrator arrived, she remained in the cramped 4' by 5' foot cubicle to monitor every word.

Intimidation and humiliation are used to discourage visits. Mumia is forced to submit to a full cavity strip search before and after each completely non-contact visit. There is a price exacted to see and talk with another human being. During the interview Mumia remained handcuffed, and at times also shackled at the waist.

Mumia's deep baritone voice, palpable humanity, and wry laugh illuminates his surroundings and the lives of the men with whom he shares his life. Images give us a glimpse of a man whose humanity remains intact, having endured 15 years of brutal solitary confinement.

This battle with censorship is not the first. It is part of an ongoing struggle to make Mumia's voice be heard. On Sunday May 15th, 1994, the *New York Times* ran an AP article "From Death Row: A Radio Show," which highlighted the next day's premier of Mumia Abu-Jamal's radio commentaries on *All Things Considered*. Most major dailies ran the article. That same day, *NPR News* managing editor Bruce Drake (who was left in charge while his boss was on vacation) stunned NPR weekend staff by canceling the debut. This was after the Prison Radio Project and NPR staff had selected, recorded, and NPR had launched a nationwide publicity campaign highlighting the debut of these "unique" commentaries. In fact, NPR does not usually set an air date for commentaries, but the press interest was so high they scheduled an air date of Monday, May 16th.

Since July of 1992, as the director of the Prison Radio Project, I have been recording and producing Mumia's commentaries for public radio. In February, 1993, I went to Washington D.C. and scheduled auditions of Mumia's demo tape with Gail Christian, executive director of Pacifica National Programming, and Ellen Weiss, executive director of *All Things Considered*. I was accompanied by Jane Henderson of Equal Justice U.S.A./Quixote Center. NPR was immediately interested. Ellen Weiss was very impressed with Mumia's work. She said "I am honored. Let's make this happen....My audience needs to hear about these issues, this is a unique perspective...Thank you."

In May 1994, Mumia's battle to be heard intensified when Robert Dole (former Republican senator and 1996 presidential candidate and senator) and the National Fraternal Order of Police forced National Public Radio to censor Mumia's regularly scheduled commentaries on *All Things Considered*/NPR. These essays would have reached 17 million people on 500 stations across the U.S., Canada, Mexico, Europe, and South Africa.

The state in effect has confiscated these new recordings of Mumia, and it has been able to compel NPR to keep them from being aired. Ten unique and irreplaceable essays, some of the last recordings of Mumia, remain under lock and key. Although under great pressure, NPR has refused to air or release them.

"The state would rather give me an Uzi, than a microphone," commented Mumia. And the major network journalists are complicit in this censorship. No recordings of Mumia's voice have ever been aired on a national network news broadcast. "My offense is painting an uncomplimentary picture of a prison system that eats hundreds of millions of dollars a year to torture and maim tens of thousands of men and women, a system that teaches bitterness and hones hatred." Why is the simple truth of life in prison perceived as such a threat? The answer lies in the fact that Mumia's words, spoken in the King's English, if heard, would threaten the smooth and orderly function of both state-sanctioned murder and modern slavery.

Mumia Abu-Jamal's perspective is a serious threat to the hegemony of the "corrections industry." He humanizes over one-and-a-half million prisoners in America. Disclosure of torture and human rights abuses would slow productivity and expansion in one of the U.S.'s largest growth industries: human storage and slave labor.

Five million one hundred thousand American citizens are under correctional control of prisons, jails, parole and probation; the highest per capita rate of imprisonment and state control in the world.

At the current rate of incarceration, by 2010 the majority of all African-American men between the ages of 18 and 40 will be in prison: the state as their captor and their labor on the auction block.

Whether Mumia Abu-Jamal's voice will reach the airwaves, and ultimately whether he lives or dies, will be a true test of whether freedom of the press exists. It will also depend on our independence, the depth of our courage, and our will to organize.

SPOON-FED MEDIA EATS WELL OFF OF PRISON OFFICIALS' HANDOUTS

California Prisoners Assault Office

Dan Pens, September 1995

On May 5, 1995, at 9:45 a.m., five prisoners at California's Calipatria maximum security prison walked into an "A Facility" program office and stabbed a sergeant. Three other guards rushed to her aid and they too were stabbed in a brawl that rolled through the office. It was not until four other guards arrived on the scene that they were finally able to disarm the prisoners. In all, five guards were stabbed and three others suffered various minor injuries. We have no information on what, if any, injuries were suffered by the five prisoners. The prison was put on indefinite lockdown status.

Calipatria State Prison spokesman Lieutenant Tom Deschler said to the press that prison officials are "not really sure" why the prisoners launched the assault. "I don't think they were trying to take over anything, but it's a scary thought," Deschler said.

He said the attack "seemed planned," but that "we have no motive or anything like that."

The above comments, reported in the *Sacramento Bee,* were made weeks after the incident, so Lt. "Spin Doctor" had plenty of time to gather information upon which to base his comments about the apparently senseless attack.[1] As usual, the mainstream press gets its version of events from the prisoncrats. Whatever the government spin doctors have to say is "news" and the mainstream press accepts it and prints it, without question. So why would five prisoners, in what appeared to be a "planned attack" storm a prison office and start stabbing guards without having a "motive or anything like that"? They must be mad dogs.

The *Bee* reported that the prisoners were "later identified as members of a South Central Los Angeles street gang." Not reported by the *Bee*, however, is the fact that earlier that morning another member of the same gang, the East Side Crips, was beaten by Calipatria prison guards. The assault on the prison office, then, was apparently a calculated response in retaliation for the earlier beating.

To the *Bee's* credit, they did dig a little bit in an attempt to make some kind of sense out of what may have appeared to be a totally senseless assault. They pointed out that fourteen California prisons are filled to over 180 percent capacity, and five are stuffed with over 200 percent of their rated capacity. They also cited a 1994 California Department of Corrections (CDC) Emergency Operations Unit report that compared current conditions in California's prisons to those that presaged violent, bloody uprisings in Attica, Santa Fe and Lucasville. The *Bee* also interviewed a number of "experts" on the California prison system as well as several state assembly members. One assembly budget committee analyst said that taking away prison "perks" like family visits and weight-lifting, both of which experts say can serve as a measure to control prisoners if rationed in accordance with good behavior, amount to "emotive policy making" that places politics over "good penology."

The *Bee* article made some sound points, but by failing to interview some "experts" about the CDC—those who live within its belly—the *Bee* missed the mark on this one.

1 *Sacramento Bee,* June 1, 1995.

Clallam Prisoners—"No Grievances"?

Paul Wright, January 1996

On September 26, 1995, some 25 prisoners in A-unit of the Clallam Bay Corrections Center (CBCC) in Clallam Bay, Washington attacked two guards and then attempted to barricade themselves and the guards within the 33-cell pod unit. The guards succeeded in escaping after being sprayed in the face with spray cleaner. The unit was placed on lockdown and remained that way until the morning of September 29, 1995. A prison spokesperson stated that at least two prisoners would be referred to the Clallam County prosecutor for criminal prosecution. The spokesperson claimed that the prisoners had tried to take the two guards hostage.

This is not the first time CBCC prisoners have rebelled. On April 16, 1995, prisoners at CBCC caused well over $30,000 in damages by totally demolishing a unit pod with cleaning utensils. That uprising was suppressed three hours later by guards with stun grenades. Back in 1990 there was another uprising at CBCC. Prisoners who were being beaten by guards were defended by other prisoners and the prison's Close Custody Unit was seized and held by prisoners for three hours.[1] Basically, not much has changed at Clallam Bay.

The amazing thing about this latest incident wasn't so much that it received little attention from the corporate media, but the blatantly untrue headline "Prison Riot Lacks Motive" in the *Peninsula Daily News* article by Mike Dawson.[2] The subheading read: "Corrections: Probe Shows Inmates Were Without Grievances." Upon reading Dawson's article it is readily apparent that he never contacted any prisoners or spoke to any of them, not even the ones being charged with criminal offenses. *Prison Legal News* contacted CBCC prisoners and found, not surprisingly, that they had plenty of grievances.

A CBCC prisoner reported: "There is no way I could list each and every reason that prisoners here 'act up...'" The complaints are:

- **Recreation:** At one point we had a hobby craft room, but it was taken from us so the [guards] would have some place to train new [guards]. The same is true with our bandroom. The yard is constantly closed due to some mysterious fog that no one can see except the [guards].

- **Chow Halls**: The chow halls are tiny, there is only enough room for approximately 90 prisoners but the [guards] pack 198 prisoners in there at once on a daily basis. The menu that was sent from Olympia as to how much food we are supposed to get is drastically reduced, i.e. fruit juice, fresh fruit and the main course is usually cut in half.

- **Religious Programs**: Any religion other than Christianity is heavily scrutinized by chapel staff and the [guards], making it extremely difficult, often times impossible to properly fulfill religious obligations or ceremonies.

- **Store Prices**: The store prices here are about 20-40 percent higher than any other joint. The [guards] have recently pulled all radios from the store list, promising to replace them with walkmans. None have been located and when they are they will cost about $90 each, not to mention a lame store list.

- **Staff Corruption**: The staff here is really fucked up, and what makes it worse is that they are all related to each other and make sure to cover each other's tracks. None of the staff follow WAC [Washington Administrative Code] rules. They make up shoe string policies daily. They force prisoners to program [i.e., participate in programs] and don't provide enough jobs or school slots. When a prisoner is unable to program he is locked in his cell for most of the day and his good time is taken. Prisoners' property is consistently stolen by the [guards]. There is constant misuse of the Inmate Betterment Fund. The grievance system is a joke, no steps are ever taken within the institution to correct any problems. Any prisoner complaints of staff misconduct result in the prisoner being infracted and harshly punished for "lying."[3] The unit counselors never make any attempts to work with prisoners to help them better themselves, all they do is push through loss of good time paperwork. Legal mail is unlawfully opened and regular mail is constantly stolen. Harassment of visitors is common-

place. The [guards] are [everywhere]... and are constantly physically and verbally abusive towards prisoners.[4]

- **Legal Library**: The law library is small. It only has room for 16
people at a time.

Did the newspaper say prisoners "were without grievances"? With
journalism like Dawson's he should just put "DOC handout" as the
by-line. Other CBCC prisoners reported that one guard, Schneider,
had contributed to the uprising by instituting even more repressive
policies, such as denial of TV and radio during cell confinement. This
is at a prison where some 25 percent of the prison population is routinely on "cell confinement" at any given time for petty rule violations and the cell confinement can and does last for periods of up to
180 days.

With regards to the September 26 incident one CBCC prisoner
summarized:

> There was no attempt to take any hostages. Basically a few pris-
> oners were sick of all this shit and attempted to assault a few [guards]
> who entered their living quarters. When the [guards] fled the doors
> were barricaded and some fires were set. The prisoners were gooned
> after about 15 minutes and taken to IMU [Intensive Management
> Unit] where I am sure they will be buried. Basically it was just a mes-
> sage to tell the [guards] "We ain't going for it anymore and some
> changes better be made. Who knows what will happen next?"

The ongoing series of events at CBCC, which include several
shootings of prisoners, a counselor being taken hostage, beatings of
prisoners, etc., can easily be attributed to the fact that contrary to
public opinion, CBCC is "managed like a Nazi concentration camp"
(a direct quote from a senior Washington DOC official, who asked
that his name not be used) where confrontation is actively sought
and any type of peaceful protest or dissent is ruthlessly crushed. The
federal courts in Seattle have given their rubber-stamp to this process
by refusing to address the ongoing series of civil and human rights
violations at CBCC. Hard-hitting investigative reporting by the likes
of Dawson doesn't help matters.

1 See: "'Disruption' At Clallam Bay Report," *PLN*, May 1990, p. 6.
2 *Peninsula Daily News* (Port Angeles, WA), Sept. 29, 1995.
3 See: "Prisoners and the Grievance System," *PLN*, July 1991.
4 This is a long-standing practice. See: Paul Wright, "Clallam Bay Prisoner Brutalized," *PLN*, February 1991, p. 8.

CALIFORNIA BANS MEDIA INTERVIEWS WITH PRISONERS

Willie Wisely, March 1997

California Governor Pete Wilson issued an executive order banning face-to-face media interviews with prisoners. The ban comes at a time when most civil rights for the state's 142,000 prisoners have been taken and violence is on the rise in the world's largest prison system. At the obligatory public hearing held at the Department of Corrections, representatives of the media and public strongly opposed the proposed new policies. In its public notice for that hearing, the Department claimed the ban was necessary to prevent individual prisoners from becoming celebrities and gaining access to contraband.

Saying that prisons represent "the most expansionist sector" of state spending, Terry Francke, Executive Director of the California First Amendment Coalition, said, "the individual stories and accounts that only inmates can provide" make up a critical component in determining how smoothly the state's prison system is run. For some stories about prison life and administration, Francke continued, "there is no substitute for the opportunity to talk directly and candidly with specific individuals who either know the facts or can point to those who do." When prison guards boiled a mentally ill prisoner alive at Pelican Bay and beat, kicked and shot prisoners for sport at Corcoran, prisoners relayed the stories to the media. Critics of the ban believe it's exactly that type of information Department of Corrections Director James Gomez hopes to suppress with the new policy.

Department officials point to the alleged escape attempt by Black Panther George Jackson at San Quentin prison in 1971 and the regular *Geraldo* sideshows featuring Charles Manson as justification for refusing to permit the media to interview specific prisoners any longer. In addition, prisoners will no longer be allowed to send mail to representatives of the media confidentially. Now, such mail will be read by guards before it's allowed out of the prison. Reporters will only be permitted to speak to prisoners selected by officials during approved tours of prisons. Prison officials could offer no examples of how face-to-face media interviews actually compromised the security of any prison.

"Why should some guy benefit from committing a crime? We did this because we didn't want to have inmates becoming celebrities and heroes," J.P. Tremblay, Assistant Secretary of the Youth and Adult Corrections Agency said in an interview with the San Francisco *Daily Recorder* last January. He claimed that the principle of preventing criminals from profiting from their crimes necessarily "includes the intangible profit that certain inmates acquire by receiving the attention they crave and the attendant opportunity for a public forum in which they can espouse their often sociopathic philosophies." Tremblay failed to explain why any prisoner bent on promoting "sociopathic philosophies" couldn't simply do so in regular, non-confidential letters mailed to the media.

While prisoners might express their viewpoints to the media in open letters, few will be willing to risk the consequences of exposing beatings, shootings, theft and other misconduct by prison staff. Prison guards who screen all outgoing prisoner mail routinely seize letters addressed to the media which are critical of prison employees. Photocopies of such letters are placed in the prisoner's file for other staff to read and disciplinary action or other retaliation is taken against the author. The possibility of such retaliation will have a chilling effect on the flow of information about abuses in prison to the media.

Peter Sussman, co-author of *Committing Journalism: The Prison Writings of Red Hog* and President of the Northern California Chapter of the Society of Professional Journalists, recalls once receiving a confidential letter from a prisoner which contained a copy of a lab report showing high levels of human fecal matter contamination in a prison water supply. With many prisons located in the state's agricultural based Central Valley, it has long been suspected that drinking water supplied to prisoners is contaminated with nitrogens, pesticides and sometimes even fecal matter, but hard evidence has been difficult to obtain. With a report in hand, Sussman could insure the story was told. Under the new policy, it's doubtful the report would have made it out of the prison.

In 1994, Governor Wilson signed into law legislation which stripped California prisoners of most civil rights. That law provided the Department of Corrections with an excuse to implement restrictions on access to the media, something they had on their agenda for a long time. State Senator Quentin Kopp, San Francisco independent, co-authored the legislation, but said it provides, "no authority to change or terminate prior departmental policy in regard to media interviews of prisoners." Director Gomez wrote March 19, 1996, that, "Nothing is contemplated to alter media access" to department facilities. Just ten days after that letter was written, media access to prisons in the state was radically altered.

The Department's self-serving rationalizations for the new media policy ignore the public's interest in being informed about what goes on in the world's largest prison system. Some courts have recognized the importance of a prisoner's ability to communicate with the media. As one judge put it, "In a civilized society, governed by the rule of law, voices of dissent cannot and should not be suppressed. History has been punctuated by writers who have emerged from prison cells to become spokesmen for humanity."[1] However, the right-wing dominated United States Supreme Court has upheld prison restrictions on the media's face to face interviews with specific prisoners as long as those prisoners have some ability to communicate with reporters.[2]

Prison officials were quick to punish the first prisoner to challenge the restrictions on access to the media. Boston Woodard, who has spent some 15 years at California Men's Colony near San Luis Obispo, was editor of the prison newspaper, *The Commentator*, until last December. He was relieved of his position and disciplined for allegedly advising reporters on possible strategies to circumvent the prohibition against interviews with specific prisoners. Woodard scoffs at that claim and says his removal from the newspaper staff was retaliation for an article he wrote criticizing the new policy. In an interview with the *Recorder*, Woodard said prisoners fear the restrictions are part of an effort to shut the public out of the prison system altogether. He said the rule allowing media representatives to interview only those prisoners chosen by prison officials during random tours means "They'll make sure you're in an area where all the inmates [the press] talk to will have the IQ of a cinder block."

Lifers fear the interview ban has even darker implications. California's prison population is 180 percent over capacity. The Director's policy of housing known enemies on the same prison yard has led to escalating violence. Many privileges, such as family visits and weights, and programs, such as education and vocational classes, have been either taken or drastically reduced in response to pressure from special interest groups. Without such incentives, the large and growing number of young lifers, often street gang members, feel they have nothing to lose and this is raising the level of tension in prisons statewide. As Ken Hartman, a writer serving life without parole at Lancaster's maximum security prison put it, prison officials "know what's coming and they want to be able to control the flow of information."

The California Office of Administrative Law issued its formal ruling December 11, 1996, disapproving the Department of Corrections' proposed regulations banning face-to-face media interviews with prisoners and eliminating confidential correspondence between people in prison and representatives of the media. The CDC immediately re-filed the regulation change as an emergency which allows them to enforce the ban for 120 days without a public hearing. Prison administrators must amend their regulation change application and resubmit it to the OAL within the four month period barring any additional extensions of time.

The OAL found that CDC officials failed to respond to many of the comments received from the public during a June hearing and in writing. A total of 100 comments were acknowledged by prisoncrats, 99 opposed to the media ban and one in favor.

The Society of Professional Journalists, the American Civil Liberties Union, the American Jewish Congress, the California First Amendment Coalition, the Prison Law Office, PEN Center USA West, California Broadcasters Association, California Senator Kopp, an attorney representing national news organizations, a reporter for the *Orange County Register* and several others opposed the proposed ban on media interviews with prisoners.

The CDC's initial response to the comments in opposition to their regulation change application was superficial and arrogant in places. With regard to one comment concerning brutality by prison staff, the OAL said, "The Department's response simply assumes that mistreatment of prisoners does not occur because it is prohibited by Penal Code §§2650, 2651 and 2652. That response does not address the commentator's assertion that confidential media access is the only effective remedy to protect prisoners from abuse should that abuse occur."

The CDC's attempt to shut out the media from the largest prison system in the world is part of a well-coordinated effort in several other states. California's regulations are closely monitored by other prison administrators because the state's prison rules are often used as a model for prison systems in the remainder of the country. Prison systems in Virginia, Missouri and South Carolina have also banned media access to prisoners.

1 *Martin v. Rison* (N.D. Cal. 1990) 741 F. Supp. 1406, 1425.
2 *Pell v. Procunier* (1974) 417 U.S. 817.

PRISON WEIGHT-LIFTING IS A NONSENSE ISSUE

Paul Wright, March 1995

Across the country Republicans have seized on prison weight-lifting as a no-risk political "issue" which they can make a big hoopla over. The corporate media has abetted this by running sensationalist stories of prisoners bulking up and getting scarier by pumping iron. So far Arizona, Mississippi, South Carolina and Wisconsin have banned weights in prison. The California legislature has required that the DOC submit a plan so prisoners can use weights but not build strength or bulk. The Washington state legislature is going to consider the matter this term. It is being pushed by Mike Padden, the anti-abortion Republican from Spokane, and Ida Ballasiotes, the professional prisoner basher who heads the "Corrections Committee" in the State House.

Prisoners have been lifting weights in Washington for over forty years. How many people outside prison knew or cared about this until the Republicans and media made it an issue? None. weight-lifting has been popular in prison for decades with both prisoners and their keepers for several reasons.

Prisoners like to pump iron because it represents an opportunity for intense workouts and solid exercise year round, even when prison yards are closed due to rain, fog, or snow. Prisoners lift weights to, among other things, release tension and build discipline. In other words, basically the same reasons non-prisoners lift weights. Where Washington state prisoners in population are locked in their cells 20 or 22 hours a day, an hour on the weight deck is the only meaningful exercise they will get. Prisons tend to be sedentary in nature with little opportunity for movement or activity. Without exercise the health problems associated with such a lifestyle, combined with the

environmental dangers associated with prisons (inadequate ventilation, fat- and cholesterol-saturated food, etc.) are amplified. Regular exercise such as weight-lifting boosts the immune systems,
reduces the risks of cardiovascular disease and improves people's
overall health. With a rapidly aging prisoner population prisoners
should be encouraged to maintain their health—not deprived of the
opportunity to do so.

For prison officials, weight-lifting is popular because it takes up
very little room, is easy to supervise by guards, and it gives prisoners something to do that isn't illegal or dangerous. It also provides
a privilege that can be withdrawn for misbehavior. By constitutional
law prisoners must be provided with an opportunity for at least one
hour of exercise which allows for strenuous workouts to reduce large
muscle deterioration. weight-lifting allows prison officials to meet
this legal obligation.

Another reason that weight-lifting is popular in prisons is because
it is extremely cheap, consisting mainly of iron weights that rarely
need to be replaced. Politicians wanting to take the weights claim
they are concerned about "costs" and that taxpayers shouldn't be
paying for weights. They know full well that is a lie. All recreation
equipment in Washington state prisons, as well as in most other prisons in the country, is bought and paid for by the prisoners themselves.
The money comes from the profits made by selling goods to prisoners from a commissary (soda pop, cigarettes, etc.) at inflated
prices. Not a penny of taxpayer money goes towards weights and
other recreation items.

The reality is that prison weight rooms are not equipped with any
state of the art exercise equipment. Prison weight rooms are hardly
comparable to a free world gym or exercise club. When politicians
claim that prisoners shouldn't be able to lift weights when free people
have to pay for membership in a gym to do so, remember that we
are paying to lift weights, quite literally with years of our lives. Nothing is "free" in prison, it is all paid for in one way or another.

So, if the two parties most affected by prison weight-lifting—
guards and prisoners—support it, why is it an issue at all? Because
politicians see it as an easy slam dunk to garner publicity and distract voters from real issues such as their agenda to reduce taxes for
the wealthy, limit access to safe abortions, and otherwise make the

rich richer and the poor poorer. No politicians are going to take any type of stand on this issue because prisoners aren't a constituency anyone has to cater to, as they are mostly poor, and unable to vote to boot. The real agenda is take away what modest privileges prisoners have and replace them with idleness. This has historically led to violence and the level of overcrowding in prisons today will only exacerbate the level of conflict.

The political cover is that weight-lifting is a public safety hazard because "criminals are bulking up." Anyone familiar with weight-lifting or exercise knows this is a crock. First off, when was the last time someone was attacked by a weight-lifting ex-con? Secondly, however much bulk someone puts on (many weight lifters train for tone and not bulk) is quickly lost if the person doesn't continue working out. Most released prisoners quickly lose any bulk they gained when locked-up, as weight-lifting, for whatever reason, is not a part of their outside lifestyle. Given the proven health benefits of over 40 years of prison weight-lifting, its detractors have speculation and sheer demagoguery. But, like all other aspects of the hoopla, I can't bring myself to call it a "debate." Facts and reason have nothing to do with the matter. Will a ban on weight-lifting stop prisoners from "bulking up"? I'll keep on doing push ups and calisthenics, as will many others who want to stay in shape. The best shape I've ever been in was after getting out of any basic training, and did we lift weights then? No, just a lot of calisthenics. Guess what legislators have prisoners in so called "boot camps" doing? You got it, a lot of calisthenics. So what's next? A law banning push ups in prison, but not boot camp? Once the weights are gone, what next? Within a year what voter or free person will even remember anything about weights in prison? We know the answer to that one. None.

PRISON TV

LUXURY OR MANAGEMENT TOOL?

Aid and Comfort to the Enemy

Adrian Lomax, June 1995

I've been serving time in Wisconsin prisons since 1980. A lot of
changes in the way these joints are run have come down the pike in
that time, almost all of them for the worse: less recreation, less visiting, less educational and counseling opportunities, more overcrowding, more lockdown time in the cells, and lower wages for
prison jobs. Last October the Wisconsin Department of Corrections
removed all weight-lifting equipment from state prisons. In 1992,
prison officials here imposed a draconian new scheme of property
rules that drastically reduced what prisoners could have. Everything
that prisoners own, aside from their televisions, must now fit inside
a footlocker measuring 16" x 16" x 32".

TVs are not only excepted from the 1992 property rules, they are
excepted from the entire trend toward less and less. Wisconsin prison
officials have steadily expanded opportunities for television view-
ing. The Waupun prison now shows five uncut movies daily on its
closed-circuit institution channel, and the Portage prison offers prisoners basic cable service, ESPN and all. The Green Bay prison,
where I'm now confined, provides state-owned TVs, at no charge,
for prisoners who can't afford to buy their own sets.

It's no coincidence that TV privileges have grown during the same
period when everything else has been cut back. Prison officials gave
us more and more TV precisely for the purpose of keeping prisoners
pacified while the DOC took everything else. In essence, prisoners
have sold their souls for television. We've said to the keep: "Look, you
all can do anything you want to us, so long as you let us watch TV."

When prisoners and their supporters began campaigning to get
televisions into the prisons back in the 1970s, correctional adminis-

trators resisted the idea. But twenty years of observing the effects of television on prisoners has caused the keepers to change their minds. Nowadays, when elected politicians rail against prison TV in order to get votes, prison officials vigorously defend the "need" to keep television in the joint.

The administrators know that television is the most powerful tool they have for keeping convicts docile and submissive. TV privileges are suspended as punishment for infractions, and television is completely denied to convicts in the hole. Prisoners who spend most of their waking hours staring at the tube, as an embarrassingly large number do, pose no threat to the keep. A definite trend I've noticed over the course of my term is that the level of resistance to oppressive actions by prison staff has decreased in direct proportion to the increase in television privileges.

Whenever I pull a stretch in the hole, I'm struck by the huge difference in the extent of social interaction between prisoners in the segregation units and those on the main-line. Convicts in seg talk for hours on end, discussing everything imaginable. In the hole I'll often read interesting articles aloud on the tier, and spirited debate always follows. Prisoners from all different sets and races contribute their views and respond to others. Nothing approaching that level of community can be found in the main-line cell blocks, where prisoners mostly interact with their TVs.

Reading material is like gold in the seg units. All books and magazines that make it into the hole are eagerly devoured and passed from prisoner to prisoner. I've seen convicts perform astonishing feats of fishing, skipping lines from tier to tier and even around corners in order to retrieve printed matter. I've also spent several years working in prison libraries. I can't begin to count the number of times I've seen a main-line prisoner show up in the library, grab a newspaper, turn to the TV listings, write down the times and channels for all the shows, and then leave, never to be seen in the library again.

There is yet another way the presence of television in the joint harms prisoners. The general public firmly believes that anyone who watches TV is living in the lap of luxury, even if they're also packed like sardines into filth-ridden, vermin-infested cells, fed slop, enslaved and forced to work for pennies an hour, deprived of family and friends, and denied all freedom. That belief is incomprehensible to me, but it's very real and extremely popular out there in the world. The fact that we watch cable TV and rented videos sets people's blood boiling, no matter how badly we're treated otherwise. Right-wing cranks continuously scream that the justice system is way too soft on criminals, citing as evidence the fact that prisoners are sitting around watching color TV. Many people are even moved to support capital punishment because they so loath the notion of convicted murders watching TV in prison.

The presence of television carves away at our interests from opposite directions at the same time. TVs allow prison administrators to roll back our rights and impose conditions harsher than they would otherwise be able to get away with, and prison TV also convinces the public that we're living far too comfortably in these joints. A more devastating double-whammy is hard to imagine. Those whose goals are hostile to the cause of prisoners have no more potent a weapon in their arsenal than prison TV.

Just as the prison administration establishment changed its view on TV, prisoners and their supporters must do the same. It's time for us to recognize the real purposes prison TV serves. Nothing gives more aid and comfort to our enemies.

Paul Wright says in these pages that the prisoners' rights movement can be characterized as the struggle for more: more visiting, more education, more access to the courts... I accept that characterization, but the most effective step we can take toward accomplishing our ends is to dump the TVs. It is only because we have television that prison officials have been able to get away with taking everything else. So long as our adversaries can tell the public that we're sitting around watching cable, no grievance we have, regardless how just, will get a fair hearing in the public discourse. Let us bar the gate to this Trojan horse our enemies so deviously offer. Give television back to the keepers; let them watch it.

We Need Social Consciousness, Not Fewer Privileges

Paul Wright, September 1994

In March of 1994 the Florida state legislature passed a law severely restricting how the Department of Corrections could spend prisoner welfare funds. It specifically prohibited the expenditure of welfare funds for cable television, to rent movie videos, televisions, VCRs or purchase other electronic entertainment equipment for prisoners. The law passed on a 37 to 1 vote in the state senate. Corrections officials predicted the move would lead to more violence in state prisons unless the legislature provides other activities to keep prisoners busy.

The Florida DOC does not allow its prisoners to privately own television sets. This law effectively removes all televisions from Florida state prisons.[1] Only a handful of the state's 65 prisons had cable TV. Lawmakers claimed not to like the idea of prisoners watching TV, movies or playing video games.

In Massachusetts former federal prosecutor William Weld was elected Governor as a hardline republican vowing to "get tough on crime." One of his campaign pledges was to rid the state's prisons of television sets. (He didn't accomplish it.)

In Michigan state prisoners recently sought, and obtained, an injunction from Ingham County Circuit Court Judge James Giddings ordering televisions to be made available for purchase. For years the Michigan DOC had allowed prisoners to purchase televisions, then in the months before June, 1994, the DOC did not make televisions available for purchase on its commissary. Judge Giddings ordered on June 8, 1994, "A prisoner may purchase a television set selected by the Department through the institution, equipped with earplugs or earphones, with a price limit of $140."

In Washington state one of the little noticed provisions of the so-called "Youth Violence Initiative," signed into law by Governor Lowry during the 1994 legislative session, was language which prohibits the DOC from showing "X" or "NC-17" rated and non-rated movies in adult prisons. "R" rated movies cannot be shown in juvenile prisons.

Martin Tankleff, a prisoner in Dannemora, New York, reported:

Effective May 26, 1994, the Clinton Main Facility implemented the in-cell TV program and sold the first units. The program is in place at other New York state prisons; Wende, Southport-Cadre, and Attica... After the program was initiated in the other prisons, the administration at Clinton put the vote to the prisoners in August of 1993. What was funny was that within an hour of taking a paper ballot vote, the prison administration came up with numbers in favor of the in-cell TV program.

The program has a catch. Once the in-cell TV program is in effect, packages from family and friends are limited to only two a year. A prisoner can now receive only 20 pounds of food on a birthday and the holiday of his choice. All other packages—such as clothing and toiletries—must come from approved sources: manufacturers, stores and mail order catalogs, etc.

It is my opinion that the reason for the enactment of the in-cell TV program is to reduce the amount of violence inside prison walls. Perhaps that explains why the only other New York state prisons with personal televisions are those that have a history of violence. Administrators feel that if a prisoner has a TV the likelihood of that prisoner violating prison rules will be minimized. Why? Because one of the rules of having a TV is that if the prisoner gets a Tier II or Tier III ticket (the most serious levels of disciplinary violations), he loses his televisions privileges. Also, there will be no violence concerning crowded yard TV's, and more time will be spent in cells, avoiding contact with other prisoners. So far, it appears to have worked in the other prisons. Now let's see how it works in New York's most violent prison.

In 1992 while I was at the Clallam Bay Correction Center (CBCC) in Washington state, the administration began a program of providing free state-owned televisions to those prisoners unable to afford one of their own. CBCC was then in the process of being converted into a maximum security prison with the accompanying restrictions on prisoner movement and recreation activities. A similar program was implemented in 1993 by officials at the Washington Corrections Center in Shelton.

While legislators in Florida are removing TVs, prison officials in Washington are giving them away (albeit with money from the Inmate Welfare Fund). And in New York they are being allowed at selected facilities.

So is TV the opiate of the prisoner masses or the lap of luxury? A number of people, including some prisoner activists, believe it is the former.

Adrian Lomax, a prisoner activist in Wisconsin, would like to actively seek the removal of all televisions from that state's prisons. He is of the view that television results in prisoners sitting in their cells, stupefied, and not taking any steps to improve themselves or their situation. It is easy to say that prison officials must agree with this view or they would not allow TVs in prison. The drawback to this type of approach is that just having the state take away televisions does not build any type of social consciousness. I asked a prisoner who's been doing time since the mid-50's "what did prisoners do before TV?" and he replied "We listened to the radio." All the complaints leveled against TV in prison now were said about the radio then. The problem lies not with television as such but rather what is shown on it. To the extent that programming reflects the dominant political and economic structure and values, then of course it is an indoctrination tool of the worst sort, witness the proliferation of right-wing corporate ideology masquerading as news, i.e. the *McNeil/Lehrer Hour*, the *Rush Limbaugh Show*, etc. Whether or not prisoners watch TV has nothing to do with their level of political consciousness. Political consciousness comes from study and struggle.

The prisoners' rights movement can be characterized as the struggle for "more." Whether it is more rights in the way of mail, religion, court access or more privileges such as recreation, visits, and yes, television. While I myself wouldn't lose any sleep if TVs were removed from all prisons, including my own, I don't think that prison activists should support anything that eliminates any of the privileges or rights that have been gained over decades of struggle.

One point about television is that anyone who wants to be in tune with what passes for popular culture and debate needs to be aware of what is going on, that is reflected on television which is where the majority of Americans get all their information and news. I watch virtually all programs purporting to deal with prison or criminal justice issues simply because I have to be aware of what images are feeding the public's perception of prisons and prisoners. I've come up with more than one article from this habit: to counteract the mainstream media's distortions you have to know what they're saying in the first place.

So far most legislatures are taking away education, weights, visits, etc., but keeping the televisions. It's obvious where their goals lay.

1 The Florida DOC sidestepped the intent of the law by interpreting it to mean the DOC couldn't spend money to buy new TVs. The DOC now repairs and refurbishes the TVs it had in its posession as of 1994. Obviously the DOC is loathe to part with its prisoner TVs.

NOT ALL PRISONER LAWSUITS ARE "FRIVOLOUS"

Chief Judge Jon O. Newman
Second Circuit Court of Appeals, April 1996[1]

There exists today in this country a concerted effort to disparage the vindication of prisoners' rights and to limit opportunities for legal redress. Many in the legal, political, law enforcement and corrections fields are calling for restrictions on prisoner lawsuits. However, the accounts are often misleading.

Individuals and groups throughout this nation are desperately in need of legal representation but cannot afford it. They have important legal rights, but unless a lawyer steps forward to assert their rights, there will be no vindication. One example of such a group are the inmates of our prisons, a group that is understandably not too popular with the public and frequently the object of either neglect or abuse.

Please do not misunderstand. I have no general objection to their confinement. Perhaps a rare few are innocent, and, if so, appropriate avenues of redress should be pursued. Rather, my concern is for the prison population as a whole, nearly all of whom, I accept, have committed crimes for which they must be punished.

But while serving their prison sentences, they retain legal rights. Most fundamentally, the right not to be victims of abuse, as many of them are, and the right to minimum standards of sanitation and habitation, and ancillary rights to practice their religion and maintain access to courts.

A bill is pending in Congress to curtail prisoner litigation and the need for effective representation of prisoners was forcefully illustrated earlier this year by an endorsement of this bill by the attorneys general of four states, including New York.[2] They sent a joint letter which appeared in *The New York Times* which cited three prisoner suits and contended that these are "typical" of prisoner suits.[3] Here is the way they described these three suits:

> Typical of such suits is the case where an inmate sued, claiming cruel and unusual punishment because he received one jar of chunky and one jar of creamy peanut butter after ordering two jars of chunky from the prison canteen. Or the inmate who sued because there were no salad bars or brunches on weekends and holidays. Or the case where a prisoner is suing New York because his prison towels are white instead of his preferred beige.

I wondered about the characterization of these suits, because, though I have seen many prisoner suits that lacked merit, it has not been my experience in 23 years as a federal judge that what the attorneys general described was at all "typical" of prisoner litigation.

New York Attorney General Dennis Vacco was kind enough to respond to my request for copies of the complaints in these three cases. Here is what I learned:

In the peanut butter case, the prisoner did order two jars of peanut butter from the canteen and one was the wrong kind. But he did not sue because he received the wrong product. He sued because, after the correctional officer quite willingly took back the wrong product and assured him that the item he had ordered would be sent the next day, the authorities transferred the prisoner that night to another prison, and his account remained charged $2.50 for the item that he ordered but never received. Maybe $2.50 doesn't seem like much money, but out of a prisoner's commissary account, it is not a trivial loss, and it was for loss of those funds that the prisoner sued.

As for the case of the beige and white towels, the suit was not brought just because of a color preference. The core of the prisoner's claim was that the prison confiscated the towels and a jacket that the prisoner's family had sent him, and disciplined him with loss of privileges. In the case, the prisoner stated, the confiscation, "cause[d] a burden on my family who work hard and had to make sacrifices to buy me the items mention[ed] in this claim."

Lastly, the salad bar claim allegation turns out to be a minor aspect of a 27-page complaint alleging major prison deficiencies including overcrowding, lack of proper ventilation, lack of sufficient food, confinement of prisoners with contagious diseases and food contamination by rodents. The inmate's reference to the food was to point out that basic nutritional needs are not being met. The claim mentioned that the salad bar was available to corrections officers and to prisoners in other state prisons. It is hardly a suit about lack of a salad bar.

I do not mention these cases and the letter of the four attorneys general to pass judgment on their merits, but to remind you that while there are many frivolous claims, those in responsible positions ought not to ridicule all prisoner lawsuits by perpetuating myths about them.

1 The following article is based on Judge Newman's commencement speech to the graduating class of the Brooklyn Law School. We extend our thanks to Judge Newman for granting us permission to reprint his article. -eds.

2 The bill Judge Newman is referring to is the Prison Litigation Reform Act. It was signed into law April, 1996. See: Paul Wright, "Prison Litigation Reform Act Passed," *PLN*, July 1996, p. 1, and: The National Prison Project (of the ACLU), "Prison Litigation Reform Act News," *PLN*, Nov. 1996, p. 6.

3 The letter to *The New York Times* which Judge Newman refers to was sent by the attorneys general of four states: Washington, New York, Indiana and Nevada. Needless to say, *NYT* printed the letter without checking the underlying facts behind it, as Judge Newman did. But the facts are immaterial; the concerted effort by the National Association of Attorney Generals to push legislation eliminating prisoners' ability to access the courts relied on lies, half-truths and misrepresentations. They are silent about the many cases where their prison official clients are found guilty of violating prisoner rights. After all, if responsibility were a concern of theirs, losing prison employee defendants would pay damage awards and defense fees from their own pockets. Instead, taxpayers get stuck with the tab for the state defending prison staff; and the defendants keep their jobs to boot—even after courts rule that they grossly abuse prisoners' human and civil rights! -eds.

PRISON LEGAL NEWS'S TOP TEN NON-FRIVOLOUS PRISONER LAWSUITS

Paul Wright and Dan Pens

Everyone has heard about the Attorney General's infamous list of "Top Ten Frivolous Suits" filed by prisoners. Aside from lying or distorting the facts, the reality is that a great many suits filed by prisoners—usually proceeding without assistance from counsel and with no legal education of their own—do have merit and do win. Every year *Prison Legal News* reports literally hundreds of such cases. The ten cases below are only a small sampling of the type of cases reported in *PLN*. They are excerpted from *just twelve issues* (August, 1995, through July, 1996). In no particular order of importance:

1. A federal court in Massachusetts found that prisoners' Eighth Amendment rights in a 150-year-old prison were violated by massive vermin infestation, fire hazards, and a lack of toilets in the cells prisoners were locked in at night. The resulting use of chemical toilets posed enormous health and sanitation hazards. The court described the sanitation at the prison: "...the unsanitary conditions that attend the use of the toilets in the cells and the emptying of them in the slop sink area call to mind the muck that 'boils up and pours over' in the gloomy second river of hell, the Styx, described by Dante." This isn't Dante, it's the United States in 1995![1]

2. The Court of Appeals for the Fifth Circuit affirmed a lower court order finding the Eighth Amendment rights of pretrial detainees (citizens too poor to afford bail who are held pending trial) were violated by massive overcrowding in the Harris County (Houston,

Texas) jail. The court put the massive overcrowding into perspective when it stated: "Harris County now has more prisoners sleeping on the floor of its detention facilities than the total number of convicted offenders incarcerated in fourteen states." An epidemic of drug resistant pneumonia was traced back to this jail as a direct result of poor ventilation from an overtaxed ventilation system. The epidemic later spread outside the jail. Absent court intervention these inhumane conditions would have continued.[2]

3. On April 5, 1996, a Denver, Colorado district court jury awarded former prisoner Arthur Nieto $1.44 million in damages against Colorado state prison officials for showing deliberate indifference to his serious medical needs. Nieto was imprisoned at the Delta Correctional Facility in 1991 when he developed a cold and sinusitis. The head cold developed into a sinus infection and the infection then spread to Nieto's brain. The prison medical staff ignored Nieto's worsening medical condition despite obvious symptoms, until he was taken to a hospital with a 105 degree temperature and "his eye had bulged out of the socket and was discharging green pus," according to his attorney Robert Ozer. Despite several surgeries and hospitalizations Nieto suffered permanent brain damage that caused his left side to be paralyzed and he has "major cognitive deficiencies." The six member jury awarded Nieto $1.8 million in damages but reduced the award because Nieto had failed to take medication. Ozer noted "he was too disoriented to do that."

4. A federal court in the District of Columbia found prison officials liable for the systematic sexual harassment, rape, sodomy, assaults, insults and other abuses by prison staff of women prisoners in a District of Columbia prison. The court found the physical facilities were dilapidated and a health hazard, medical care woefully inadequate and women prisoners were discriminated against on the basis of their gender by being provided with inferior programs than those available to similarly situated male prisoners.[3]

5. A federal court in California condemned a massive pattern of brutality at the Pelican Bay state Supermax prison. This brutality included: fatally shooting unarmed prisoners in order to break up minor scuffles; placing naked prisoners in phone booth-sized wire mesh cages outside in low temperatures; non-existent medical and mental health care; hog-tying prisoners to their toilets for up to twelve hours as punishment for making noise; and many, many more examples of inhumane treatment. One prisoner was stripped by guards and forced into a tub of 160 degree water. The court held that the pervasive pattern of brutality was known and condoned by high ranking California prison officials. The litigation was initially filed by prisoners; the court later appointed counsel.[4]

6. A jury in Indiana awarded a quadriplegic prisoner $30,000 in damages, finding his rights under the Americans with Disabilities Act were violated. The prisoner was kept in a prison hospital and denied access to all rehabilitative and educational programs offered by the prison, which he was qualified and able to participate in.[5]

7. In a six year period eight different federal court rulings found 27 New York state prison employees in the Clinton Correctional Facility in Dannemora, NY, guilty of assaulting prisoners in such a severe manner that the prisoners' constitutional rights were violated. Damage awards have ranged from $18,000 to $40,000 per beaten prisoner. Different judges have termed the actions of prison guards in these cases "excessive," "cowardly" as well as "quick, efficient, savage beatings." The prisoners suffered injuries ranging from a perforated eardrum, lacerations, bruises and contusions. All the guards sued remain employed at the prison.[6]

8. A jury in Ohio awarded two prisoners $460,800 in damages after finding they had been savagely beaten, without any provocation by prison guards. The jury found that prison guards had "created an atmosphere of reprisal and retaliation at the prison" where the prisoners suffered massive injuries, bruises, contusions and lacerations.[7]

9. A federal appeals court affirmed $150,000 in damages awarded by a jury to a New York state prisoner who was brutally beaten, threatened, stripped naked, placed in a feces smeared cell for eight days, and then denied medical attention for the beating.[8]

10. A federal judge in California ruled that the state's entire prison mental health care system suffered from "gross inadequacies" and "serious constitutional deficiencies." Problems included inadequate staffing and keeping of medical records, no quality assurance, the use of stun guns and tasers on mentally ill prisoners, delays in prescribing medication, and much more. The court found that prison officials, in a court battle lasting over five years, vigorously disputed their liability "even in the face of overwhelming evidence to the contrary."[9]

Between 1992 and 1995 all five of the prisoner cases that were heard by the U.S. Supreme Court—several of which the Supreme Court ruled in the prisoner's favor—were begun as suits filed by prisoners without the assistance of a lawyer. These cases included: prisoners' right not to be exposed to second-hand tobacco smoke; not having to suffer serious physical injury in order to sue guards over beatings; and a right to be protected from sexual assault by other prisoners when there is an obvious danger to the prisoner. These are the cases not mentioned by the Attorney Generals or the DOC's when they talk about prisoner litigation.

1 See: "Chemical Toilets May Violate Eight Amendment in Massachusetts Class Action," *PLN*, June 1996, p. 18. See also: *Masonoff v. DuBois*, 899 F. Supp. 782 (D M 1995).

2 See: "Population Cap, Fines Affirmed," *PLN*, Oct. 1995, p. 17. See also: *Alberti v. Klevenhagen*, 46 F.3d 1347 (5th Cir. 1995).

3 See: "Sexual Harassment Violates Eighth Amendment," *PLN*, Dec. 1995, p. 14. See also: *Women Prisoners of the District of Columbia DOC v. District of Columbia*, 877 F. Supp. 634 (DC DC 1994).

4 See: "Pelican Bay Ruling Issued," *PLN*, August 1995, p. 3. See also: *Madrid v. Gomez*, 889 F.Supp. 1146 (ND CA 1995).

5 See: John Emry, "Prisoner ADA Suit Wins at Trial," *PLN*, March 1996, p. 1. See also: *Love v. Westville Correctional Center*, Case No. 3:94-CV-0371-RM.

6 See: "NY Prisoners Awarded Damages in Beatings," *PLN*, Sept. 1995.

7 See: "$460,800 Verdict in Ohio Beating Affirmed," *PLN*, April 1996, p. 18. See also: *Grimm v. Lane*, 895 F. Supp. 907 (SD OH 1995).

8 See: "$150,000 Jury Award in Beating Case Affirmed," *PLN*, April 1996, p. 21. See also: *Blissett v. Coughlin,* 66 F. 3d 531 (2nd Cir. 1995).

9 See: *Coleman v. Wilson*, 912 F. Supp. 1282 (ED CA 1995) *PLN*, May 1996.

Part III
THE DOWNWARD SPIRAL

Prisons Do Their Damnedest
to Increase the Misery

The legal and moral "principle of lesser eligibility" took root when the English Poor Laws were written. When the Poor Laws were reformed in 1834, the principle was applied to criminals in a somewhat modified form, this time advocating that convicts should be treated *no better* than the least fortunate law-abiding citizen.

That principle is enforced in the U.S. prison system today. As the wages, rights, and living conditions of unimprisoned workers have entered a downward spiral over the last two decades, it has become necessary for the Establishment to re-examine the living conditions of prisoners and exert a downward pressure upon them. If not, you have such uncomfortable happenings as sick members of the urban poor committing crimes so that they can take advantage of what miserable health care opportunities exist in prisons. Cold homeless people intentionally getting arrested so as not to freeze to death. Such events raise disturbing questions about a society. How can prison keep its force as a deterrent, when the lives of so many Americans are already so miserable?

Increasingly, at the urging of politicians and corporate media, the U.S. public demands harsher conditions for prisoners. If the unimprisoned, however, were to question why their own living and working conditions are spiraling downward... Well the answers to that question would pose a considerable threat to the profit-reaping status quo of the bond- and stock-holding class. Indeed, the mean-spirited resentfulness with which many working Americans view prisoners' lives—along the "I wish all I had to do was sit and watch TV all day long" line—is a grim comment on the quality of life of the American working class. It has reached the point where the denial of basic freedoms is no longer even considered a punishment: a fair bit of unpleasantness, preferably bordering on the cruel and unusual, should be thrown in for good measure.

As long as the public's attention is focused on the conditions of prisoners, and they are made to feel that prisoners "have it too good," their own drop in living conditions can be made to seem less intolerable by comparison.

OPPRESSION ON THE RISE IN ARIZONA

O'Neil Stough and Dan Pens, August 1994–April 1996

Arizona has joined the ranks of many other prisons nationwide where oppressive and tried-and-failed barbaric methods of the distant past are being re-instituted.

Neo-fascist Governor Fife Symington[1] and Director of Corrections, Sam Lewis have spearheaded the drive to make the Arizona prison system an environment of suffering, rage and cruelty. Both have no previous experience in corrections.

At a 1994 Republican fund raising dinner, Symington, with Lewis in the wings, announced a new "get tough" program. Symington bragged of the cruelty of one of the facilities being planned: "It will be a hellhole [to which] no man will ever want to go." Lewis boasted later that the catch-all category "troublemakers" will be forced to perform hard labor in the hot Arizona desert without benefit of tools. "They will literally be breaking rocks with their bare hands," Lewis stated. Such "leadership" from the top has given rise to an increase in threats towards and abuse of prisoners by guards who perceive the "get-tough" philosophy as a green light to act out their basest hostilities.

Lewis has consistently demonstrated that he has little regard for the suffering and abuse of prisoners. He has shown equally little understanding of law, and has leaned strongly to the street cop mentality of power and brute force—instead of reason or intelligence—end of the law and justice spectrum. He has faced no less than two contempt of court violations, both for refusing to obey court orders aimed at the prisons under his rule.[2] At a 1994 hearing regarding the *Casey v. Lewis* case—which was designed to provide, among other things, proper law libraries in the state's 29 penal institutions, and assure prisoners' right to access of the courts—his demeanor was defiant and smug. He openly admitted that he told staff not to worry about any fines that might be assessed against them for refusing to obey court orders in *Casey*, assuring them that any fines would be paid by the state.

During the contempt hearing, Special Master Dan Pachoda said that Lewis was being "contemptuous." Pachoda reminded the prison director that he, not Lewis, was running the hearing.

In a separate contempt hearing, Lewis was severely scolded by the court for attempting to impose an adult magazine ban. Any magazines which showed exposed breasts, whether *Playboy*, *Easy Rider*, or *National Geographic*, were slated to be taken in a massive shakedown, and forever banned. This action was in direct defiance of the 1973 *Hook* decree which affirmed First Amendment rights to receive such publications. Attorney John P. Franks, on behalf of the plaintiffs in *Hook*, called Lewis a "tinhorn dictator." "I've never seen a grosser defiance of the federal court in all my life," stated Franks to U.S. District Judge Carl Muecke. Three days before the ban was to go into effect Lewis was forced to rescind the directive. He vowed to reverse the 1973 ruling.

Lewis soon went on a spree of bannings. Taken were:

- Hot pots—and the foodstuffs for them—from the commissary. Other store items, not only those for hot pot use, have been severely reduced. A list of permissible items that was once four pages long is now one page. Large numbers of prisoners go hungry—and get irritated—between sparse prison meals;

- Personal clothing prisoners could obtain with their own funds, such as t-shirts, underwear, socks and blue jeans. Now only state-issue—used and/or soiled—of the very same items is allowed, at a cost to the taxpayer;

- Fans, which prisoners bought or had their families buy for them. In the intensely hot conditions of Arizona, in the poorly ventilated state institutions, fans are very much a necessity, not a luxury;

- CD players and tape recorders. Any radio with a cassette player taping capability is now forbidden. This poses a tremendous strain on those who are illiterate (roughly 72 percent in 1994), whose only means of communication with family was a correspondence tape.

In keeping with this mentality, bills have been taken before the legislature aiming to charge prisoners for medical care. For the few prisoners who have jobs, the average pay is 20 cents an hour.

The system is destined to reach epidemic overcrowding as the new "no parole" law took effect in January, 1994. Anyone sentenced after that date must serve 85 percent of their mandatory sentence before being considered for parole. Another parole-related law now in effect mandates that a parole panel must vote unanimously—not just a majority—for parole, or the parole is denied.

Under Lewis, halfway houses have been closed and most all programs which aided a prisoner's rehabilitation or reintegration into society have either been discontinued or severely cut back.

The 1995 Arizona legislature passed a law that requires the DOC to establish a plan wherein prisoners will be charged a monthly "utility fee." The statute directs the DOC to collect a monthly fee, "not to exceed two dollars per month," from any "prisoner who possesses at least one major electrical appliance." The legislation is purportedly meant to "offset the cost of the department's [of corrections]'s utility expenses." But it is doubtful that the monies thus extorted from prisoners would more than offset the accounting/clerical expenses required to collect the fees.

What "major appliances" do Arizona prisoners have in their cells? Electric ranges? Washer and dryers? No, what the law euphemistically refers to as "major electrical appliances" are television sets—Sam Lewis's electronic baby-sitters. (The fact that the Department of Corrections would take away virtually every other "privilege," yet they allow prisoners to retain their TV sets, speaks volumes about the value that prisoncrats place on television as a mind-numbing prisoner pacifier).

The Coming of the Inevitable

The inevitable prisoner rebellions arrived in early 1995.

In February, the prisoners at the Florence South Unit had a full sit-down work strike in response to the dictatorial rule of the new deputy warden, Angelo Daniel, and his oppressive and unfair practices. Mike Arra, Arizona's champion spin doctor, stated the disturbance would not be tolerated and that "inmates had better learn who is running things."

Following the sit-down strike in Florence, prisoners at the Winslow Kaibab facility staged an uprising that resulted in injuries to three prisoners and one prison guard. About seventy-five prisoners barricaded themselves inside the kitchen after a tactical team fired tear gas and assaulted them with "stingball" grenades, devices that shoot out hard rubber pellets designed to inflict pain. After barricading themselves, the prisoners set fires. The siege lasted approximately six hours. It was evident from the quick use of excessive force by prison guards that they enjoy these kinds of incidents. Many were heard bragging in the following days about how they had pained and injured prisoners. That is precisely the type of attitude that has been instilled in staff by Director Lewis, and condoned by Governor Symington. What neither realize is that the word is spreading of these abuses, and prisoners are likely to respond in kind, returning the same level of brutality and callous disregard being shown to them.

In March 1995 another prisoner uprising erupted. Prisoners at the Safford Graham Unit used rocks and sticks to assault guards and set fires to several living areas and administrative offices. For over five hours the prisoners had free run of the facility. Several shotgun blasts were fired into crowds of prisoners with no regard as to who was in the line of fire and whether or not they were taking part in the melee. Several guards and numerous prisoners sustained injuries during this uprising. Arizona DOC officials have claimed this was "a racial incident between Hispanics and Blacks." The cause, obviously enough, was the level of tension caused by the restrictive policies that have been implemented over the previous year. Everyone had become increasingly fed-up and disgusted, and was ready to do something about it.

New Dictator, Same as the Old Dictator

The tyrannical rule of Sam Lewis came to an end with his resignation in December, 1995. While Lewis proclaimed that treating prisoners harshly would be a deterrent to crime, the opposite appears to be true. The recidivism rate during his reign steadily increased. Many prisoners are leaving Arizona's prisons bent on destruction as they feel that society has supported Lewis's repressive policies, so they will now show society no mercy in turn.

The new prison director, Terry Stewart, is cut from the same mold as Lewis. Already in the short time since Stewart was appointed, he is being termed "just another tin-horn dictator." Shortly after he took the reins of office, Stewart ordered all movies forfeited, and that no future movies be bought or rented. He also canceled all premium cable channels. The movies and cable channels were paid for by the Activities and Recreation fund. This fund receives its revenue from the profits of services paid for by prisoners themselves (commissary purchases, telephone calls, etc.) and not from tax-payer money. He further ordered that all TV systems have a master cut-off switch which "shall be under the direct control of the warden of each facility." As of January 16, 1996, all TV's are cut-off from midnight to 6:00 am, and on weekends from 2:00-6:00 a.m. Each warden can cut off all TV's at his or her discretion, facilitating censorship of various kinds.

Stewart's next focus was on food services. On a state-wide scale any food items that could possibly cause prisoners some degree of pleasure, were removed, with blander fare taking their place.

On December 27, 1995, just days after the new policies were announced, 200-plus prisoners at the Safford Tonto Unit, a medium security facility, went on a rampage, causing extensive damage. Mike Arra, giving the same old line, said it was "a racial incident between Blacks and Whites."

The claim by Symington, Lewis, and Stewart that so called "get-tough" measures somehow deter crime or criminals are supported by no data whatsoever, past or present. Quite to the contrary, ill treatment breeds ill behavior.

Some ranking staff have resigned in protest of the barbaric and cruel policies being implemented. Escapes are rising in response to intolerable conditions, hunger strikes have taken place and the early signs of mass protests—and revolt—are emerging. Human suffering in a barren and desolate environment breeds hostility and rage. Sooner or later it will seek expression such as the massive riots of the late 1960's and early 1970's in prisons nationally; a fact Symington and Stewart obviously lack the experience or basic intelligence to understand.

While such tough talk and actions sounds good to a fed-up public in these troubled times, it rings hollow. It is counter-productive, dangerous, expensive and a waste of people's hard-earned tax dollars. More prisoners do not a safer community make. And, for those who occupy these cells, harsher and tougher policies and restrictions do not reform, but rather, deform.

1 In September, 1997, Symington was convicted in federal court on multiple charges of fraud. He resigned as governor shortly thereafter.
2 See: *Hook v. Arizona*, 907 F. Supp. 1326 (DC AZ 1995)

THE RESURGENCE OF CHAIN GANGS

Dan Pens and Paul Wright, July 1995 - July 1996

In early 1995, Ron Jones, then-Commissioner of the Alabama Department of Corrections, announced that the DOC ordered 300 sets of leg irons to the tune of $17,000 so prisoners could be put to work for the first 90 days of their sentences. Jones was carrying out a directive from Republican Governor Fob James that new prisoners be denied television and put to work—as well as subject to a number of other torments—so that their first impression of prison "be so unpleasant that they never come back."

Previously, Alabama only used minimum security prisoners, without shackles, to pick up litter around highways. But over half of Alabama's prisoners had medium and maximum security classifications which did not allow them to work outside of prison compounds. "With leg shackles, we can put higher risk inmates to work on the outside," said Jones. He stated the chains would allow five prisoners to work in a group with eight feet of chain between the prisoners.

The first 320 prisoners forced to labor were transferred to the Limestone Correctional Facility in Capshaw from other prisons in Alabama. Upon laboring on chain gangs for a given period of time, prisoners are transferred back to their prison of origin.

The idea for bringing back chain gangs was first broached—where else?—on a radio talk show by Fob James during his campaign for governor in November of 1994. The chain gangs are used along heavily traveled interstate highways in full view of motorists. This would indicate that the actual purpose of the chain gangs is as a political propaganda tool of the Republican Governor rather than any penological goal of impressing newcomers to the Alabama state prison system.

Chain gangs were originally used in Alabama as a means of building roads for the automobile age. Indeed, prisoners on chain gangs did much of the work of "modernizing" the South after the Civil War. There is an unbroken line between slavery and the use of prisoner slave labor, and this is especially apparent with chain gangs. The "Black codes," a group of laws governing the behavior of newly freed African-Americans, criminalized a broad spectrum of harmless behavior to assure the state and private interests a continued source of slave labor.

In the first incarnation of chain gangs prisoners were chained together in groups of five and forced to labor for twelve hours a day along Alabama roadsides. Prisoners were given axes, shovels, blades and bush hacks to cut grass and pick up litter alongside roadways. Prisoners who refused to work on the chain gang were handcuffed to a metal post, with their arms above their heads, and were forced to stand on an uneven surface all day in the hot sun. Chain gangs were abolished throughout the South by the early 1960s. But when asked by the media, no one in the Alabama Department of Corrections could recall when or why they had done away with chain gangs in the first place.

Human rights groups have a better memory. In response to the announcement by the state of Alabama that it was reintroducing chain gangs, Amnesty International called on the U.S. government to investigate the practice, saying that it possibly violated international treaties on human rights and the treatment of prisoners. The use of leg irons for example is clearly outlawed under United Nations Standard Minimum Rules for the Treatment of Prisoners. Amnesty also called on Alabama to halt the practice. The statement read: "This is the first time in recent history that the practice of shackling inmates together in chain gangs has been sanctioned by a U. S. state, and is clearly a retrograde step in human rights."

Human rights notwithstanding, politicians know a good sound-bite when they see one. As states try to outdo each other in the ill treatment of their prisoners, it follows that when someone comes up with a doozie others will copy it. So it was when Alabama announced that it would reintroduce prison chain gangs. Media from around the world descended on Alabama to catch the spectacle of prisoners shackled together working in the sun. Other states jumped at the chance to obtain similarly favorable photo-ops.

In June of 1995 Arizona became the second state to reinstate prison chain gangs. On May 15, 1995, the Arizona DOC began putting prisoners in shackles along Interstate 191 at the prison near Douglas. Some 26 minimum and medium security prisoners were put to work cutting weeds alongside the road. The prisoners were shackled individually. Inside the prison, some 20 prisoners from protective custody used sledgehammers to break up concrete for erosion and flood control projects. The prisoners were dressed in blue long-sleeved shirts with vertical orange stripes. A two foot piece of steel chain was padlocked to each prisoner's ankle.

By July of '95 anti-prisoner demagoguery had gone so far that reactionary Arizona Governor Fife Symington announced his intention to implement a program in which the state's 119 death row prisoners would be put to work breaking rocks and digging holes. Also instituted were chain gangs for prisoners in lock down units throughout the state. Symington announced this scheme on the heels of a state Supreme Court stay of execution for death row prisoner Luis Mata. Symington made the chain gang announcement at a press conference, flanked by the parents of the woman Mata was convicted of killing.

"This is clearly a campaign speech aimed at getting votes," asserted Denise Young, of the Arizona Capital Representation Project. She criticized Symington for turning a purely legal matter into a political issue and for exploiting the victims of Mata's crime for his political purposes.

In November 22, 1995, a memo was distributed to Arizona's death row prisoners, relating to an order issued by then-DOC chief Sam Lewis. The memo stated in part:

> Arizona Revised Statute 31-151 gives the Director of Corrections authority to require that each able bodied prisoner in the department engage in hard labor for not less than forty hours per week... Be advised that the statutes *do not* exempt you, because of your Death Sentence, from performing work or hard labor, nor is it unconstitutional. This program is an opportunity for you to improve your status while on Death Row. Even though hard work may be considered as punishment, it does provide you with a means to earn some money [10 cents an hour -*eds.*], and you are able to perform an assignment

that is beneficial to the inmate population as a whole, while working in the garden growing vegetables.

Inmates refusing to turn out for work assignments shall be forcibly
removed from their cells and taken to the work site, secured accord-
ingly [chained to a post under the hot Arizona sun-*eds*.], and then be
subjected to the disciplinary process. (emphasis in original)

Donna Hamm, a prisoners' rights activist in Arizona, noted at the
time that the program is certain to be challenged in court and could
spur "a physical protest in the form of a riot or disturbance... I'm
just astounded they would open themselves, their staff, not to mention the public, to that type of risk, all for the sake of [Symington's]
self-aggrandizement. It's just an insane idea."

Douglas Cole, Symington's Press Secretary, provided a justification for the forced-labor program: "The food they grow, the taxpayers
don't have to pay for. Before, these guys were costing us lots of
money because they were sitting idly in their cells."

Not surprisingly, this reasoning is complete bunk: On December
7, 1995, the first work crew of 23 death row prisoners was put to
work weeding and hoeing a 19-acre field within the State Prison
Complex in Florence. The 23 prisoners were supervised by nine
armed guards on horseback. The prisoners are paid 10 cents an hour.
The total pay for 23 prisoners for 8 hours is then $18.40. Assuming
the cost for the guards is $11 per hour (not to mention the cost for
boarding and feeding the horses), the total pay for nine guards for
8 hours is $792. Mike Arra, the Arizona DOC spokesman, said the
vegetables raised on the 19-acre plot would supplement food purchased by the DOC to feed prisoners. Considering the labor cost for
the death row vegetable patch averages $800 a day, those are some
mighty expensive vegetables.

One must look to the "political capital" Symington reaps from
this "get tough" program—widely covered by the Arizona press—
to understand that $800 a day is a bargain. Especially considering
that it is a campaign expense footed by Arizona taxpayers.

By November '95 Florida had become the third state to institute
prison chain gangs. The prisoners work in 20 man crews, supervised
by three gun-toting guards. Prisoners are assigned to serve on the
chain gang as punishment for disciplinary infractions. Florida's "lib-

eral" Governor Lawton Chiles was supportive of the plan, despite some tepid opposition voiced by DOC officials.

The prisoners wear ankle chains, but are not shackled together. This infuriated Republican state Senator "Chain Gang" Charlie Crist, who wrote the legislation. Crist had wanted five prisoners chained to each other, the way Alabama did it. "We said chain gangs, and that means chained together."

But Crist was overruled by Florida DOC Secretary Harry Singletary, who deemed that more work could be done if prisoners were not shackled together. "This is the whole reason to send people out to work every day," said a DOC spokesman. "You can get more work done if people are not chained together."

The Executive Director of the National Prison Project of the ACLU, Alvin Bronstein, said the ACLU would not file suit against the Florida chain gang law. He said the Alabama chain gang led to more injuries among prisoners—such as when someone tripped and fell, dragging others down with them. Bronstein said the Arizona and Florida versions were more humane, but they were still a step backward to a long discredited practice.

"It has nothing to do with public safety," Mr. Bronstein said. "It has to do with treating people harshly, as if this would have an impact on crimes, which it won't."

Stan Czemiak, Assistant Secretary for operations at the Florida DOC, said he was unsure the chain gangs would be the deterrent "Chain Gang" Charlie wants, and questioned whether they were worth the extra manpower they necessitate: inside prison, two guards oversee 144 prisoners, on the chain gangs, three guards are required for 20 prisoners.

By early December there were 140 prisoners working on what the DOC calls "restricted work crews" at seven prisons across Florida. DOC officials said that 200 prisoners would soon be working on the chain gangs. By this time prison officials were eagerly discussing expanding the program for the following year, and petitioned the legislature to approve the required additional funding.

It should be noted that it is seemingly possible for prison officials to go too far. With all his effort to cause prisoners tremendous pain, it seems that Alabama's prison commissioner, Ron Jones, finally passed the acceptable limits of hateful zealotry. On April 26th, 1996, Jones was abruptly fired after announcing plans to put female prisoners on chain gangs. Jones had ordered the warden at Julia Tutwiler State Prison for Women to develop a chain gang policy. He said the plan was in reaction to male prisoners who had filed lawsuits challenging (among other things) that Alabama's chain gangs were exclusively applied to male prisoners. "There's no real defense for not doing the females," said Jones.

Governor Fob James apparently thought there was no real defense for putting the women in chains, and announced Jones' resignation the following day. "There will be no women on any chain gang in the state of Alabama today, tomorrow or any other time under my watch," the governor said.

Governor James first learned of Jones's plan by reading about it in the morning papers. James, who had taken a hands-off policy on the prison chief's "get tough on prisoners" initiatives, decided it was time for Jones to step down. He announced that Jones would return to his old job of warden at the Elmore Correctional Facility near Montgomery.

Chain Gangs Challenged

The new wave of chain gangs was not uniformly popular among state citizenry, nor its prison population. Arizona, after Symington and Lewis revived the chain gang there—and tacked on the idiotic practice of making the participation of both death row and prisoners in lock down units mandatory—is a good example.

In one instance of citizen resistance, on June 12, 1995, Donna Hamm—a long time prisoner rights activist, former judge, and organizer for the prisoners' rights group Middle Ground—grabbed a bullhorn, jumped in her car, and drove to the roadside where prisoners were being paraded in chains for an ogling contingent of media. The prisoners were working alongside Wilmot Road, not far from the Arizona State Prison (ASP) Complex in Tucson. She parked her car legally along the shoulder of the road beyond a parked DOC truck with an armed guard.

Ms. Hamm was soon told to move her car by DOC hacks, and refused twice, telling them that she was legally parked and as a free citizen had every right to be there. The guards reported the incident to ASP Warden Sam Sublett, who had the Pima County Sheriff's office called.

Donna spoke to the 20-prisoner chain gang through a bullhorn for about an hour, with reporters present. After the media left, two Pima County deputies told her she was being placed into "administrative detention" while they handcuffed and pat-searched her. When the prisoners saw her being handcuffed they sat down and refused to work. A second work crew inside the prison also sat down and refused to break rocks for the media contingent who had arrived to collect footage of the spectacle.

Ms. Hamm was released after a brief spell in "administrative detention." She was told that if she returned to the chain gang site with her bullhorn she would be arrested.

"I am going to exercise my First Amendment rights," with a court order if necessary, she said. "I will not be intimidated by the Department of Corrections or, quite frankly, the Pima County Sheriff's Office." Ms. Hamm quickly sued the DOC and Pima County Sheriff for their harassment of her.

On the death row chain gangs there have been several violent incidents. DOC spokesman Mike Arra recounted to the Arizona media that on that December 20, 1995, one prisoner was grazed in the cheek by a birdshot pellet fired to break up a quarrel. Arra said a second incident occurred on January 10, 1996, when a fight broke out between prisoners Jake Hughes, 33, and Aryon Williams, 34. He recounted the incident to the Arizona media: "A mounted corrections officer, who was armed with a shotgun ordered Hughes and Williams to stop fighting, but they ignored his repeated orders. The officer then fired a warning shot to get their attention. Williams raised his arms over his head, but Hughes took the opportunity to choke Williams with a handle of a hoe. The officer then shot Hughes below one knee, hitting him with more than 50 birdshot pellets. One pellet struck Williams in the leg." Arizona prisoners recount a different story. As one prisoner noted, "You must understand that the newspaper here doesn't report everything that happens."

In regards to the December 10th incident in which Arra claims one prisoner was merely grazed in the cheek: "The newspaper reported only one prisoner was shot, when four were shot! One was pretty bad. Three pellets cannot be removed from that prisoner's back because they are too close to his spinal cord. The newspaper won't print that because it may cause people to rethink working death row prisoners [on the chain gang]."

Another reason that chain gangs originally fell into disuse that no one seems to remember was that prisoners tended to scamper off when given the opportunity. Within the first month one prisoner escaped from Alabama's chain gang, and two escaped in the first two weeks of Arizona's program by riding off in a DOC vehicle. As more prisoners escape, or are ferried off by motorists, we'll see how popular the chain gang remains with reactionary politicians, or what vicious means they develop to keep prisoners in their place.

DYING FOR ATTENTION

The Atrocity of Prison Health Care

Paul Wright, April 1994 - June 1996

Washington's Murderous Medicine

On May 16, 1994, Gertrude Barrow, a prisoner at Washington Corrections Center for Women (WCCW) at Purdy, died of a perforated, chronic gastric ulcer with acute peritonitis. Essentially this means she died because a hole in her stomach permitted fluids to leak out, causing inflammation and eventually fatal infection in the surrounding areas. Barrow had been convicted of a narcotics charge with a 31-month sentence and was due to be released September 14, 1994.

Barrow had sought medical care in the days before her death. Her symptoms included severe pain, inability to keep down food, and the vomiting of blood. She was turned away from the infirmary and sent back to her cell.

Two days before her death she was admitted to the prison infirmary, where she was treated with contempt and disrespect. On one occasion a few hours before Barrow's death, Barrow vomited and a nurse gave her a towel and told her to "clean it up yourself." Barrow was not even seen by a physician until the day before she died. Prison doctor Christopher Badger diagnosed her pains as due to gas, constipation, and, after an x-ray, kidney stones.

On April 19, 1994, Barrow was returned to Purdy from a pre-release center suffering from chills, vomiting, and an inability to eat. Despite the kidney stone diagnosis she received no pain medication. On May 3, 1994, she contacted attorneys at Evergreen Legal Services. Attorney Patricia Arthur wrote to the state Attorney General's office about Barrow's condition, requesting that Barrow be provided with prompt medical attention. Assistant Attorney General Cheryl Casey claimed the letter was forwarded to the prison. Later, after Barrow's death, prison spokesperson Kim Shafter stated Casey had instructed her not to comment on prison officials' inaction.

Patricia Arthur referred to Barrow's death as a "preventable tragedy. It's really indicative of the problems with the health care system there at the WCCW."

After this embarrassing incident the Washington Department of Corrections contracted with David Dugdale, its medical consultant, to determine which errors resulted in Barrow's death and how such deaths could be prevented in the future. Dugdale, an assistant medicine professor at the University of Washington, familiar with treating such conditions, stated that the standard treatment for Barrow's case would have included placing Barrow in an intensive care unit, taking of blood samples, and prescribing powerful antibiotics to fight infection, combined with medication to reduce the risk of Barrow going into shock. Instead, the only medication Barrow received before she died was a mild painkiller. And, due to Dr. Badger's faulty diagnosis of her condition, she was also given medications which were potentially harmful.

Along with Dugdale the DOC contracted Larry Pogue, a doctor with the Group Health Cooperative and Holly Wallaston, a nurse practitioner and director of nursing at the King County, Seattle, jail. After visiting the WCCW, interviewing the medical staff and warden, the trio issued a report.

The report cited:

- Communication difficulties between Dr. Badger and nursing staff. It stated that better communication would have likely led to better monitoring of Barrow's condition, and hence an earlier detection of her deteriorating condition.

- Misinterpretation of the clinical findings in the case. This was due to the fact that most of the clinical management was done by a physician's assistant (PA) with "at a distance" oversight by Dr. Badger. A small calcification in Barrow's left kidney which was misdiagnosed as evidence of a kidney stone, was cited as an example. The report concludes this was due to lax oversight of the PA— named Ingram—by Dr. Badger. It said: "Dr. Badger feels that PA Ingram needs close supervision while acknowledging that he does not provide it. This is a recipe for continued, potentially life-threatening, yet preventable problems."

- There were numerous errors of omission in Barrow's medical records. For example, her last three admissions to the WCCW infirmary did not have an evaluation—medical history and physical—by either PA Ingram or Badger. Such evaluations are standard practice in hospitals and are mandated by WCCW policy.

- The report also found "...[A] serious shortage of health care providers capable of independent diagnosis and treatment of patients." For 540 prisoners WCCW had one physician, one PA and one contract physician. "The sick call load of 40 to 60 patients per day makes it essentially impossible to do thorough evaluations of each inmate, errors of omission that occurred in Ms. Barrow's case are essentially guaranteed in such a setting."

The report concluded: "Dr. Badger is ill-prepared for the position as medical director of a correctional facility. Based on a review of his job application and our interview with him, it is apparent that it has been a long time since he has been engaged in a primary care medical practice." Badger also lacked experience in administering programs. "His orientation to the special aspects of medical care behind bars was essentially non-existent—it is no surprise things have not gone well." It was recommended that Badger receive orientation from other DOC doctors on how to administer the WCCW medical program and have his clinical load lightened so that he could better administer the medical section and implement operation changes in the WCCW infirmary.

The Washington state Department of Health (DOH), which inspects DOC facilities, also conducted a report on Barrow's death. The DOH reached a similar conclusion as the DOC. The DOH report stated that the WCCW health care system did not offer "safe, appropriate" care for prisoners. DOH investigators found 16 deficiencies when they compared the prison's policies with actual practices. The DOH also concluded that WCCW staffing levels did not allow for "reasonable" workloads. Medical personnel did not keep complete records, failed to track Barrow's ulcer condition and did not follow up on previous medical problems. The report also described WCCW hospital staff's flippant attitude towards Barrow. The DOH recommended that the DOC come up with a plan to correct WCCW infirmary deficiencies within 10 days. However, there was no way for the DOH to compel the DOC to comply with its orders, nor to take any action to ensure that Washington state prisoners receive safe, adequate health care.

More Murder by Negligence

Another preventable tragedy occurred later in the same year. On December 12, 1994, Stanley Watson died of a heart attack at the Washington State Reformatory (WSR) in Monroe. While heart attacks do happen and can be fatal, Watson's death could have easily prevented. So easily that his death smacks of negligent homicide.

On December 11, 1994, Watson went to the WSR hospital on two separate occasions complaining of chest and back pains. The first time he was given no treatment whatsoever by Dr. Meloche—the physician on duty. Watson was given an appointment to see a physician's assistant the next day, but he was dead by then.

After dismissing Watson, the WSR hospital staff had instructed him to return to the clinic if his symptoms got worse. Watson duly returned the same day, and was seen by nurse Yeager. He complained of continued chest pain, and classical heart attack symptoms. He was given nitroglycerin and Nifedipine and sent back to his cell. The next time Watson was seen by WSR medical staff it was in response to Watson's collapse at his work place, the kitchen. His lifeless body was transported from there to Valley General Hospital. Efforts to resuscitate him were unsuccessful and he was pronounced dead at 8:11 a.m. on December 12.

That would have probably been the end of it, except for a complaint filed with the DOH. The complaint was supported by affidavits from two prisoners stating that Watson, in the last hours of his life, had complained to them about not receiving appropriate medical treatment. The DOH initiated an investigation that revealed shoddy treatment and gross negligence.

On March 8, 1995, the DOH issued its final report. The five-page summary stated:

> Documentation in the medical record did not meet Washington State Reformatory infirmary standards as evidenced through lack of dated entries and order, missing authentication of entries and failure to record self-administered medication distribution.... Appropriate

follow through with inmate's hypertension and medication was not documented in the inmate's medical record.... Facility did not have policies/procedures/protocols for handling of the life threatening emergency of myocradial infarction [(MI), i.e., a heart attack.]

In addition the "Facility lacked documentation of appropriate licensure and CPR/First Aid of two personnel involved with inmate's care."

The report referred to a "statement of deficiencies," which was four pages long. The statement revealed that Watson was given an electrocardiogram—or EKG, a device to measure heartbeats—on the eleventh. The DOH stated:

> [I]t was learned that at the time of the inmate's death, it was policy to have EKGs read by a computer. The computer system was old and had a history of significant problems in accurately interpreting EKGs. No qualified staff read the EKG that was completed in the clinic on 12/11/94. The EKG was determined 'normal' by the computer when it was not normal. This policy and practice did not support safe care.

Among the other deficiencies found were:

- "Two of the four personnel involved with the investigated case did not have current licenses on file at WSR. One was a physician assistant and the other a Registered Nurse. The PA license on file had expired on 9/9/93 and the facility had no verification of any license for the RN."

- "Three of the four medical personnel attending the deceased inmate did not have documentation of current CPR/First Aid. During this complaint investigation, a notice was observed posted in the infirmary nursing station asking how many staff needed CPR/First Aid updates. Six (6) of the seven (7) names of those responding stated they needed an update."

- "The facility did not have protocols/procedures for the assessment, care and transfer of inmates who might be at risk for infarction (MI). This patient showed typical symptoms of MI. No assessment except vital signs was documented on the first clinic visit of 12/11/94. Differential screening was done on the second visit including administration of Nifedipine, nitroglycerin, monitoring of vital signs and a computer read EKG. All documentation, except the computer read EKG, suggested a possible MI, yet the patient was not transferred to a hospital where further assessment, not provided at the infirmary, could have been provided."

- Despite having a history of hypertension, Watson was given no follow-up care upon arrival at WSR. "Documentation and practice did not support continuity of care and physician orders for medication were not followed."

Other problems with WSR medical records were: illegible signature; undated infirmary entries and medication records; and many hospital entries—including Watson's last two—which were not timed.

The DOH report also noted: "None of the four medical personnel who attended [Watson] were available for these surveyors to interview during the investigation survey." At least one of these medical personnel were not qualified to be practicing medicine. One of the PAs who attended to Watson in his dying hours began working at WSR after being "asked to leave" his prior place of employment at Fircrest, a home for the developmentally disabled. He was asked to leave due to his inept care of patients. Unfortunately for prisoners, he was then hired by the DOC.

What makes deaths like Barrow's and Watson's all the more tragic is the fact that they were easily treatable and completely preventable. All that was required was a minimum amount of medical care. Instead, a confluence of untrained, incompetent, and—more importantly—uncaring, DOC medical personnel condemned these, and other, prisoners to death as surely as if they had pointed a gun at their heads and pulled the trigger.

Washington Doctors Fit Only for Prisoners

The terrible quality of care dispensed in Washington state prisons becomes more understandable when one examines the hiring practices of the DOC.

In September, 1994, the DOC hired James McGuire to work as a psychiatrist at the McNeil Island Corrections Center

(MICC). His work involves diagnosing and prescribing drugs, conducting mental health counseling to sex offenders, referrals, and crisis intervention.

Before landing the Washington job, McGuire was a practicing psychiatrist in Alaska. There, he entered into a sexual relationship with one of his patients, Karma VanGelder. The sexual relationship violated ethical and professional standards, and lasted some five and a half years. As a result, McGuire lost his license to practice psychiatry in Alaska and moved to Washington, where he was promptly hired by the DOC. Because the loss of a medical license in one state doesn't affect the license in another, McGuire was able to practice psychiatry in Washington.

On June 2, 1995 the Medical Quality Assurance Commission held a hearing to determine whether McGuire's license should be suspended. In an ironic situation, the Department of Health was the party seeking revocation of McGuire's license and was represented by the Attorney General's office. All the while McGuire is working for another state agency, the DOC. To further complicate the situation, both parties appeared before yet another state agency—the Commission—to consider the matter.

VanGelder, a former Alaska state trooper, testified before the hearing that while treating her for multiple personality syndrome McGuire forced her to have sex with him. McGuire admitted to having had sex with VanGelder. He was in group therapy at the time of the hearing. Kevin McGovern, McGuire's psychologist, said he thought McGuire was gaining insights into his problem and could safely handle the work at McNeil. McGovern supported this statement by saying that McGuire isn't interested in having sex with grown men.

DOC spokesman Veltry Johnson stated that the DOC had been fully aware of McGuire's Alaska suspension, but had hired him anyway based on his "qualifications," as well as the fact that his Washington license hadn't been suspended, yet. Patricia Robinson-Martin, an assistant to DOC boss Chase Riveland, further stated that the DOC was well aware of the Alaska incident, but McGuire was the only applicant for the position. She noted: "It is difficult to attract psychiatrists to work in prisons."

The state asked the medical board to suspend McGuire's license to practice medicine in Washington based on the Alaska suspension. The DOH asked that McGuire's license be suspended, but that he be allowed to continue a limited practice treating adult male prisoners with close supervision and continued psychiatric treatment for himself. The medical commission rejected both requests pending a full hearing.

On July 10, 1995, the Commission issued its report. In its findings of fact, conclusions of law and final order, the Commission made some interesting comments. Among them were that: Dr. McGuire is taking 20 milligrams of Prozac a day to treat his own mental illness and has to attend sex offender therapy sessions once a week with his therapist in Portland, Oregon. He and his wife of 17 years, Janice McCrimmon, have also undergone marriage therapy.

The Commission concluded that McGuire had "clearly committed unprofessional conduct" and had lowered the public perception of all medical professionals. The Commission held: "The Respondent, however, should neither be allowed to provide individual psychotherapy to any male inmates nor to provide psychotherapy to patients in a private practice setting. The Respondent's limited practice of treating only the male inmates at the Corrections Center does contribute to the public welfare and does not represent a danger to the public." The Commission held that revoking McGuire's license would be a "purely punitive act."

In its final order the Commission indefinitely suspended McGuire's authorization to practice as a physician and surgeon but then stayed the suspension as long as McGuire complies with the Commission's terms and conditions. Under the order McGuire can only treat male prisoners at MICC and can only practice psychopharmacology and diagnostic psychiatry; he is forbidden to give individual or group therapy. He is to be supervised by a psychiatrist who will submit quarterly reports to the Commission, and must continue his sex offender therapy. McGuire was fined $1,000 and prohibited from using alcohol or mood altering drugs as long as he is in therapy. In essence, the Commission held that McGuire is fit only to treat prisoners.

Another Winner

In October, 1994, the Washington state Medial Quality Assurance Commission began an investigation into the qualifications of Dr. Thomas McDonnell, the supervising physician at the Washington Corrections Center (WCC) in Shelton. The investigation began after the Commission received two anonymous complaints. On April 8, 1996, the Commission suspended McDonnell's medical license, finding he had exposed prisoners and employees at WCC to "an unreasonable risk of harm" due to poor quality of care, misdiagnosis or failure to supervise care. The Commission stated that it had "determined that an immediate suspension was necessary to prevent the likelihood of harming patients."

In suspending his license, the Commission cited the cases of seven prisoners where McDonnell acted, or failed to act, in a way that caused the prisoners to be hospitalized. One patient was given such large quantities of drugs by McDonnell after a dental procedure that he stopped breathing twice. He was resuscitated and transferred to an Olympia hospital.

In another case a prisoner, Mike Langford, reported to the infirmary with symptoms of blurred vision, increased urination, thirst, weakness and headaches. A PA examined the prisoner and noted symptoms for diabetes, even though Langford was taking medication for high blood pressure. McDonnell was told of the Langford's condition and, without examining him, began insulin treatment, despite the PA saying that he personally had had no experience treating diabetes. McDonnell went home and did not monitor the patient's condition. Langford went into spasms and had severe abdominal pain as his kidney functions collapsed. He was transferred to a hospital. When he returned to WCC, McDonnell did not examine him. The Commission concluded that a reasonable physician would not have relied on a PA to examine, treat and diagnose such a patient.

Another prisoner showed signs of respiratory failure after McDonnell prescribed medication, again without examining the patient. The prisoner suffered a seizure en route to the hospital. The Commission scheduled a hearing for McDonnell on April 29, 1996.

This was not the first time McDonnell has had a brush with the medical regulatory establishment. McDonnell, who is paid $80,000 a year by the DOC, had his license suspended in 1986 after he admitted abusing controlled substances during and after office hours. He also admitted to fraudulently using his position to obtain large quantities of controlled substances. The DOC hired McDonnell in 1993 after he completed substance abuse treatment and regained his medical license. DOC spin doctor Veltry Johnson told reporters he did not know when the DOC first became aware of allegations of poor quality medical care. One would think it would have begun with the first patient to be hospitalized due to McDonnel's negligence and incompetence.

That the DOC would hire a sex offender for a shrink and a drug addict as its chief medical doctor should come as no surprise. As described above, medical care for Washington state prisoners is disastrous.

The Washington DOC has begun charging Washington prisoners at least $3 each time they seek medical care or treatment. That such "treatment" is being provided by an assortment of incompetents seems to be of little consequence to lawmakers despite the fact that these people are being paid salaries—like McDonnell's—in the $80,000 range. Can't a "real" doctor without a drug or sex problem be hired for that amount? In legislative posturing political hacks whine about prisoners getting "free health care." Given the choice, few prisoners would willingly seek treatment from people like McGuire, McDonnell, the people who were undeniably instrumental in the deaths of Barrow, Watson and others. Yet the fact of incarceration deprives prisoners of that choice. The result is medical murder at $3 a pop.

The current Washington DOC budget calls for a reduction in the amount spent on prisoner health care. It is likely that medical treatment will only get worse. And Washington State is by no means unique in its quality of prisoner health care. Similar horror stories are played out in prisons across the country. The media pays little attention to the deaths of prisoners, however, so the scope of the problem remains below the radar screen of public attention, and well below warranting popular outrage.

"JUST SAY NO"?

Philip McLaughlin, September 1994

Imagine if you will, a syringe in my hand. I am coming toward you. I have six men in riot gear, armed with gas canisters and hand-cuffs, to back me up. You will take my mind-altering drugs or you will pay for your decision not to! I don't care if you don't under-stand what it is you're taking. I don't care if it muddles your brain, tranquilizes or zombifies you. I don't care about your fears or the painful side effects. I have no moral problems with invading your body with mind-altering drugs. You will take these drugs now or we will attack!

You have a question? Hmm. No, I'm sorry—you cannot "Just Say No."

How many people are aware of the practice of administering mind-altering drugs against a person's will by the staff of U.S. pris-ons and mental institutions today? I am talking about psychotropic drugs prescribed by state-employed psychiatrists. These drugs are supposedly for the use of "helping" prisoners with a variety of mental ailments from minor depression to schizophrenia.

I first became aware of the practice of forcing drugs on prisoners when I came to the Special Offenders Center (SOC) in Monroe, Washington. I was transferred from an Intensive Management Unit at Washington Corrections Center in Shelton where I had been housed for several months. They suspected I was suffering from a severe depression, so they sent me to SOC for an evaluation period of 3-4 months. As of this writing, I have been at SOC over three months, and will soon be leaving since my depression has disappeared. This startling change in my psyche happened "miraculously" once I was taken out of the hole at Shelton—where conditions were, and remain, inhumane and—not surprisingly—*incredibly depressing*!

While at SOC I have witnessed a nightmarish process in which various prisoners have been forced to take drugs. Many of these psychotropic drugs cause mild to severe side-effects. Common side-effects include, but are not limited to: muscle spasms; restricted or delayed movement; blurred vision; nausea; extreme thirst and "cotton mouth"; memory loss; extreme fatigue; loss of concentration; and slowed thought processes. In rare instances death has occurred as a result of taking new and dangerous drugs because either the testing on these experimental drugs was not thorough enough to discover possible serious side-effects, or the side-effect medication supposed to accompany the drug was either not administered, administered too late, or administered in too low a dosage.

The process of placing a prisoner on involuntary medication status involves the recommendation of the prisoner's assigned counselor and then an involuntary medication hearing. The hearing is a mere formality, a kangaroo court composed of a panel of biased state-employed staff. The panel includes two psychologists, one psychiatrist, one hearing officer, and the prisoner's designated counselor. The counselor states his/her case to the doctors. The prisoner is allowed to make a statement. The hearing officer operates the tape recorder, and is responsible for ensuring that the hearing is conducted properly. Two of the doctors must vote in favor of the involuntary medication status, and one of the doctors must be the psychiatrist. Once enacted, the involuntary medication status is reviewed once every six months by the same panel. The determining factors the doctors are supposed to go by are whether or not the prisoner presents a "serious threat to the safety of himself, others or property" when not on medication.

And what actions by a prisoner are commonly defined as being serious safety threats? Unpredictable violent episodes? Breaking windows? Assaults? Perhaps in some cases these reasons are used, but the instances I have witnessed were much less serious.

One prisoner by the name of Mike threatened to punch a guard during a heated argument. He never did so and has no history of assaultive behavior, but was placed on involuntary medication status nonetheless. Now, as a result of the drugs, he looks and acts like a zombie; his thought process is much slower and he has stiff muscles which curl his wrists back. When he walks he has the swinging arm motions of an ape.

Another man by the name of Bill was recently placed on involuntary medication status because he informed the superintendent that his "psychic employers" would have him taken care of if he was not released from SOC immediately. Bill believes he is a psychic general employed by a secret psychic forces agency in Washington, DC, under the supervision of the President himself. He repeatedly informs the counselor and officers that the President has ordered his immediate release, and that he is currently being kept at SOC illegally. Admittedly, he's a little loony. But the "threat" he supposedly poses to the institution is no more than the delusional ramblings of a harmless old man.

Another prisoner, Pat, was placed on involuntary medication status because he ripped up some of his generic state-issued clothing. For this act he was considered to be "a serious threat to property."

And the list goes on.

Obviously, the stated justifications in the above-mentioned examples are not reason enough to force a man or woman to ingest mind altering drugs against their will. But in my opinion, even if these prisoners were actually threatening and assaultive, it still would not justify playing God with another human being and forcing that person to ingest mind-altering drugs. This is a basic human right that should never be violated for any reason. If someone is assaultive, and it is absolutely necessary that they be controlled, then isolate them from others. If someone is suicidal, then watch that person closely or change the circumstances which make them miserable. If someone is a threat to property, then limit that person's access to damageable property. But never should any man have a right to force another man or woman to ingest mind-altering drugs against their will. Never!

And what happens to those prisoners who exercise their choice to "Just Say No"? If a person on involuntary medication status refuses to take his prescribed drugs, he will be forced to do so by the "goon squad." A group of five or six guards gear themselves up in black jump suits, combat boots, helmets, shields, and gas masks. They then proceed to the prisoner's cell. If the prisoner refuses to cuff-up so a shot can be administered to him, then the goon squad sprays him with a powerful gas that, on contact with skin, literally gives the victim the sensation of being on fire. It also burns the lungs and blinds. The goons spray again and again until the prisoner complies or passes out. They then hold the prisoner down while a nurse administers a shot with a hypodermic needle in the man's behind. All this is done in the name of "mental heath," part of a supposed "benevolent" effort to help people with mental illnesses. What it really is, is a legal way to exert total control over people through the use of drugs. And who's to stop it? If prisoners have very little support or sympathy from the public, or defenders of any kind, then mentally ill prisoners and patients—most of whom have no concerned family or friends to help from the outside—have even less.

The legal background for this torturous treatment is a 1989 Washington State Supreme Court case *Washington v. Harper,* which held that before a prisoner could be drugged he or she had to be found incompetent by a court and the drugging had to be necessary for medical reasons. The state appealed and in 1990 the U.S. Supreme Court held that it does not violate due process to forcibly drug prisoners, even those who have never been found incompetent and are not mentally ill, as long as prison doctors claim it is necessary. They did this while acknowledging the severe and permanent damage that powerful psychotropic drugs inflict. Since then, there have been numerous cases which have upheld prison officials' ability to forcibly and indefinitely drug prisoners.

STATE MURDER MACHINES PICK UP SPEED

Dan Pens, May 1996

Fifty-six people were executed by sixteen states in 1995. That was the highest national figure since 1957. Between 1976, when the Supreme Court reinstated the death penalty, and September of 1995, there have been 313 executions in the U.S. The 1995 total of 56 executions is a distinct increase from recent years. There were 23 in 1990, 14 in 1991, 31 in 1992, 38 in 1993, and 31 in 1994. The total for the first half of this decade, 193, already surpasses the 117 carried out in all of the 1980's. There were only three in the '70's, and 191 in the '60's.

Congress eliminated the $20 million in federal funds for all 21 death penalty legal resource centers across the U.S. Opponents of the post-conviction centers say they needlessly delay justice. "The centers have functioned like brakes," says Michael Rushford of the Criminal Justice Legal Foundation. "Congress is taking the brakes off."

The death penalty centers opened in 1988 in response to a rising death row population and an inadequate number of lawyers to handle the cases. Proponents of the federally funded centers proclaimed that they would speed-up the execution process. Now many of those same people support closing the centers—for the same reason. Opponents of the closures, however, say that it will only slow down the process.

"The centers provide an expertise that we can't provide," says Esther Lardent of the American Bar Association's Post-Conviction Death Penalty Project, which recruits law firms to handle death penalty appeals. "Nobody practices this area of law except for people in these centers, and a few other people scattered in the country."

Steve Hall, administrator of the Texas Resource Center's Austin office, says that capital punishment laws are ever-shifting, so recruiting experienced counsel is "tough work. People do two or three [death penalty appeals] and feel like they've done their civic duty."

About half of the 3,029 prisoners on death row were being represented or assisted by experienced capital punishment attorneys from the 21 centers at the time of the center's closures. That is probably the crux of the issue. After those experienced attorneys were scattered to the winds, death row prisoners have a more difficult time mounting effective challenges to the legal issues in their cases.

HOUSTON, TEXAS

Death Penalty Capital of the U.S.A.

Dan Pens, December 1994

In one week of September 1994, six separate capital murder cases were tried in Harris County, Texas. Some legal observers consider this to be a national record.

Houston is the largest city in Harris County. "They may have done this in the Old West, but there's been nothing like this in modern times," said a law professor at the University of Houston. The six capital murder cases tried in one week in Houston were more than any other Texas county tried in an entire year. Dallas County, which encompasses Dallas-Fort Worth, tried only one capital murder case up to September of 1994. In Harris County the number was over twenty.

District attorney John B. Holmes, Jr., who has been referred to as the "killingest man" in America, vows to continue his murderous ways: "I am not about to alter my rigid views on capital justice, and if the public doesn't like it, they know what they can do about it."

By the end of 1995, there were a total of 313 state sponsored murders in the U.S. since the United States Supreme Court reinstated the death penalty in 1976. In that same period of time the State of Texas murdered 104 of its citizens. That's 33 percent of all U.S. executions since 1976! (Texas didn't resume executions until 1982). Of the 104 put to death in Texas, Harris County proudly claims 33. As of December, 1995, there were 404 people on death row in Texas, at least 111 of whom were tried in Houston.

These figures clearly make Texas the leading state murderer in the U.S., and Harris County has the distinction of leading any other county in Texas. If you are put to death by the government in this country, there is a better than one-in-ten chance that your case was tried in Houston, Texas!

The practice will probably continue, or even accelerate in the years to come. Former Texas governor, Ann Richards (D), never issued a death row pardon. The new governor, George W. Bush (R), son of the former president, is a staunch supporter of the death penalty. Both candidates called for "speeding up" the appeals process in death penalty cases, presumably so the state can murder its citizens faster and with less "interference" from federal courts.

Fast Food Style Death Penalty Defense

What better place than Harris County for a lawyer to develop and market the same techniques that made fast food a commercial success in this country? Joe Frank Cannon, acting as a court-appointed attorney, has "defended" eight men who currently await execution in Texas. Two other former clients have already been put to death. His strategy for those capital punishment cases is simple: work fast.

"Juries don't like a lot of questioning, all of these jack-in-the-box objections, going into every little detail, so I've never done it," explains the veteran lawyer. He openly boasts of hurrying through trials like "greased lightening."

Harris County judges are elected by popular vote, rather than being appointed to the bench. The judges have complete control over appointing and supervising attorneys in death penalty cases. Some judges, concerned about budgets and docket backlogs, appoint attorneys who are known for trying cases rapidly rather than zealously. District Judge Miron Love has said, "The number of death penalty cases currently pending could cost taxpayers a minimum of $60 million."

Mr. Cannon discovered that by working as fast as possible, he could gain more appointments from those judges worried about budgets and crowded dockets. He has explicitly marketed his fast approach to trying murder cases.

Veryl Brown, a former Harris County prosecutor, swore in a 1988 affidavit filed in the Houston federal district court, about a conversation he had witnessed between Cannon and then-Judge Joseph Guarino four years earlier. In this conversation Cannon asked to be appointed to the capital murder trial of Jeffrey Modey. "Mr. Cannon represented to the judge that if he was appointed he could have the case completely tried within two weeks," Mr. Brown stated in his affidavit. Cannon was subsequently appointed to the case, which was tried in 19 days, and resulted in a death sentence for Modey.

Candelario Elizondo, a past president of the Harris County Criminal Lawyers Association, swore in a 1988 federal court affidavit that it is "generally reputed in the Harris County legal community" that Mr. Cannon received capital appointments "because he delivers on his promises to move the courts' dockets."

In a how-to article written by Mr. Cannon years ago, he scorned death penalty defense attorneys who "slavishly 'follow the book' for weeks or months" in the courtroom. To illustrate his fast food approach to capital defense, he pointed to the 1981 case of Willie Williams. With relatively light questioning by Cannon and his junior co-counsel, a jury was selected in just five days—three or four times faster than was, or is, typical in the Harris County Courthouse. The trial consumed only parts of two days. After deliberating for only four hours, the jury returned a death sentence.

As America watched with fascination how the criminal justice system works in the O.J. Simpson murder trial, they saw a rich defendant buttressed by the best attorneys that money can buy. Most people fail to realize that the vast majority of defendants in death penalty cases are too poor to retain their own attorney. They must rely on whatever defense is put up by the attorney appointed to their defense by the court. In Texas, these publicly paid attorneys receive only a modest fee, just $10,000 for a typical murder trial, or up to $40,000 for one that lasts several months.

Stephen Bright, an Atlanta based capital-punishment defense expert, wrote in the *Yale Law Journal* that "Poor people accused of capital crimes are often defended by lawyers who lack the skills, resources and commitment to handle such serious matters." Citing court records, he gave several examples including:

• An Alabama lawyer who was so drunk during a capital trial that the judge found him in contempt and sent him to jail. After a day's delay, the lawyer returned, the trial proceeded and the death penalty was imposed.

• A Georgia lawyer who missed key testimony of a witness he subsequently cross-examined because he was outside the courthouse parking his car.

• Attorneys from Texas and elsewhere who, in front of juries, referred to their clients as "niggers" or "wetbacks."

Mr. Cannon, now 75 years old, has been known to sleep in court during more than one of his capital murder trials. He denies this, but the allegations are supported by affidavits from, among others, a former assistant who at the time of the trial was only a few weeks out of law school. Appellate lawyers trying to have the 1984 conviction of Calvin Burdine overturned noted that Mr. Cannon's case file contained only three pages of handwritten notes. Cannon asserts that the appellate attorneys intentionally lost or destroyed the rest of his notes, though he concedes that "nobody would believe me."

In the Burdine case, Cannon made plain legal blunders. In one meandering cross examination of a police detective he opened the door to otherwise inadmissible testimony portraying his client as the leader, rather than the follower, in a two-man robbery that resulted in murder. "It was an incredible blunder, which there is no justification for," says Randy McDonald, a former prosecutor who defended Burdine's crime partner. Burdine is now on death row. His partner, even though evidence indicated he was responsible for at least one of the fatal knife thrusts, got a 40-year sentence.

Critics point to sloppy work on vital legal procedures in other cases tried by Cannon. Consider the case of Carl Johnson, now on death row, who was another Cannon client. Johnson was convicted of robbing a convenience store and fatally shooting a security guard, who had fired his weapon at Johnson first. Johnson claimed he pulled the trigger only out of reflex and didn't mean to kill. But Mr. Cannon failed to inform jurors that they could spare his life if they found his actions to be a "reasonable" response to provocation. In its opinion reviewing the case, the Texas Court of Criminal Appeals said unequivocally that the evidence "raised the issue of provocation" and that the trial judge should have explained this potentially life-saving point to the jury. Ordinarily such a clear mistake would be grounds for setting aside a death sentence. But because Mr. Cannon failed to mention the concept of provocation at trial, the court said, Mr. Johnson was barred from bringing the issue up on appeal.

Harris County continues to try capital murder cases at a record pace. Although Mr. Cannon is no longer taking capital murder cases, his low-budget, fast food approach to trying cases must still be used by his successors. How else can Harris County try capital cases at such a record setting pace? Maybe they should put a sign out front of the courthouse that says "33 Fried So Far." But maybe their already strapped budget would not be able to support the labor incurred changing the numbers on the sign every time the executioner murders a new victim.

DEMANDING DEATH

Mumia Abu-Jamal, September 1994

Michael Alan Durocher, of Florida's Death Row, wrote to the Governor, literally begging for death. Governor. Lawton Chiles agreed, signed his death warrant, and Durocher sent him a thank you note.

On August 25, 1993, at 7:15 a.m., Durocher, 33, got his wish.

California's death row convict, David Mason, fired his appellate lawyers, saying he was both willing and ready to breathe his last in the gas chamber. Mason, 36, angrily decried what he called the "industry" of lawyers who capitalize off of appeals in capital cases. Even after his last ditch change of heart, where he sought life, his case came to symbolize the growing incidence of death row prisoners who demand death. There is, however, a critical difference between perception and reality.

There are approximately 2,600 men and women on Death Row in the U.S. [The figure was 3,054 by December, 1996 -eds.] To date, only 26 people have volunteered to be executed; less than one percent. The Washington, DC-based National Coalition to Abolish the Death Penalty has assembled facts on this phenomenon detailing the race of those persons choosing execution and found that twenty-one Whites have done so, while only two Black, two Latino, and one man of unknown ethnicity have done so. Whites have made up over eighty-percent of those who have demanded their own death.

No meaningful analysis of the incidence of volunteer executions can take place without noting who does so. Whites constitute less than 51 percent of all Death Row prisoners in the U.S., so why are over 80 percent of the volunteers White? How does a bare minority of Death Row, become an overwhelming majority?

Nationally, Blacks constitute roughly 46 percent of state prisoners. In 35 states, new court commitments for Blacks entering prison stands at 51.3 percent of all admissions, according to the U.S. Department of Justice Statistics. Increasingly, since the rebellions of the '60s, prisons have become Blacker and Blacker. A threatening milieu to White prisoners, among them, those on an increasingly Blacker Death Row.

For far too many African-Americans, imprisonment has become a warped rite of passage, a malevolent mark of "manhood" that denies Black men entry into more socially acceptable realms of economic activity. For Whites, however, even working class ones, it is a mark of social expulsion, and affirmation of one's outcast status. Alienated from a social order that has prescribed death, and further alienated from a younger, Blacker, more militant prisoner either on death row or in general population, is there any wonder that the majority of prisoners who have opted for death have been White? To this must be added the onslaught from the federal judiciary which has eviscerated the Writ of Habeas, thereby thickening the atmosphere of despair that pervades Death Row. For all on Death Row— White, Hispanic, Asian, Native American, women—the regime of lockdown, loneliness, and hopeless waits for death exacts a terrible psychic, spiritual, psychological toll. Fear of approaching, advancing lassitude, the loosening bonds of loved ones, the specter of prison as a foreboding old folk's home—all these things play a part, more crucial than admitted, in the headlong rush for death.

As long as conditions on the Row are soul-killing by design, there will continually be those who would rather die than live another day in these man made hells.

Part IV
WORKIN' FOR THE MAN

Prison Labor in the U.S.A.

Perhaps no aspect of penology is more germane to the understanding of the U.S. penal system than the use of prisoner labor. Yet it remains rife with complexities.

First and foremost, no prison in the country could function without the use of prisoner labor in the kitchen, laundry, groundskeeping, maintenance, and janitorial duties. It is for this reason that Supermax and control unit prisons—in which the imprisoned are confined in their cells for 22-24 hours a day—are always built near a minimum-security prison. The lower security prisoners are made to perform the labor necessary to keep the control unit functioning. Were it not for these prisoner workers, the cost of hiring "free world" wage earners to operate every aspect of a control unit—or of any high security prison for that matter—would quickly skyrocket.

Most mainline prisons, however, require only about a quarter to a third of their imprisoned to perform the day-to-day upkeep chores. What, then, to do with the remaining "idle hands"?

The articles in this chapter explore some of the emerging trends that answer this question. But the "answers" have ramifications which reach far beyond the prison walls. While imprisonment itself is obviously a form of social control, various side-effects of mass imprisonment are being used in subtler ways to control society at large. The effect of prison labor in undermining the solidarity of outside workers and eroding whatever strength outside labor may have is a prime example. Not only are the jobs of U.S. workers being moved by corporations to lower costing labor in Third World countries, but increasingly they are being moved into U.S. prisons.

SLAVES OF THE STATE

Paul Wright, May 1994

Many people have the mistaken impression that slavery was outlawed or abolished in the United States after the civil war by the passage of the Thirteenth Amendment. Unfortunately, that was not the case. The Thirteenth Amendment reads: "Neither slavery nor involuntary servitude, except as punishment for crimes whereof the party shall have been duly convicted, shall exist within the United States, or any place subject to their jurisdiction." The effect of the Thirteenth Amendment was not to abolish slavery but to limit it to those who had been convicted of a crime.

The reality was made apparent in the aftermath of the civil war when large numbers of newly freed Black slaves found themselves "duly convicted" of crimes and in state prisons where, once again, they labored without pay. It was common practice for state prisons to "lease" prison labor out to private contractors in a modern form of chattel slavery. This situation led the Virginia Supreme Court to remark in an 1871 case, *Ruffin v. Commomwealth*, that prisoners were "slaves of the state." All that has changed since then is that the state is less honest about its slaveholding practices.

Until the 1930s most state and federal prisons were largely self-sufficient, producing most of the goods and food they consumed and even producing a surplus, for sale, of food and some industrial products. In many states prisoners even served as armed guards (until the mid-1970s the state of Arkansas held some 3,000 prisoners with only 27 civilian employees) and many other functions which required minimal investment by the state. Prison self-sufficiency and excess production for profit largely ended during the mid-1930s when the U.S. was in the midst of the depression and both unions and manufacturers complained about competing against prison-made products on the open market.

One of the laws passed was the Ashurst-Sumners Act (1935) which prohibited the transport in interstate commerce of prison-made goods unless the prisoners were paid at least minimum wage.

Prison labor did not start to become a major issue again until the 1980s. Until then most prison-produced goods were either for use within the prison system or sold to other state agencies, license plates being the most familiar example. This began to change with the massive prison building and incarceration binge. In a 1986 study designed to reduce the cost to the government of its prison policies, former Supreme Court Justice Warren Burger issued the call for transforming prisons into "factories with fences." In essence, prisons should once again become self-sustaining, even profit-producing, entities requiring minimal financial input from the state.

While some think that slavery—i.e., unpaid, forced labor—offers enormous profit potential for the slave owner, there are historical reasons slavery is no longer the dominant mode of economic production. First, the slave owner has a capital investment in his slave: regardless of whether the slave is working or producing profit he must be fed, housed, and so on, in minimal conditions to ensure the slave's value as a labor producer remains. With the rise of industrial capitalism in the 18th and 19th century capitalists discovered that capitalism has its boom and bust cycles characterized by over-production. Thus idle slaves would become a drain on the owner's finance because they would still require feeding, housing, etc., regardless of whether they were working. However, if the slave were "free" he could be employed at low wages and then laid off when not producing profit for the employer, the wage slave was free to starve, free to be homeless, and so on, with no consequences for the owner.

Another reason chattel slavery was inefficient compared to wage slavery was that the slaves would occasionally revolt, destroying the means of production and/or killing the slave owner. More common and less dramatic were the acts of sabotage and destruction that made machinery, with its attendant capital investment, impractical for use by slaves. So by the middle of the 19th century wage slaves employing machines could out produce, at greater profit for the factory owner, chattel slaves using less easily damaged, more primitive machinery.

The problem slave owners of old faced was what to do with non-producing slaves. Today's slave owner—the state—faces the opposite problem of having idle slaves who must be fed, clothed and housed whether or not they produce anything of value. The current thinking goes that any potential profit produced by prison slaves is better than none.

Some of the proponents of prison slavery try to disguise it as a "rehabilitation" or "vocational" program designed to give prisoners job skills or a trade which can be used upon their release. This is not the case. First, almost without exception the jobs available in prison industries are labor intensive, menial, low skill jobs which tend to be performed by exploited workers in three places: Third World dictatorships, and in the U.S., by illegal immigrants or prisoners. Clothes and textile manufacturing are the biggest example of this. Second, because the jobs don't exist in the first place the job skills acquired are hardly useful. Does anyone expect a released prisoner to go to Guatemala or El Salvador to get a job sewing clothes for the U.S. market at a dollar a day? Third, if it's rehabilitation then why not pay the prisoner at least minimum wage for his/her work? Fourth, it ignores the reality that the U.S. has at least 8 or 9 million unemployed workers at any given time, many of them highly skilled, who cannot find jobs that pay a meaningful wage to support themselves. So-called "job retraining" programs are a failure because all the training in the world won't create jobs with decent wages. In pursuit of higher profits—by paying lower salaries— U.S. and transnational corporations have transferred virtually all labor intensive production jobs to Third World countries.

The U.S. has little problem condemning the export of prison-made goods from China. What makes this blatant hypocrisy is the fact that the same criticisms leveled by the U.S. government against Chinese prison-made goods can be leveled at U.S. prison-made goods. Prison-made goods from California and Oregon are being exported for retail sales. In a supreme irony, the California DOC is marketing its clothing lines in Asia, competing against the sweatshops of Indonesia, Hong Kong, Thailand and of course, China. The Prison Blues brand of clothes, made by prisoners in Oregon, has annual projected sales of over $1.2 million in export revenues. U.S. State department officials were quoted saying they wished prison-made goods were not exported by state DOC's because it is being raised as an issue by other governments. Namely the Chinese, which have cited U.S. practices in response to criticisms. For their part, the Chinese have announced a ban on their export of prison-made goods while the U.S. is stepping up such exports.

California prisoners making clothes for export are paid between 35 cents and $1 an hour. The Oregon prisoners are paid between $6 to $8 an hour but have to pay back up to 80 percent of that to cover the cost of their captivity. As they are employed by a DOC-owned company this is essentially an accounting exercise where the prisoners' real wages are between $1.20 to $1.80 an hour. Still competitive with the wages paid to illegal immigrant sweatshop workers here in the U.S. and wages paid to garment workers in the Far East and Central America.

Fred Nichols, the administrator of Unigroup, the Oregon DOC prison industries, has said: "We want them to work in the same environment as on the outside" in terms of hiring interviews and such. Yet obviously this does not include the right to collective bargaining and union representation.

While the particulars may change, the trend continues towards increased exploitation of prison slave labor. Some states, especially those in the South—such as Texas, Arkansas, Louisiana—still have unpaid prisoners laboring in fields supervised by armed guards on horseback, with no pretense of "rehabilitation" or "job training." In those states the labor is mandatory, refusal to work brings harsh punishment and increases prison sentences served.

In 1977 the Supreme Court decided *Jones v. North Carolina Prisoner's Labor Union,* which removed court protection for prison union organizing. Efforts to obtain the minimum wage for prisoners through litigation have been largely unsuccessful, with courts bending over backwards to read exemptions (which are not written) into the federal Fair Labor and Standards Act (FLSA).

In Washington the state offers a lot of incentives for private businesses to employ prison slaves. Class I venture industries pay no rent, electricity, water or similar costs. They are exempt from state and federal workplace safety standards and pay no medical, unemployment or vacation/sick leave to slaves who have no right to collective organizing or bargaining. In a case like this we are seeing welfare capitalism where private business is getting a handout from the state at taxpayer expense. One which, will largely swallow the profit paid back to the state under guise of taxes, room and board, etc., by the prisoner. To the extent that prison slaves are forced to pay state and federal taxes there arises the question, linked to the right to vote, of taxation without representation. If forced to pay taxes like any other citizen, under the guise of rehabilitative or vocational employment, then why not the right to vote given other workers and taxpayers?

Workers on the outside should also be aware of the consequences that prison slave labor poses for their jobs. Ironically, as unemployment on the outside increases, crime and the concomitant incarceration rate increases. It may be that before too long people can only find menial labor intensive production jobs in prisons or Third World countries where people labor under similar conditions. The factory with fences meets the prison without walls.

TEXAS PRISONERS BUILD THEIR OWN CAGES

Dan Pens, September 1996

Texas increased its prison population over the past ten years from 37,000 to a soon-to-be 145,000. At one point, the lack of prison space kept a backlog of 35,000 state prisoners in county jails. All told, the state paid more than $650 million in court-imposed fines because of overcrowded prison conditions.

In the early 1990's Texas voters approved $2 billion in bonds for an unprecedented prison expansion program, but according to Wayne Scott, director of the TDCJ Institutional Division, the new beds were brought on-line for $1.5 billion.

"We built 75,000 prison beds in four years—that's like building the fourth largest prison system in the country," said Scott. "And we were able to do it ahead of schedule and under budget."

There were two main reasons the state was able to accomplish this gargantuan feat, and do so at a cost estimated to be one-half of the national average for prison construction: the use of a prototypical (cookie-cutter) design done by in-house architectural teams, and the extensive use of unpaid prisoner labor.

"Almost all of the finished items that go into the prisons are manufactured by the prison inmates in our state, including the bed, mattress, the pillow, the combination sink and toilet, the stainless steel chase wall, the light fixture, and the door that fits into the cell," said Scott. "The only thing that we didn't manufacture that goes into the cell are the walls and the floors that are poured-in-place concrete."

That will soon change, however, in the next round of construction. Because the state expects to fill up its remaining 10,000 empty beds by the fall of 1996, it has already embarked on further expansion. The state plans to add 12,000 new beds at existing facilities.

According to Scott, the TDCJ has set up batch plants at each of the proposed construction sites where unpaid prisoner laborers will actually manufacture the concrete cells.

"By doing that, we're able to make a maximum security cell for about $35,000 per cell," says Scott. "The national average for such a cell runs between $80,000 and $100,000."

According to Scott, prisoners will be trained to make the forms, put them in place, and pour the concrete walls and floors. They will also provide the labor for putting up the cells as well as support facilities, and will do almost all of the painting and landscaping for new facilities.

Texas currently has more than forty prison industries, including a steel furniture plant that produces parts for new prisons. In 1995, these prison industries produced more than $100 million worth of goods and services—all with unpaid, virtual slave labor, not only for prisons but also for other state agencies, cities and counties.

As far as the latest construction effort goes, Scott says that the only work that will be contracted out to private entities will be some construction management functions and some of the electrical and plumbing work. All electronic devices will be installed by the manufacturer in order for the warranties to apply.

THE GLOBAL ECONOMY BEHIND OHIO PRISON WALLS

Danny Cahill, March 1995 - April 1996[1]

In an effort to market prisoners as cheap labor the Ohio government has unveiled the Ohio Offshore Industries Project (OSSI). This marketing campaign offers companies a vast pool of cheap prison labor as an attractive alternative to foreign-based production. Companies have been moving overseas to take advantage of cheap labor, and the government hopes to keep these companies in the U.S. or lure them back by offering prison laborers. Overall the project is an effort to stop economic decline, and to help reduce the cost of mass incarceration.

Ohio's Department of Rehabilitation and Corrections (DORC)[2] has entered into a contract to supply space and laborers to a private firm named Unibase. Unibase is a data processing company that has eighteen of these work programs in prisons across the country.

The work involves entering data into computers, and prisoners are paid a base rate of $0.47 an hour, plus an incentive pay based on keying speed. The incentive pay rate was repeatedly lowered until it reached a point where workers cannot key in data fast enough to earn more than the base pay of $0.47 an hour. Unibase is attracted to this cheap labor, as well as the fact that prisoners cannot legally organize unions, and are not covered by Workers Compensation or the federal Fair Labor Standards Act (FLSA). Prisoners can't voice complaints except at the risk of incurring the arbitrary discipline of prison officials, and can be hired, fired or temporarily laid-off at will.

At the Lebanon Correctional Institution, Unibase has the highest disciplinary rate of any job assignment. Prisoners working for Unibase forfeit educational, treatment and religious programs. Unibase workers at Lebanon must even forgo laundry services because the laundry schedule interferes with the Unibase workers' schedule. They have difficulty getting showers or going to commissary for the same reason.

Prison officials are telling the public that this type of work program is helping the economy by preventing the loss of U.S. jobs to cheap foreign labor markets. They say they aren't taking jobs away from U.S. workers on the outside, but creating new jobs for staff and supervisors. However, before Unibase opened the work program at the Lebanon prison, the same general manager who runs that program closed a data processing office in Kentucky and let go of all of the workers. The equipment and work was shipped directly from the closed Kentucky office to the prison in Ohio. So in this case it did cost free U.S. workers their jobs.

A number of other companies have voiced their interest in the prospect of exploiting Ohio's prison labor force. Two companies have already signed private person contracts with Ohio Penal Industries (OPI) to use prison labor at the Chillicothe Correctional Institution (CCI). (OPI differs from OSSI in that state employees supervise prisoner laborers and operate the work program themselves, instead of the work programs being run directly by outside contractors and companies, as with OSSI.)

In April of 1993, Konica Business Machines, Inc.—a Windsor, Connecticut-based company—signed a private person contract with OPI to use prison labor to recondition Konica copiers. Prisoners fresh out of a vocational training program for Office Machine Repair at CCI were recruited to work under the OPI-Konica contract. Prisoners were paid between 35¢ and 47¢ an hour for their labor. The reconditioned copiers were eventually sold or leased by Konica to other companies in Ohio and other states.

The contract between OPI and Konica was terminated in May of 1994 because Konica experienced legal problems related to the contract. Evidently, there was some concern about the legality of an out-of-state company using prison labor to produce products which were sold or leased on the open market in Ohio. In addition, the reconditioned copiers were labeled as "Reconditioned By Konica," when in fact the copiers were reconditioned by prison labor. There were no markings or other indications on the finished products to show that prisoners had done the work.

In August of 1995 OPI signed a private person contract with Perry Corporation, a copier dealership based in Lima, Ohio, to recondition copiers. The OPI work area for reconditioning copiers is being retooled and prisoners reorganized to begin reconditioning copiers for Perry. The prisoners will be paid the same wages as in the past for private person contracts. The contract with Perry is for OPI to initially recondition 200 copiers. Perry has promised to use OPI and prison labor in the future to recondition several hundred copiers. With the passing of Senate Bill 2 in 1995, Ohio greatly increased the number of Community Corrections Programs, and will have an ever-increasing number of prisoners available to anyone who wants to profit from their labor.

[*Editors' Note*: In mid-1997 Ohio Department of Rehabilitation and Corrections media contact Joe Andrews stated that the Ohio Off-shore Industries Program had been terminated due to "public outcry," and Ohio no longer operated any joint-venture programs using prison labor. A call to Unibase, however, found that Unibase continues to operate in Lebanon, Warren and Orient Correctional Institutions through Ohio Penal Industries.[3]]

1 Some of this material appeared in William Ridenour, "Exploitation of Ohio Prison Labor," *PLN*, April 1996, p. 10.
2 Ohio's Department of Rehabilitation and Corrections uses the acronym "ODRC." Some Ohio prison activists prefer DORC. -eds.
3 Interviews with Joe Andrews and Lynn Blodgett, Unibase president, by Daniel Burton-Rose, June, 1997.

WORKED TO DEATH

Danny Cahill and Paul Wright, October 1995

The unprotected use of prison labor leaves prisoners open to the possibility of extreme abuse. One example is the prisoners from the Franklin County Workhouse who were paid about $5.00 an hour to separate metal with their bare hands from the ash stream at a trash-burning power plant run by Shaneway in Columbus, Ohio. The Workhouse was directly across the road from the plant, making the supply of work-release prisoners even more convenient. The prisoners worked without any protective clothing or equipment. Work-release prisoners were actually working directly in the ash stream from a power plant, the largest known source of dioxin in the United States. Prisoners worked in toxic ash which contained arsenic levels of 2 1/2 times those allowed by OSHA standards; cadmium levels at 5 times; lead at 138 times; and dioxin at levels 770 times the ambient air in the community. All the work-release prisoners working in the ash stream had visible skin problems consistent with symptoms of chloracne caused by dioxin exposure. The Workhouse used the prisoners for at least a year and a half, and possibly as long as four years. Nonviolent offenders serving short sentences of 6 months or less in county or city jails are a perfect marginal transient population for deadly work.[1]

Another related horror story took place in the Eastern Oregon Correction Institution (EOCI). Prisoners in one work detail were ordered to remove asbestos which was hanging off of pipes and bag it for disposal, without any type of protective clothing for either the prisoners or the guard who was supervising them. A state fire marshal had ordered the material to be removed, and prisoners were assigned to do so. The prisoners spent about 45 hours removing the asbestos dressed only in prison khakis and cotton work gloves.

Both the prisoners and their supervisor experienced pain in their lungs, coughed up black fluid and had other health problems shortly thereafter. One prisoner, Clarence Wallis, attempted to notify EOCI officials of the asbestos and filed a grievance requesting removal from the work detail or that he be provided with adequate protective clothing. After this and other complaints, the prison hired a professional asbestos removal company to remove the asbestos, and they took more than 1,130 pounds of it from the prison attics.

One year prior to this incident an asbestos assessment report had been completed alerting prison officials to the fact that the asbestos in the prison attics pose a serious health risks to the inhabitants and employees of the prison. The Ninth Circuit Court of Appeals later found prison administrators deliberately indifferent to the danger the asbestos posed to prisoners and staff. In such conditions, even a relatively short prison sentence can turn into a lingering death sentence.[2]

1 Prisoners forced to work in toxic conditions may wish to read, *Fruit v. Norris*, 905 F.2d 1148 (8th Cir. 1990), which held that "Prison inmates are protected from punishment for refusing to perform an unconstitutional assignment. For prison officials to knowingly compel convicts to perform physical labor which constitutes a danger to their health, or which is unduly painful, constitutes an infliction of cruel and unusual punishment." The court went on to say that certain "acts or omissions [are] so dangerous (in respect to health and safety) that knowledge of the risk can be inferred."-eds.

2 *Wallis v. Baldwin*, 70 F.3d 1074 (9th Cir. 1995).

MICROSOFT "OUTCELLS" COMPETITION

Dan Pens, April 1996

In the Seattle area, home to software giant Microsoft, it's not uncommon to hear the phrase "Microsoft Millionaire." There exists a large number of ex-Microsoft employees who made their millions, quit the company, and are now free to enjoy other pursuits. Many of them are quite young, in their thirties or forties.

Not everybody who toils for Microsoft, however, can hope to become a millionaire as a result. Many of Microsoft's products are packaged and shrink-wrapped by prisoners at Washington's Twin Rivers Corrections Center (TRCC).

According to one prisoner who works for Exmark, a company specializing in product packaging, approximately 90 prisoners at TRCC packaged 50,000 units of Windows '95 demo disks and direct-mail promotional packets.

"Those were good times for us," he recalls fondly. "Everybody had plenty of work then." That same worker says he was laid off after the Microsoft contract, and he hasn't worked since. Each day, he says, he checks the bulletin board: Exmark posts a "call-out" list with the names of those workers fortunate enough to have a job the following day. He explains that those prisoners with the least seniority or who have fallen into disfavor—for anything from back-talking to poor work habits—will appear on the call-out list only for the largest contracts.

Exmark is a subsidiary of Pac Services, a Washington company which also employs non-prisoner, or "free world" workers. Steve Curly, a "free world" supervisor at Exmark, denied the company had packed any Windows '95 units. But he said that Exmark's TRCC operation had packed tens of thousands of units of Microsoft Office, and had wrapped and shipped as many as 40,000 Microsoft mice in one week.

Many of Exmark's prison workers are employed mainly—as one prisoner puts it—"when they have a big contract and need the extra workers." When work is plentiful, Exmark's prison workers shift into high gear, often working both day and swing shifts. At other times the crew is called back and most workers remain idle in their cells.

Exmark workers say that Microsoft is not the only beneficiary of Exmark's "flexible" labor force; they also claim to have regularly packaged goods for Costco, Starbucks and JanSport. They also say that Exmark not only packages retail goods, but also stuffs envelopes for mass mailings, something they claim to have often done for telecommunications giant US WEST.

Most people are surprised to learn that private corporations use prison labor. After the initial shock, however, many think it's a terrific new idea. There has been considerable debate as to whether or not it's a "terrific" idea, but rare is the challenge to the premise that it's a "new" one. Most people assume that corporate use of prison labor is a recent innovation. Nothing could be further from the truth.

Beginning in 1817 with New York's Auburn prison, the predominate U.S. prison model was based on a scheme generally referred to as "lease prisons." Sometimes private business entities contracted with states to operate their entire prison system; other times the state would operate the prisons and "lease" the prisoner labor to businesses.

Nineteenth-century prisons were essentially forced labor camps. Prisoners were made to produce a wide array of goods, including shoes, furniture, wagons, and stoves. For the sake of profit they were often housed in squalid conditions, fed spoiled food, and given scant clothing or shoes. Whippings were commonplace, and medical care was non-existent.

Dr. Lewis Wynne, executive director of the Florida Historical Society, says that since states rarely monitored conditions, operators of lease prisons often worked prisoners to death. Mortality rates, Dr. Wynne said, ran as high as 40 percent.

From almost the very start of the lease system, there were scattered protests from manufacturers' associations and organized labor. The states were addicted to the cost savings, however, and refused

to dismantle the lease system. Events in Tennessee provide an illus-
trative example.

In the 1870's competitors of the Tennessee Coal, Iron and Rail-
road Company charged that convict labor gave that company an
unfair competitive advantage. Their protests fell on the deaf ears of
state lawmakers, and the lease system continued.

In 1891, the company locked out all of its union workers for refusing to sign a "yellow dog" contract that would have barred them from
union membership. The company replaced the locked-out union
workers entirely with lease convicts. In what was dubbed the "Coal
Creek Rebellion," angry union miners stormed the lease prisons,
released over 400 prisoners, and loaded them onto trains headed for
the state capitol. The company filled up the work camps with more
convicts. The miners released those prisoners, too, and this time they
burned the prison stockades to the ground. Shortly thereafter, Tennessee finally dismantled the lease labor system.

By the beginning of this century most other states had followed
suit, enacting a patchwork of state laws abolishing or restricting
the use of prison labor by private enterprises. Two New Deal-era
federal laws, the 1929 Hawes-Cooper Act and the 1935 Ashurst-
Sumners Act, effectively ended the private business-convict labor
relationship. Hawes-Cooper authorized states to pass legislation
prohibiting the entrance of prison-made goods from other states,
and Ashurst-Sumners made it a federal offense to move prison-
made goods across state boundaries, irrespective of individual state
laws. Thus ended this first round of prison labor profiteering.

In the 1970s Chief Justice Warren Burger, born 16 years after
the Coal Creek Rebellion, began proselytizing for conversion of
U.S. prisons into "factories with fences." Congress was a willing
convert. As part of the Justice System Improvement Act of 1979,
Congress passed an amendment which established seven Prison
Industry Enhancement (PIE) pilot projects which would be
exempted from the provisions of Ashurst-Sumners. By 1984, PIE
had grown to 20 pilot projects, and the definition of project was
changed to encompass not just a single business, but all businesses
set up in prisons by either a county or a state. The law was again
amended in 1990 to allow up to 50 pilot "projects" (e.g., states) to
participate. Today all of the prison products from as many as 50

states or counties may legally enter the stream of interstate commerce. And so begins round two of the prison labor profiteering racket, with a PIE big enough for any business in any state to start grabbing a piece of the action.

For companies like Exmark, it is an attractive proposition. Exmark pays its prison workers the minimum wage ($4.90/hr in Washington), but that figure is misleading. The Department of Corrections deducts twenty percent of prisoners' wages to recover "cost of corrections." (Calculations indicate that the twenty percent deduction from the wages of 100 such prisoner workers is enough to subsidize the salary and benefits of eight guards.) Another ten percent is deducted and placed in a non-interest bearing "mandatory savings account." Five percent is deducted for a "Victims' Compensation Fund" administered by the state. Federal income tax, social security tax, and Medicare tax are also withheld. The DOC can deduct an additional twenty percent to pay court-ordered restitution, court costs, and other debts. When all is said and done prisoners can see a spendable wage of $1.80 to $2.80 per hour. But even this amount is generous, because the law actually authorizes up to eighty percent of a prisoners' wages to be deducted, meaning they could actually "take home" less than one dollar an hour.

Exmark and other private industries operating in Washington's prisons do not have to provide their prison workers with any benefits such as health insurance workers' compensation, or retirement (although the state offers a comprehensive "Three Strikes" retirement plan!). These operations are further subsidized by the state in that they usually pay little or nothing for the factory, office, or warehouse space in the state's prisons.

Exmark has a "lease" (sound familiar?) with Washington state wherein they pay only one dollar per year for an impressive amount of factory and warehouse space. The DOC often subsidizes other overhead expenses (like 24-hour security) that a private company would have to pay in a non-prison setting.

Many of the prisoner workers claim the arrangement offers them tremendous benefits, and these claims are backed up by a waiting list of at least one year for TRCC prisoners hoping to get an Exmark job. Workers say that since they have no real living expenses, most of the money they earn in industry jobs can be sent home to help support their families. Many of them express a fierce sense of pride in the fact that they provide for their families, even while they are imprisoned. Since most prison jobs in Washington state pay 25-42 cents an hour, the prospect of working at Exmark is considered by most prisoners to be a tremendous opportunity.

Some prisoners' rights activists also think that private industry jobs are a boon to prisoners. Charlie Sullivan, Co-Director of Citizens United for the Rehabilitation of Errants (CURE), a national prison reform organization, when asked in a 1995 interview about CURE's accomplishments over the past five years, said:

> I think in general it seems like where we've been successful is concerned with employment. We've been working on prison-based industries, which involves a philosophical argument going on in the prison reform community—particularly the left wing, which is worried about exploitation of prisoners. But I feel very strongly that we should be moving in the direction of supporting the idea, though certainly there should be caution in setting them up... As I've said, the whole goal of the system should be to make prisoners employable upon release.

But what kind of jobs will await these "employable" prisoners when they are released? Many of the jobs that might otherwise be available to them may have moved into prisons. Lockhart Technologies, Inc. is one example of a company which eliminated 130 "free world" jobs. They closed their Austin, Texas, circuit board assembly plant, moved all of their machinery inside of a "private" prison (operated by the Wackenhut Corporation) 30 miles away, and used state prisoners to replace the 130 workers they laid off in Austin. The prison actually designed their factory space to Lockhart Technology's specifications and charges the company one dollar a year rent.

In 1994 the Washington DOC built, with taxpayer money, a 56,000 square foot "industries building" adjacent to the Washington State Reformatory. The state has worked hard to attract private industries to move into the factory space. So far they have attracted Elliot Bay Metal Fabrication, A&I Manufacturing, Inc., and Redwood Outdoors, Inc.[1]

Elliot Bay manufactures micro-brewery vats and commercial fishing equipment such as pans, conveyor belts and storage tanks. They employ eleven highly-skilled welders and metal fabricators, but as with most prison industry jobs, the applicants must bring these skills to the job before they are hired. Elliot Bay does not run a job-training program, and they are not in the business of providing job skills to prisoners. They operate in the prison solely to make a profit.

A&I manufacturing fabricates window blinds, mini-blinds, cell shades (blinds made out of cloth), wire shelving, and are expanding into other window coverings such as curtains. All of their output is sold to De-El Enterprises, Inc., a local company who in turn deals with construction contractors to outfit entire buildings with blinds, shelves, etc.

Redwood Outdoors is a garment manufacturer, employing about twenty prisoners. Prison workers at Redwood say they make clothing for Eddie Bauer, Kelly-Hanson, Planet Hollywood and Brooks, among others. Most Redwood workers are reluctant to talk about their jobs, especially about whose labels they sew into the garments they make. "Eddie Bauer doesn't want anyone to know they use prison labor," one said in a hushed tone.

Considering the cost of the 56,000 square foot building, the salaries of guards and DOC supervisors, maintenance and administrative costs, it is debatable as to whether the DOC makes any money with prison industries, especially considering that they charge a paltry $1 a year to lease out the factory space.

The state legislature is nevertheless committed to expanding private prison industries. In its 1993 session, the Washington legislature passed Senate Bill 5989, codified as RCW 72.09.111. The law mandates that the Washington DOC increase the number of prisoners employed in "Free Venture Industries" by 300 jobs a year, with a net increase of 1,500 new prison industry jobs by the year 2000.

There is language in the statute that alludes to a concern that state prison industry jobs don't displace free workers, stating that the industries shall "provide Washington state manufacturers or business with products or services currently produced by out-of-state or foreign suppliers." The law also says that the DOC is supposed to conduct "an analysis of the potential impact of the proposed products or services on the Washington state business community and labor market."

One could argue that some prison-made goods, like the garments sewn for Redwood Outdoors, may indeed fall into a category of goods "currently produced...by...foreign suppliers," such as the infamous *maquiladora* sweatshops in Mexico and Central America. But what about the micro-brewery and fishing equipment fabricated by Elliot Bay? Are there no Washington state metal fabricators who might produce those goods? What about the blinds and window shades manufactured by A&I? Is there not one Washington state company that could offer those jobs to unemployed free workers?

The law requires the DOC to conduct an analysis of the potential impact of prison industry jobs on the local labor market. But the law is silent about what that analysis might show, or whether the DOC should be prevented from creating prison industry jobs that displace outside workers. The question is: Why should companies like Elliot Bay or A&I Manufacturing offer real-world jobs to unemployed free workers? Not when they can move into factory space provided by the state, and employ a "captive work force" at minimum-wage which they can hire, fire, and lay-off at whim. And how can other local companies compete with these prison industries? The answer is they can't. Companies like Elliot Bay and A&I drive out local jobs and drive down the wages of free workers.

One Elliot Bay worker was talking the other day, boasting that "Elliot Bay is the best program in the joint." He claims that working there allows him to hone his welding skills and prepare for a job on the outside. When it was pointed out to him that Elliot Bay probably takes jobs away from workers in society, he replied, "Fuck society! Society locked me up."

But which segment of society is truly being screwed by prison industry jobs? Those who own stock in Microsoft, US WEST, Costco, and Starbucks are probably satisfied with the arrangement. But unemployed welders, metal fabricators, factory workers, and laborers might see it differently, especially when they realize that the only way they can get a job might be by going to prison.

[*Editors' Note:* Exmark employees report that Microsoft canceled its packaging contract with the prison-based company in December, 1996, ostensibly due to "quality control" issues. The above article, however, was reprinted locally and nationally, and may have been a factor in the termination. Corporations have no qualms about exploiting prison labor, but they don't relish the publicity.]

1 Boeing, the world's largest civil aviation manufacturing, has also discovered the benefits of captive labor. MicroJet, a small company which makes aircraft components which are sold to Boeing, employs eight prisoners paid significantly less than the outside prevailing wage, at the Washington State Reformatory in Monroe. See: Paul Wright, "Making Slave Labor Fly: Boeing Goes to Prison," *PLN,* March 1997, p.1.

ARMED AND DANGEROUS

Raymond Luc Levasseur, May 1995

When I was transferred to the U.S. Penitentiary (USP) in Marion, Illinois in December, 1989, Panama was being invaded by U.S. forces. Amidst the wholesale destruction, mass graves, and lies by U.S. politicians and military leaders, was an awesome display of American firepower designed to impose its will on yet another Central American nation. Weapons systems from land, sea, and air were utilized, along with the basic M-16 to kill whoever stood in the line of fire. Whether technologically advanced or as simple as a grenade, this war material is made in the U.S.A—some of it by federal prisoners.

The Federal Prison Industries, Inc. (UNICOR) is one of the manufacturers that supplies military equipment to the bloated U.S. war machine. UNICOR has served this function since 1934 under contract to the War Department, now known euphemistically as the Department of Defense. The Federal Bureau of Prisons boasts that the slave labor of prisoners—often under hazardous conditions, and at an entry level wage of 23 cents an hour—has and continues to make significant contributions towards supplying the needs of the military. It also boasts of using UNICOR to control prisoners within its grossly overcrowded system.

UNICOR's military production ranges from TOW and other missile cables, munitions components, communications equipment, bomb parts, engine overhauls, uniform sewing, etc. In its brochures, the BOP proudly displays photographs of prisoners working hard producing this material. As a Vietnam veteran, I was particularly struck by a photo of federal prisoners producing equipment destined for Vietnam. Unlike most prisoners, I got to see with my own eyes the lethal effect of the end product.

It is the priority of UNICOR to provide for the military's needs, whether it was during the Korean War—when 80 percent of

UNICOR sales went to the military—or the Gulf War—when prisoners were pressed into overtime. In fact, the military has its own representative on UNICOR's Board of Directors to advise how to better harness prison labor for military purposes.

Being contracted to the War Department means supplying more than just U.S. forces. It means that this military equipment is rerouted by the U.S. to its client states—from Israel to Indonesia—and into the hands of the worlds' most degenerate and bloodthirsty regimes. In cases like El Salvador, the recipients of the U.S. war supplies used them to kill their own people.

USP Marion is a control unit prison where abuse of prisoners is well documented by Amnesty International, Human Rights Watch, congressional committee hearings, and elsewhere. In the neverending lockdown there is little to engage the intellect, an abysmal lack of stimulation and recreation, and no work with which to labor. With one exception. The prison administration has designed a scheme whereby prisoners deemed suitable must enter a period of involuntary servitude in the "pre-transfer" unit before they can be transferred to a less brutal prison. It is a scheme the administration exploits to the hilt because they understand that Marion prisoners are so desperate to leave its punishment cells, isolation, and tomb-like conditions, that they will submit to almost anything.

While all federal prisoners are required to work, they are not required to work in UNICOR. Twenty-six percent do. Most prisoners opt to work in other areas such as food service or maintenance, or to pursue the very limited educational or vocational programs available. USP Marion—and now USP Florence—are the only facilities in the federal prison system which demand that prisoners work for UNICOR as a condition of transfer. The only work at Marion's UNICOR is military production.

The Bureau of Prisons has parried Freedom of Information Act (FOIA) requests to disclose detailed information about war production at Marion. However, it is known that UNICOR Marion produces electronics communication cables which it sells to the War Department. These cables are used in various ground vehicles, such as tanks and armored personnel carriers, and production line supervisors have bragged that the cables are used in helicopters. During the Gulf War, the prisoners working at UNICOR Marion were compelled to do overtime production. Whatever its finite specifics, the military applications of the electronics cables is essential to many weapons systems and platforms.

Marion's operation is an extension of a larger operation at the federal prison in Lexington, Kentucky, so its production and profit figures are not individually computed. In a typical year, Lexington fills 800-1,200 orders for the military, totaling $12 million.

In modern warfare, the term "military hardware" encompasses advanced weapons systems in which electronics often provide a more destructive function than the soldier's rifle. During the U.S. war on Iraq, for example, bombardment by electronically-enhanced munitions on water treatment plants spread a bacteriological assault on all those people whose lives depended on that water. An estimated 46,900 Iraqi children died in the first seven months of 1991 as a result of U.S. attacks on the country's infrastructure. Besides pilots and gunners who never see their victims, what's used to coordinate and propel mass destruction are the essential components of war, right down to the vital electronics and communications cables.

Military equipment is not produced in a vacuum. Those prisoners who produced material during the Vietnam War certainly knew there was a war raging. U.S. military conquests, past and present, are well documented. Perhaps less well known, though equally significant and well documented, is the government's diversion of weapons and military equipment to the serial killers disguised as heads of state. UNICOR's military production is part of an extensive pipeline that feeds the world's largest weapon exporter.

The U.S. has made much of China's use of prison labor for textile and other exports to the U.S. market. This is said to be a human rights abuse (i.e., that it cuts into the profits of U.S. corporations). One controversy revolved around Christmas tree ornaments manufactured by Chinese prisoners and exported to the U.S. To my knowledge no one has ever been killed by an attack from a Christmas tree ornament, yet tons of military equipment for which U.S. prisoners have provided essential components are exported to bomb, blast, and terrorize their ultimate recipients.

For me, being a revolutionary is the best way to live. Capture and imprisonment involve adjustments, but have not made me repentant for a life time of anti-imperialism and struggle for justice. I was sent to Marion because of my political beliefs and associations and will likely remain here unless I repudiate them, which I will not do. For me to engage in the production of military equipment as a condition for transfer would be a repudiation of my political beliefs and principles. *I will not do it.*

Refusing to be an accomplice to U.S. militarism is an act rooted deep in conscience and solidarity with those fighting U.S. imperialism and trying to survive its onslaught. It is largely a symbolic act, yet necessary in confronting the collaborative nature of the system. During the most recent attack against Lebanon by U.S.-supplied Israeli forces, every newspaper, magazine, and newsreel image of the subsequent atrocities—hundreds killed and wounded; hundreds of thousands made refugees—showed a steady movement of U.S. manufactured weapons and equipment.

For the political prisoner, putting principles into practice may be largely symbolic, but demonstrating who we are and what we stand for is better than accommodating the government's agenda. It's important to remember that however small the resistance, someone always steps forward. The magnitude of crimes perpetuated by the U.S. must be opposed, and this cannot be done without risk and sacrifice. The lack of an organized and wider resistance, though lamented, does not negate individual and small group action. History is replete with their examples and their corpses: from the White Rose activists who opposed German fascism to the first and few guerrillas of the Sandinista Front for National Liberation; from John Brown to the Industrial Workers of the World; to Malcolm X and the indomitable George Jackson. For each of them there are the countless unnamed. The only reward short of victory is the sustenance obtained from the spirit of resistance.

It is not a decision made without consequences. The government and Bureau of Prisons' iron fist gives no quarter to revolutionaries, rebels, and dissenters. It's part of Marion's mission to destroy an individual's identity and community ties. One warden, Ralph Aaron, stated that "The purpose of Marion is to control revolutionary attitudes in the prison system and at large." Rather overstated from a bureaucratic windbag, but the fact remains that Marion is repression personified in a social experiment. Any outward indication that a prisoner does not conform to Marion's dictates and he is condemned

to incessant isolation. For the transgressor there will be no relief—
no step closer to personal freedom; no embrace of family and loved
ones, no access to expanded work, education, or recreational opportunities; no shot at parole. Added to the burden is the public's indifference and the response of the liberal left, who view prisoners with
contempt and political prisoners with hostility.

There's an axiom in Marion: "All who enter these walls will eat much
shit before leaving." It's inherent in Marion's mission. But eating shit is
qualitatively different from producing war material that's used to put
someone else in their grave. Someone else who also experiences a steady
diet of oppression. Someone who does me no harm.

It's been 29 years since I moved as a soldier among the Vietnamese
people, rifle in hand, desecrating their land and seeing the ill, the infirm,
wounded and dying of those I was assigned to enlighten—or light up—
about the virtues of U.S. imperialism. After my discharge, I joined
Vietnam Veterans Against the War, a group of conscience-ridden and
war-weary vets who rejuvenated a lethargic anti-war movement when
the U.S. bombing of Vietnam was at its extreme. Overlapping with
Vietnam was the war in amerika's streets, fought in places like Newark,
Detroit, Pine Ridge, Attica, Humbolt Park, East L.A. Within *this* war
were internecine battles provoked by police spies and provocateurs and
the rapid proliferation of snitches in a drug saturated, "me first" society. And beyond S.E. Asia, U.S. wars of intervention left their bloody
footprints in Chile, Argentina, Nicaragua, El Salvador, Angola, South
Africa, Cuba and Puerto Rico, to name but a few. As in Vietnam, the
victims have been mostly civilians.

Always at war, the world's policeman, this omnipotent and ubiquitous United States military is charged with enforcing capitalism's
code of conduct. Troops were mobilized during the rebellion in Los
Angeles. Troops are deployed in Somalia where they soon stood
accused of human rights violations by the humanitarian relief agencies and the Somali people themselves.

Vietnam changed my view of liberation to mean a constant and pro-
tracted struggle against those forces that impose their will on others for
power and profit. Freedom is the ultimate expression and condition of
a people who control their own destiny. Once before, the government
put me in uniform and used me for military purposes. Being young
and naive was no excuse for my complicity. They'll not do it again.

SOLIDARITY IN STILLWATER

The Oak Park Heights Prisoner Work Strike

Daniel Burton-Rose, October 1996

On March 4, 1996, one of the most impressive recent examples of prisoner solidarity and political cohesion occurred at the Oak Park Heights Maximum Security prison in Stillwater, Minnesota. In the early morning, roughly one hundred and twenty prisoners refused to show up for work at Minncor, the Minnesota state prison industry. The list of demands of the striking workers included: the minimum wage; an end to the restricted visiting policy, systematic brutality in the segregation complex, excessive medical and phone costs, poor air ventilation, inflated canteen prices; improvement of the inadequate and substandard law library; and the return of the recently removed cable television.[1]

Minncor CEO Guy Piras stated that prisoner workers' wages started at 40 cents an hour, with 10 cent an hour raises, up to one dollar an hour. The average prisoner wage at Oak Park Heights was about 95 cents an hour.[2] Up to 80 percent of those wages went to court-ordered restitution, victims' support funds, child support, and room and board fees. Additionally, a three dollar charge per medical visit was to be instituted that July, 1996.[3]

Six hours after the strike began the prison was placed on lockdown status. Prisoners' cells were ransacked and alleged ringleaders were sent to disciplinary segregation—the Security Housing Unit (SHU). More prisoners refused to work. By dinner of the next day more than half of the prisoners in the SHU refused to eat their dinner in an act of solidarity with the striking workers. The OPH administration took this opportunity to create a second 52-person SHU to house the strikers, a new unit where prisoners were placed explicitly for their refusal to work. The only way the prisoners could be released from the twenty-three hour a day solitary confinement was to agree to work again.

It is important to mention that the prisoners' demands, as one journalist observed:

> ...for the most part merely request[ed] a restoration of the prison conditions prior to 1994. Increased restrictions over the last two years include the elimination of Pell Grants, the sealing of all windows in the institution, a severe limit to the number of clothes and books per prisoner, new restrictions in the visitation policy, charges for medical visits, the elimination of cable television, and a new 25 cent telephone call fee.[4]

As with most prisoner strikes and rebellions, the prisoners' demands were very reasonable. But the concession to prisoners of any power over their own lives is antithetical to the way prisons are run in this country.

After just over a week, with the prison still on lockdown, OPH warden Erik Skon sent staff members to interview the locked-down prisoners. The prisoners had been denied all exercise and access to telephones, as well as having been forced to bathe in their metal sinks. The purpose of the interviews was to see who was "ready" to go back to work.

The staff asked the strikers: "What are your issues? Are you ready to go back to work? And if you could be placed in a unit with other people who wanted to return to work, would you then?" If the strikers said yes, the next round of questions was "[What] if you could feel a little more protected? Is it just peer group pressure holding you back?" After the interviews there were still twenty-six prisoners who refused to work.[5] They were moved to the new SHU.

Skon was quite clear that the recently implemented restrictions which prompted the strike were in the response to the public's perceived "tough on crime" sentiment. In a memo circulated to all OPH prisoners after more than a week of lockdown, Skon stated:

> Many of these changes [restrictions] have occurred in the last few years because of increasing public and legislative attention with regard to the cost of operating Minnesota prisons. An additional factor

is the public perception that inmates in Minnesota prisons are treated far too well. It has become increasingly apparent that the public is losing patience with increasing crime and less and less interested in rehabilitation... If DOC officials are to maintain the management and control of the department's institutions, we must demonstrate that we are willing to acknowledge the concerns of the public.

In a later interview he further added:

Keep in mind that many of the issues [the prisoners] are concerned with—pay, visiting, and I think the premium cable stations was one—this wasn't Oak Park Heights going off on its own to invoke these new policies... I'm afraid our population is out of touch with how restrictive other states are becoming.[6]

No concessions were made to the prisoner strikers. The only change was that the price mark-up at the prison canteen was changed from 20 percent mark-up to an 18 percent one. This change was due to the discontinuation of the cable stations, which prisoners had paid for themselves through a canteen price hike. Also, not surprisingly, the second SHU has stayed operational long after the strike has ended. As Pat Clark, National Director of the Criminal Justice Project of American Friends Service Committee, accurately observed: "The prison administration [at OPH] used a peaceful work stoppage as an excuse to expand the SHU unit."[7]

But the strike was a powerful show of force on the part of the prisoners. Skon himself acknowledged that the strike was "the strongest organized efforts by inmates that I've experience in my 22 years [in corrections]."[8] Though the coverage in the mainstream media was typically snide and devoid of critical thought (the headline of the Minnesota daily, the *Pioneer Press,* referring to the recently implemented visiting restrictions, read: "Oak Park Inmates Kiss Off Work To Protest New Limits On Lovin'"),[9] the strike was covered relatively well in the alternative press.

The work stoppage also showed prisoners themselves that they were capable of concerted action. One prisoner striker, who had been at OPH for eight years and had heard many grumblings and rumblings about protest actions, said simply: "This was the first time I saw everybody in industry do anything in harmony."[10]

But the most notable aspects of the strike was the level of outside support. The strikers were supported by prisoners' rights activists such as the Minneapolis chapter of the Anarchist Black Cross. The Black Student Union at the University of Wisconsin at Madison, the American Friends Service Committee, and other progressive groups from the Madison area faxed messages in support of the prisoners to the OPH administration.[11]

Established unions also supported the prisoners in their effort. AFSCME local presidents and vice presidents in Madison and Milwaukee also faxed message of support to OPH. The Milwaukee regional office of the "A Job Is A Right" campaign was instrumental in putting together a letter drive demanding that the AFL-CIO to look into and protest the growing use of prison/slave labor. Phil Wilayto, coordinator of the Milwaukee A Job is a Right office, was quoted as saying: "The use of prisoners as contract labor is a growing and dangerous phenomenon which is a threat to unions and the jobs of all non-prison workers..." He further noted: "And it's a gross exploitation of prisoners, who are some of the most oppressed workers in society. To force these workers to take the jobs they were denied on the outside for a fraction of the wages is to return to a system of institutionalized slave labor."

Longtime labor lawyer and activist Staughton Lynd reflected on the strike: "It seems critical that any direct action behind prison walls should be part of a campaign that also expresses itself in highly-publicized activity on the outside, and that inmate activists should receive immediate support from outside sources."[12] To a certain extent, this is what happened at OPH.

Prisoners have never stopped rebelling in various ways against the exploitative prison regimen. But most such rebellions cannot be maintained for long under the extreme repression which the prison environment entails. Without strong outside support, including that of organized labor, prisoners' acts of resistance will continue to be sporadic and short-lived. The Oak Park Heights strike was a landmark in a re-awakening prisoners' rights movement. Though there was not enough support to win the strikers tangible gains, the strike received more outside support than similar efforts have in the past couple decades. The solidarity between incarcerated workers and outside activists provides a model for future action.

1 Nina Dibner, "Work Strike at Oak Park Heights Prison," *Love and Rage Revolutionary Anarchist Newspaper*, June/July, 1996, 9.

2 "MN Prisoners Strike for Minimum Wage," *Workers' World*, March 21, 1996.

3 Jennifer Vogel, "Cracking Down," *City Pages* (Minneapolis, MN), April 3, 1996.

4 Dibner, "Work Strike at Oak Park Heights Prison," 9.

5 Vogel, "Cracking Down."

6 Vogel, "Cracking Down."

7 Pat Clark, unpublished observation on the Oak Park Heights work stoppage.

8 Vogel, "Cracking Down."

9 Vogel, "Cracking Down."

10 Vogel, "Cracking Down."

11 "MN Prisoners Strike for Minimum Wage."

12 Staughton Lynd, "Prison Labor: A Discussion of Organizing Strategies (First Draft)," unpublished paper, p. 4.

Part V
MONEY AND WARM BODIES

The Prison-Industrial Complex in the United States

Adolf Eichmann was hanged as a Nazi war criminal in Israel in 1961. Eichmann was one of the architects of the Holocaust. While he probably never killed anyone himself, his crime was seen as much worse: the commodification of millions of human beings. He helped create a world where people were reduced to nothing more than how many days of labor could be extracted from them before they died of exhaustion and starvation, how much soap could be made from their bodies, how much gold could be taken from their teeth, and how much it would cost to cremate each corpse.

Today in the United States the commodification of prisoners has reached new heights, if not to the extremes practiced by Eichmann and his ilk. The import of prisoners' lives and personalities are erased and they are treated as little more than chattel to be worked, traded, housed, rented and stocked at a profit. Businesses devote themselves to "prisoner placement," finding empty cells and filling them with warm bodies, at a price. Prisoners' labor is seen as a commodity to be exploited for no pay or a pittance in token wages. The insult added to injury is when impoverished prisoners are forced to pay for the privilege of their captivity in the form of "fees," "rent," and "utilities."

Those building the prison industrial complex, and profiting handsomely from it, are no strangers to the game of human exploitation. The Wall Street bond houses that underwrite prison construction; multinational corporations that build the prisons; phone companies that extort high rates from prisoners' families; security companies that arm and equip the guards: these are all old players from the military-industrial complex. Lockheed-Martin is one of the most prominent death merchants now playing the prison field, and Wackenhut, the leading American provider of "security services"—protection of property, strike-breaking consultation and execution, personal protection for the rich—is another cold war company diversifying into this growing field. With every man, woman and child in America paying an estimated $250 a year to maintain the American gulag through their state and federal taxes, one would think more attention would be paid to the financial aspects of human trade and warehousing.

With more than 30 billion dollars being spent on "corrections" alone each year, it is obvious that someone is lining their pockets. This chapter gives an overview of who's making money off the prison building boom, virtually all of it tax dollars. Accompanying this prison building bonanza has been corruption, payoffs, bribes, shortcuts in construction and plenty of other nefarious activity.

Under capitalism even human beings can be, and regularly are, reduced to a bottom line dollar sign. The "imprisonment pimps" of the 1990s merit contempt. That the prison barons tend to be well-respected members of society is not surprising. Eichmann too was hailed for lowering the cost of carrying out the social policy of his day. While American imprisonment cannot be compared to the Nazi genocide, it should be remembered that Nazis did not start out murdering millions. Their first step was imprisonment and, more importantly, the dehumanization and objectification of certain social strata. The same process that is at work today when human beings are vilified as nothing more than "prisoners," "criminals," or "illegal aliens," and their warm bodies are treated as a commodity worth just so much profit potential.

THE CALIFORNIA PRISON GUARDS' UNION

A Potent Political Interest Group

Dan Pens, March 1995

There is a well fed **P**olitical **I**nterest **G**roup feasting at the California public trough, and most taxpayers are unaware of the huge growth in this creature's appetite and political clout. It has grown from a political runt to one of the biggest hogs in the barnyard in an incredibly short span of time. This group has swelled with such swiftness and cunning that most California taxpayers would not even recognize its name, much less realize how much of an impact it is having on their pocketbooks and on the state's economy. The group I'm speaking of is the California Correctional Peace Officer's Association (CCPOA).

In 1980 there were 22,500 prisoners in California. The average salary for California prison guards was $14,400 a year. The state budget for corrections was $300 million per year. In the past, California schools and universities were the envy of the world. The state's economy was strong, bolstered by huge numbers of defense jobs. CCPOA was a politically minuscule organization vying for attention among the giants of fat defense contractors.

By 1996 there were more than 140,000 prisoners in California. The average salary for California prison guards is $44,000 per year (well over $50,000 with benefits)—$10,000 more than the average teacher's salary. Prison guards require only a high school education and a six week training course. Most teaching jobs require at least an undergraduate degree in education. In 1993 California spent a greater portion of its state budget on prisons than it did for education for the first time (compared to as recently as fiscal year 1983/84 when California spent 3.9 percent of its budget on its prison system, and 10 percent on higher education). The state corrections budget in 1994 was $3 *billion.* The demise of the Cold War meant the decline of defense jobs. According to the National Commission for Economic Conversion and Disarmament, a non-profit Washington D.C. group, there has been a decline of over 750,000 defense related jobs in the last five years alone—most of them in California. But as the military–industrial complex is waning in California, the *prison–industrial complex* is mushrooming. In this way California's wealth now comes not only from perpetuating the misery of millions of people around the world, but also from the rigidly enforced misery of thousands of its own citizens. Between 1984 and 1994 California added a whopping 25,900 prison employees, substantially more than were added to all other state departments combined (16,000). By one estimate, hiring for prisons has accounted for 45 percent of the growth in *all* California jobs in that ten year period.

The CCPOA's rise to political power can be traced to 1980, when Don Novey became the group's president. Novey is the son of a prison guard. He graduated from American River College and served in Army Intelligence in the late '60s. Before becoming the head of the union, he worked as a prison guard in Folsom.

Prior to Novey's ascendancy, the union had been a pitifully weak organization, with a membership divided between the California State Employees' Association and the California Correctional Officers' Association. In all it had only about 5,600 members. But when Novey took over its leadership, the union combined Youth Authority supervisors and parole officers with prison guards, and with the acceleration of prison building, the CCPOA membership has swelled to 23,000 members.

Recognizing not only the political importance of lobbying but the power of public relations, Novey began spending about half a million dollars on PR and on honing a public image for himself: that of the self-depreciating, fedora-wearing, blue collar labor leader. But it is in the arena of political lobbying, rather than PR, that Novey has shown true genius.

The CCPOA collects nearly $8 million a year in dues, and it expends twice as much in political contributions as the California Teachers Association, although it is only one-tenth the size. The union is now second in the state only to the California Medical Association in political contributions. But in reality it is the most powerful and influential lobbying group in the state, as there are no vested interests against spending more on prisons. Don Novey has shaped the CCPOA into a potent political force. Candidates for governor have genuflected at Novey's feet in hopes of gaining the endorsement and deep pocket largess of his association, and have submitted to grilling by the union leadership to see if they were worthy. Jack Meola, the CCPOA's executive vice president, says their questioning of candidates is intense. "Our primary goal is to protect the public," he says in his smooth PR banter to the press, "to keep thugs off the street and in jail where they belong." To fail the test, Novey maintains, could mean the difference between victory and defeat. Diane Feinstein found that out in 1990 when Novey's union gave almost $1 million to enthrone law enforcement's friend, Pete Wilson, in the California State House.

And, of course, the union not only wields the political stick, it also dispenses the carrot, and not just to Pete Wilson. Novey and his union contributed $76,000 to the 1992 re-election campaign of David Elder, the chair of the state assembly's Committee on Public Employment and Security—the very same committee that rules directly on the pay and benefits of prison guards. And they received value for their political contribution dollar. Prison guards got raises six months ahead of other state government employees. Their average salary of $44,000 per year is 58 percent above the national average for prison guards. And they now boast one of the best pension plans of any state employee. In addition to excellent medical coverage, they receive 75 percent of their salary at the time of retirement, which can be 55 after 30 years' service, and they get a 2 percent yearly increase after two years of retirement.

To ward off the critics, Novey's PR machine drums up the theme that prison guards patrol "the toughest beat in the state." But that simply is not the case. Over the past three decades 13 prison guards have been killed throughout the state, compared with 63 officers in the LAPD—an organization with half the members of the CCPOA's 14,000 who serve as guards. (The rest of the 23,000 CCPOA members work in parole or as Youth Authority supervisors.)

The slick PR is aimed mainly at the public. State politicians don't need to hear any propaganda to toe the CCPOA line. They know that one false step could result in Novey pulling a "Vasconcellos" on them. That is, the CCPOA richly endowing the campaign coffers of their opponent, as Novey's union did to John Vasconcellos, the chair of the state assembly's Ways and Means Committee and an opponent of the prison building boom. Although it was generally conceded that Vasconcellos' seat was among the more secure in the assembly, the CCPOA *still* laid more than $75,000 in the lap of Vasconcellos' 1992 opponent, just to let him know that it did not *appreciate* him signing the ballot argument against the prison bond initiative in 1990, or questioning the fat contracts being awarded to prison guards at a time when the state was in the most dire fiscal straits since the Great Depression. Vasconcellos was re-elected in 1992 with a substantial majority, but a clear, sharp message had been sent to the self-described "progressive" who has labored long and hard for a more thoughtful approach to crime and incarceration, as well to any other state politicians who might entertain the thought of publicly opposing prison-building legislation or criticize the guards' union.

The crowning glory of the CCPOA's political action campaign is without a doubt the passage of Proposition 184, the "Three Strikes" Initiative. The CCPOA contributed $101,000 to get Prop 184 on the ballot. The CCPOA donation was clearly a key factor in getting the initiative on the ballot and on getting it passed. Even though the legislature had already been cowed into passing virtually identical legislation, the fact that it was passed by voter initiative ensures that the legislature cannot easily modify this "Prison Guard Full Employment Act." CCPOA member Lt. Kevin Peters summed up the membership's position on "Three Strikes" when he said:

> You can get a job anywhere. *This* is a career. And with the upward mobility and rapid expansion of the department, there are opportunities for the people who are [already] correction staff, and opportunities for the general public to become correctional officers. We've gone from 12 institutions to 28 in 12 years, and with 'Three Strikes' and the overcrowding we're going to experience with that, we're going to need to build at least three prisons a year for the next five years. Each one of those institutions will take approximately 1,000 employees.

But Lt. Peters, like the CCPOA as a whole, can see no farther than the end of the snout he has buried in the public trough. Though the public has been hoodwinked by a crime-fear hysteria fueled by the media—and capitalized on by both political parties to gain the attention and affection of voters—critics are beginning to voice their doubt and concern over the direction these misguided policies are taking California. The once Golden State, whose public education system was the envy of the world, now ranks in the bottom 10 nationally in spending from kindergarten through high school. There are almost no meaningful drug rehabilitation programs in California, and almost no housing for the homeless; hospital emergency rooms are closing all over the state; libraries in L.A. County are closed on weekends, and many are open only two days a week; kids in some of the poorest neighborhoods have no place to go after school; and California now spends more on prisons than it does on colleges and universities. It is in a climate such as this that jack-booted reactionaries are able to sound the Nazi-like alarm that immigrants are the cause of the state's budget woes and the reason there are not enough jobs, schooling, medical and social services to go around.

Many corporations have fled California because of increased state taxes, and taken their jobs with them. Although the decrease in industrial jobs has been partly offset by increases in corrections jobs, it doesn't take a genius to see that this trend doesn't make for a viable economic strategy. As more and more working wage jobs are eliminated, the unemployed and the poor will have fewer and fewer economic opportunities. The state budget for health, education and social services will continue to be bled by the prison expansion programs.

According to James Gomez, California's former Director of Corrections, it will cost $40 *billion* to build the 21 new prisons required to house the surge in prisoners that "Three Strikes" (and similar "get tough" laws) will generate, and an additional $5.5 *billion* a year to run them. A RAND Corporation study predicts the corrections budget will double, growing from 9 percent of all state expenditures to 18 percent. It also predicts that prosecution costs will soar. "To support implementation of the law, total spending for higher education and other government services would have to fall by more than 40 percent over the next eight years," the RAND report concludes. The CCPOA is spearheading a political and economic strategy that will lead California into an abyss.

But perhaps this is the only direction that may lead to eventual social and economic justice. The prospects for *evolutionary* shifts to the left grow dimmer and dimmer. Perhaps it is only after the state drives itself into an abyss that a radical *revolutionary* shift can take place. That remains to be seen.

THE BOTTOM LINE

California's Prison Industry Authority

Willie Wisely, October 1995

Imagine a half-billion dollar manufacturing company that uses slave labor, has little overhead, ignores state and federal laws regulating workplace safety, includes hazardous materials in the construction of its products, forces customers to buy those products under penalty of law, yet loses money. Now, imagine that this company is protected from bankruptcy and government interference. Protected because the government owns and operates the company. It's California's Prison Industry Authority (PIA). Why is this company still in business?

Some 41 other prison industry programs across the nation turned a profit in 1992-93. California's PIA lost $1.4 million on sales of $128.6 million. Florida, Texas, and North Carolina have the largest prison industries outside of California, and compete with private businesses in the marketplace. Florida's Prison Rehabilitative Industries & Diversified Enterprises (PRIDE) program is a private, non-profit corporation created by the legislature in 1981. Unlike PIA, PRIDE doesn't employ civil servants.

PRIDE netted $4 million on gross sales of $77.6 million in 1994, and spent $635,000 assisting paroled prisoners. Just 18 percent of PRIDE alumni return to custody. PIA spends virtually nothing to help parolees, and the recidivism rate in California is over 75 percent.

Although the Texas Industries Division (TID) is prohibited from making money on 30 percent of its output, the program has turned a profit every year since its inception in 1963. TID employs 7,500 prisoners from a prison population of 94,000. California's PIA uses only 6,800 prisoners out of a total population of more than 130,000. North Carolina's prison industry made $5.4 million on sales of $51.2 million in 1994. But PIA has lost money five out of the twelve years it's existed. And, of these four states, only California requires government agencies, schools, libraries, and hospitals to buy prison-made goods.

From furniture to eyeglasses, PIA manufactured wares are poorly made, overpriced, and often delivered months late. Don Green, purchasing agent for California State Polytechnic University at Pomona, needed chairs for the new computer lab. He could have bought them from a local retailer for about $58 each. However, California law forced him to order the furniture from the prison manufacturing empire. He waited a year for delivery and paid twice the retail price. In 1994, state entities chose from 110 product lines and 2,000 items in the slickly printed PIA catalog, spending $135 million on prison made goods. The only ones who seem happy with the status quo are the civil service shop foremen, supervisors, salespeople, and administrators who make an average of $44,000 a year—much more than they could earn for similar jobs in the real world.

"It's a joke, absolutely, positively a joke. And everybody covers everybody's ass," said Leonard Greenstone of the PIA. Greenstone is the lone dissident on the Prison Authority Board, which oversees the PIA. A Black vocational instructor who didn't want to be identified for fear of retaliation described gross program mismanagement: "When I worked for PIA, my shop turned a profit. Pretty soon, I was warned to cut back on production. They told me it made the other supervisors look bad."

"It's like the factory system under communist rule," said Joe Harrington, a retired longshoreman from Costa Mesa, California. "The workers and supervisors got paid whether their products sold or not. There was no reason for them to build quality merchandise because they had no competition."

Private business people feel that the law forbidding state agencies and other divisions from purchasing commodities on the open market is unfair to them and should be abolished. The California Constitution forbids prisons from competing with private enterprise. Yet that's exactly what the PIA is doing. "The complaints we hear are that [PIA] is in direct competition with California business. You can't deny that," Lynn Wright, Governor Pete Wilson's government purchasing expert conceded. The competition isn't quite fair because PIA has a protected market.

PIA administrators claim the law giving them a protected market is necessary because prisons aren't permitted to sell goods to the general public. They also claim their products are more expensive because prisoners are unskilled, illiterate, and require constant supervision. While it's true PIA is barred from selling directly to the public in California, they are aggressively developing markets in foreign countries. They sell bluejeans and prison denim jackets with "California Department of Corrections" stenciled on them in Day-glo orange to Japan.

The PIA's excuses for these foreign sales were considered by the Little-Hoover Commission, a state watchdog agency, in a 1993 report on the PIA. In the Little-Hoover Commission report, prison industry managers say outdated equipment, delays in processing orders for raw materials, the high turnover rate of prisoner workers, and random lockdowns by prison administrators further drive their costs up and production levels down. The commission was skeptical. "Despite these burdens, the inability of the PIA to routinely break even or post a profit is perplexing in light of the ability to set prices without fear of losing customers," the report concluded.

One state lawmaker has proposed a change to the ineffectual PIA. California Senator Richard Polanco authored Senate Bill 617. If passed into law, the bill would free state entities from the requirement to buy only from PIA. They would be at liberty to find better deals in the private sector. On May 11, 1995, the measure easily won approval in the state senate. Joined by Senator Dan Boatwright, Polanco demanded a probe of PIA's finances and operations by the state Bureau of Audits. That investigation is expected to begin soon. At the most, insiders anticipate the ouster of Dave King, general manager of the Prison Industry Board, and executive staff loyal to him. But, mismanagement isn't the only problem with PIA.

Materials used in the manufacturing of furniture the prison industry sells to state schools and hospitals are dangerous, flammable, and destructive to the environment. For example, urethane foam is purchased by the PIA furniture factory at Tehachapi prison's maximum security facility. The large sheets of foam must be cut to size for use in chairs and couches. Cutting urethane foam in the unventilated shop poses a serious, potentially lethal, health threat to prisoners and civilian employees alike. When the foam is cut with power saws, tiny particles are dispersed into the air. Trapped inside human lungs, these particles can be deadly. "Urethane foam particles are carcinogenic. And, after accumulating in the lungs, they can cause a condition similar to asbestosis," says John Diffenbaugh, a Captain with the Kern

County Fire Department. The foam also bears a warning to consumers that it was manufactured with 1,1,1 trichloroethane, a substance known to destroy ozone in the upper atmosphere.

Urethane foam is also flammable, and once ignited produces a toxic gas which can quickly overcome and kill anyone nearby. The California Furniture Association does not approve of the use of this foam in furniture. PIA ignores the danger, causing some employees to seek other jobs. "I'm transferring out of here," said a former PIA supervisor. "My father died of emphysema, and I've seen too many people with suspicious coughs in the shop. That damn dust will kill you." Foam dust fills the air at Tehachapi's Furniture Factory, and many prisoners working there develop a chronic cough. After Captain Diffenbaugh warned that the dust could cause serious illness, prisoners demanded exhaust fans to remove the particles from the shop air. Instead, they were given disposable paper face masks with labels that read "This is not a filter. Prolonged use may be dangerous to your health."

In the Sacramento capital it's politics and deliberate indifference as usual. Governor Wilson is officially neutral on Polanco's bill, but is strongly committed to PIA. "Prison Industry needs to expand, not contract, these positive efforts toward providing job skills and lessening the financial burden of state prison costs," he said in a 1992 video message. But, because PIA uses obsolete equipment and outmoded techniques, prisoners don't learn practical skills needed in the workplace outside. PIA executives claim they save taxpayers millions of dollars by allowing prisoners to earn time off their sentences for working. According to the legislative analysis of SB 617, however, that's just not true. The conclusion that prison industry saves tax dollars by allowing prisoners to earn time off is based on the false assumption those prisoners wouldn't find other jobs and earn time off anyway. The savings guesstimate also supposes the Department of Corrections would have to create other activities for prisoners. The Little-Hoover Commission found that PIA really didn't save taxpayers any money at all. "Through the mechanism of forcing these departments to purchase from the PIA, the costs of dealing with inmates are shifted throughout the state government but are still paid by the same public-provided dollar that would cover costs if they were contained in the Department of Corrections budget." So what's the bottom line?

The bottom line is that the PIA—like the Department of Corrections itself—has become a welfare system for its employees. The sole purpose of the PIA, it seems, is to furnish civil service employees with big salaries for doing little work. It is not concerned with helping insure that prisoners stand a chance of success upon their parole. It is not concerned with producing well-made goods or turning a profit.

But no one in the PIA is bothered by this. And Governor Wilson, counting on his base of faithful civil servants at election time, will likely veto Polanco's bill just as he did other bills in 1991-92 which aimed to reform the PIA. So schools, already strapped for cash thanks to budget cuts, must continue to pay $3.56 for plastic binders they could buy at a stationery store for $1.55, and $695 for conference tables that run $279 at a furniture outlet. State hospitals will have chairs and couches in their waiting rooms made with highly flammable, toxic materials.

In a way, California's Prison Industry Authority is like the goose that laid the golden egg. As long as no one kills the goose, PIA employees, and the myriad vendors who make a living supplying the prison industry, continue getting the gold. The trouble is though, the goose is shitting all over everyone else.

TAPPING THE CAPTIVE MARKET

Dan Pens, July 1996

The U.S. prison population has tripled in the last fifteen years and now stands at over a million and a half. But the number of bodies is not the only statistic that has grown. 1995 saw record sums of money move through prisoner accounts: In California, $64 million; in Florida, $50 million; in Ohio, $33 million.

Most of the money is spent on staples such as cigarettes, coffee, snacks, and toiletries. But even after these deductions, according to calculations by Newhouse News Service, prisoner accounts added up to a staggering $100 million average daily balance. Collectively prisoners are big business. Communications giant AT&T Corp, for instance, estimates that prisoners placed about $1 billion in long-distance calls in 1995.

States are scrambling to upgrade or streamline their prisoner accounting systems. In Texas, for instance, prisoners use debit cards, similar to ATM cards, to make purchases at the commissary. These purchases are automatically deducted from their accounts by an electronic system that links the state's 100-plus prisons.

Most states, and the federal government, don't pay interest on the money in prisoners' accounts. The Federal Bureau of Prisons, for example, keeps more than $12 million of federal prisoners' money at the U.S. Treasury, which pays no interest on it. Not that interest would amount to much for most prisoners.

Nearly 70 percent of Texas prisoners have less than $5 in their accounts, said one Texas Department of Criminal Justice (TDCJ) official. In prison, just as in the free world, a few prisoners control a disproportionate share of the wealth. In Texas, 30 percent of the prisoners control 94 percent of the money on deposit. One former Texas prisoner, according to a TDCJ spokesperson, kept his balance at the maximum permitted: $99,999.

In Illinois, according to one prison official, there is no limit on the amount of money prisoners can keep on their accounts. "But once it hits a magical number—and I'm not at liberty to give you that—we start looking at it as a means of giving something back to the taxpayer."

Nationwide, according to an estimate by Newhouse News Service, the average daily balance for a prisoner's account in 1995 was $86. All this money, as well as the resources of prisoners friends and family trapped into using whatever over-priced services are forced upon them, make prisons and prisoners a quite attractive market to many business.

VITAPRO FRAUD IN TEXAS

Dan Pens, July 1995 - May 1996

Texas Department of Criminal Justice (TDCJ) has gotten itself into the fast food business in the last few years. This is a new and different kind of fast food, though. What makes it "fast" is how quickly prisoners whisk their trays to the garbage can to dump the soy-based meat substitute off of their trays.

The new product is called VitaPro. Larry Kyle, the director of the Texas prison industries, says that under what he terms a "gentleman's agreement" with VitaPro Foods, Inc., of Montreal, Canada, the Texas prison system will be the sole distributor of this new wonder-product to cost-conscious prisons and jails all over the United States. The Texas Department of Criminal Justice (TDCJ) was to purchase 36 metric tons of the product each month for five years. The TDCJ hoped to make a cool $4 million on the distribution in 1995 alone.

But the money didn't come that easy. In early 1996 Texas state prison officials asked a judge to nullify an agreement to purchase $33.6 million worth of VitaPro, saying the TDCJ had no authority to sign such a contract. Investigators for Governor George W. Bush Jr. said the arrangement between VitaPro and the TDCJ involved "fancy footwork" and was clearly not conducted in the proper manner. The FBI, Texas Rangers and internal prison investigators probed the pact, including the involvement of former TDCJ Executive Director James A. "Andy" Collins, who urged the agency to buy the powdery product while earning $1,000 a day working as a VitaPro consultant. Kyle himself was also under investigation. He was placed on administrative leave—with full pay—pending the outcome of the investigation.

Texas prisoners balked when it came to eating the product. They claim it causes diarrhea, skin rashes and other ailments. Though Kyle claimed that if any of the prisoners noticed a difference in the quality of their food, none complained, we here at *Prison Legal News* received quite a few unsolicited and less-than-positive reviews of VitaPro. One letter described the product as "looking and smelling like Alpo [dog food]." Though, it should be noted in all fairness to Kyle, the author of that letter failed to make any specific complaints about how the product *tasted*. But even if lost on Kyle, Texas prisoners made their strong dislike of VitaPro known by refusing to eat it, and as a result, tons of the product piled up in prison warehouses around the state. On top of this the state is currently defending several *pro se* lawsuits from prisoners claiming health problems related to eating the chemical and preservative-laced product.

Collins resigned as executive director of the TDCJ in the fall of 1995 after investigators linked him with a fraudulent scheme to finance several rent-a-cell jails in small Texas municipalities. Just prior to resigning, Collins approved a promotion for Kyle which raised his salary to $75,744. TDCJ spokesperson Glen Castlebury said that only one other TDCJ employee had been promoted to that level of pay, and that individual, Art Mosley, was a deputy director. Castlebury also said the TDCJ stopped taking delivery of any more VitaPro shipments in late February.

In its request to nullify the contract the state asked judge Bill McAdams not only to throw out the pact, but also to order VitaPro to refund the estimated $3 million the state has paid to date. The ongoing soap opera of official fraud and corruption in the TDCJ speaks volumes for a topsy-turvy criminal justice system wherein tens of thousands of petty thieves and drug users are being imprisoned in a system operated by multi-million dollar thieves. When a poor person robs a convenience store of $50, that is characterized as a violent crime. When senior TDCJ officials bilk the taxpayers of millions of dollars, those actions are characterized as "fancy footwork" or "shady business deals."

KIDNAPPING AND EXTORTION, TEXAS-STYLE

Dan Pens, February- May 1996

In the dead of the night, they come to your cell. You wake up with a flashlight shining in your face. You hear the rattle of chains. "Roll 'em up, boy... you're goin' for a ride." The next day you get a bedroll and make your new bunk in a county jail in some god-forsaken town in... Texas! "Why me!?" you ask. In a word: "Money."

In 1989 Texas state prisons were severely overcrowded and 9,500 state prisoners were backed up in county jails. The District of Columbia was under court orders to ease overcrowding, and was actually polling jailers by telephone prospecting for beds. Houston developer, N-Group Securities, Inc., smelled a profit.

Job-starved Texas towns were approached by developers with the sales pitch: prisons as an economic development project. It seemed like a no-lose situation. The promoters offered the prospect of a stable, growth industry with no pollution problems. Wall Street investment firms, such as Drexel Burnham Lambert, offered to underwrite the development schemes by selling high-yield "junk munis" to finance construction.

The "market" looked solid. In a 1989 press release, N-Group Securities expressed the optimism of the day: "Counties and state and federal agencies with crisis overcrowding conditions will be lining up to pay for their prisoners to stay in these new facilities."

The junk bonds were sold. The jails were built. And then the trouble began. The state of Texas went on an unprecedented $1.5 billion prison construction binge. The bulk of the new state facilities opened in 1994 and '95. In 1995 alone the Texas Department of Criminal Justice (TDCJ) announced they would hire 12,000 guards to staff the new prisons. The TDCJ now has a large surplus of prison beds.

The opening of some of the new state prisons was delayed because of the glut. Other states expanded their prison capacity, and the job-starved Texas towns who built privately financed jails were faced with disaster as payments on their bonds were coming due.

Since the "local" market of Texas state prisoners was evaporating, the enterprising counties had to man the phones. This time it was they who were polling the states, looking for takers to fill their empty rent-a-cells. So far they have lured business from Colorado, Hawaii, Oklahoma, Oregon, Massachusetts, Missouri, Montana, New Mexico, North Carolina, Utah, Virginia, Wisconsin and Wyoming.

The Colorado prisoners sought and obtained assistance from the Colorado ACLU to file suit on their behalf. In June, 1995, 500 Colorado prisoners were shipped on "the midnight express" to the Bowie County Correctional Facility in Texarkana. Bowie County collects $40 a day per prisoner—$20,000 a day total—which is far above the average per diem cost for county jails. But the Colorado prisoners are housed in substandard dormitory-style cells, are allowed very little personal property, and have almost no recreational, educational or vocational programs (not to mention the constraint on visiting!).

In a move to counter the ACLU suit, which alleges substandard living conditions, Texas sent one of their own state inspectors in to the jail. On December 4th, 1995, a report was released by the Texas Commission on Jail Standards which found no problems with the facility during the inspection. One week later the Colorado prisoners, frustrated and angry over their plight, erupted in a melee that rolled through the jail for two hours.

The riot began at 3 a.m., when guards went into one of the 24-man dorm-style living units and attempted to pull down towels and blankets that prisoners had put up to shield their eyes from the 24-hour-a-day lights. A scuffle broke out between guards and prisoners in that unit, and the rumble quickly spread to other units. Some prisoners broke into an adjacent hallway and tore out light fixtures and damaged a classroom. Prisoners in the living units ripped out plumbing and light fixtures. Additional guards had to be called in to quell the disturbance, and a helicopter hovered over the jail to watch for escaping prisoners. No injuries were reported, but past experience leads us to view such reports by prison officials to the media with a great deal of skepticism.

Five Colorado corrections officials flew to Texarkana later that same day to interview the prisoners. According to Liz McDonough, a Colorado DOC spokesperson, criminal charges may be filed in Colorado and Texas against the prisoners involved in the riot.

Paul Katsamples, a Metropolitan State College criminal justice professor who toured the Bowie County facility in August, documented numerous "critical areas." Among them: food prepared and served in extremely unsanitary conditions; poor quality drinking water; defective plumbing; insect infestation; and the excessive use of force by jail guards. Sick prisoners were placed in the hole and received no medical treatment.

At 3:00 a.m. on Tuesday, February 21, 1996, in the Crystal City Detention Center in Zavala County, about 200 frustrated and disgruntled out-of-state prisoners erupted, seizing control of the jail and setting fires. The uprising was not quelled until dawn. No injuries were reported.

The prisoners, mostly from Missouri and Utah, claimed they were angry because of a lack of Black guards, the fact that many of the jail's guards verbally harassed them in Spanish, and they were upset about the television being turned off early on Monday night.

The Crystal City Detention Center was built in 1989. The county was lured by the promise of easy profits offered by Diversified Municipal Services, Inc., of Lebanon, Indiana, which packaged the $4.4 million bond deal to build the jail. The county bought a "turnkey contract" (no pun intended) which included the financing, design, construction, and operation of the facility. It was a pretty cozy deal. Philip Packer, for example, was a vice president of Hale-Mills Construction Company, a shopping center builder from Houston who built the facility. Packer was also a registered agent for the local arm of Diversified Municipal Services, which financed the deal; he was also a vice president of Detention Services, Inc., which had the contract to operate the facility. The alarm and electrical subcontractor was former Navarro County, Texas, sheriff Bobby Ross.

The facility originally housed prisoners from the District of Columbia. When Jonathan Smith, an attorney for the D.C. Prisoners' Legal Services Project, Inc., visited the jail in June of 1990, he observed baseball bats in the dorms and "shoots" of pruno (homemade wine) fermenting openly in the shower stalls. In late 1990 the

District of Columbia declined to renew its contract. Zavala County took over management of the jail in late 1990. The financial consultants, brokers, architects, and contractors had collected their fees and left town, leaving Zavala County with an empty substandard jail that nobody seemed to need or want and a $4.4 million bond issue to pay off.

They have since worked with Dominion Management, Inc., a private Oklahoma brokerage firm dealing in state-to-state prisoner transfers, to put warm Utah and Missouri bodies in the jail, and have found another private contractor, Dove Development Corp., to operate the facility.

Now if they could only figure out a way to keep those ungrateful out-of-state exiles from burning down the joint, maybe they could get those pesky bonds paid off.

INS DETAINEES TRASH PRIVATE PRISON

Dan Pens, September 1995

Another example of the failure of prison privatization is the privately-run Esmor Immigration Detention Center in Elizabeth, New Jersey. On June 18, 1995, some 300 immigrants being held at Esmor chased out the guards, trashed the facility and held off federal, state and local law enforcement agents for nearly six hours. Police finally threw a flash grenade into a barricade the detainees had set up and stormed the facility. Twenty detainees were injured in the melee.

The Esmor facility was hastily set up in a converted warehouse just over a year ago when the U.S. government decided to "crack down" on immigrants who land at Kennedy (NY) and Newark (NJ) airports with no papers.

The 240 men and 60 women detainees at the 300-bed center included Romanians, Cubans, Chinese, Russians and Sikhs, most of them seeking political asylum in the U.S. None of the detainees had even been accused of a crime, let alone convicted of one. Many of them had been forced to flee their homelands due to poverty or political persecution. They came to this country believing in the rhetoric of freedom and democracy. What awaited them, however, was a nightmare of concentration camp imprisonment and brutal mistreatment. One young Somali woman told of being tortured and imprisoned in her homeland before fleeing to this country only to be imprisoned and brutalized yet again.

The detainees were warehoused inside the crowded, windowless facility for months while awaiting hearings. Some detainees say they were physically and sexually assaulted by guards. The female detainees complained of sexual abuse and guards spying on them while they showered. The immigrants were often shackled to their toilets or other furniture, and they were constantly taunted with ethnic slurs by Esmor guards. Former detainees say they were forced to take anti-depressant drugs, denied food or served spoiled food. Detainees objected to blaring television and bright lights kept on almost all night in crowded dormitories, as well as guards pushing them around and trying to pick fights with them.

"They were really acting in self-defense," said Peter Schey, an attorney at the Center for Human Rights and Constitutional Law. Schey filed a class action suit against Esmor in April, 1995. After the uprising the detainees were dispersed to widely-scattered prisons and county jails in an attempt to silence them and keep their story from coming out.

The detainees released a list of demands to the press, but to our knowledge the only publication to print it was the *Revolutionary Worker*. The demands were:

> 1) We should be treated as "Prisoners of Conscience" and not criminals. 2) We are entitled to a fair hearing. 3) We should not be used as an avenue to acquire wealth. 4) We need our freedom. 5) Conditions of detention are unacceptable. 6) We are covered by the 1947 United Nations Universal Declaration of Human Rights—right to life, liberty and property. 7) The INS and the U.S. government should observe the United Nations laws on refugee status. 8) Asylum seekers should not be kept in jails with hardened criminals. 9) Our trials are not democratic.

Esmor Correctional Services, the private corporation then based in Melville, Long Island, had a five-year, $54 million contract to operate the facility. Esmor manages four other correctional centers (mostly boot camps and halfway houses), and six additional INS detention centers. The other detention centers are in New York, Colorado, Texas and Washington. Esmor's stock is publicly traded, with projected earnings of $36 million in 1995.

INS officials said on June 19, 1995, that they expected the heavily damaged facility to re-open in 45 days and that it would continue to operate under Esmor's management. Union County, New Jersey prosecutor Andrew Ruotolo said that he would file a civil suit if necessary to keep that from happening. Ruotolo said that only a dozen employees—whose training lasted three hours and who earned $7 an hour—were guarding the facility at the time of the rebellion. The contract was later bought out by another private prison contractor, Corrections Corporation of America, which now operates the facility.

Esmor chairperson James F. Slattery claimed that the INS was responsible for the uprising because it ordered the center built for stays averaging 90 days, while in fact delays in processing cases meant that detainees were stuck there for much longer periods. But assistant prosecutor Michael Lapolla said: "Esmor put minimal effort into this place. If privatization is the future [of corrections] then we're all in for big trouble."[1]

[*Editors' Note:* Esmor Corrections Corporation, now based in Florida, changed its name in July, 1996, to Correctional Services Corporation (CSC), after having caused what federal officials, called "the worst disturbance ever," [referring to the New Jersey riot,] at a privately run prison. According to Prison Reform Trust, a London-based private prison watchdog group, CSC continues to run another INS facility in Seattle and twelve other facilities Arizona, Florida, New York and Texas.[2]]

1 This certainly isn't the first time that INS prisoners have rebelled. For another recent example, see: "INS Detainees Rebel," *PLN*, February, 1995
2 "Esmor Changes Name," *Private Prison Report International*, Aug. 1996, No. 3.

AMERICA'S PRIVATE GULAG

Ken Silverstein, January 1997

What is the most profitable industry in America? Weapons, oil and computer technology all offer high rates of return, but there is probably no sector of the economy so abloom with money as the privately-run prison industry.

Consider the growth of the Corrections Corporation of America, the industry leader whose stock price has climbed from $8 a share in 1992 to about $30 today and whose revenue rose by 81 percent in 1995 alone. Investors in Wackenhut Corrections Corporation have enjoyed an average return of 18 percent during the past five years and the company is rated by *Forbes* as one of the top 200 small businesses in the country. At Esmor, another big private prison contractor, revenues have soared from $4.6 million in 1990 to more than $25 million in 1995.

Ten years ago there were just five privately-run prisons in the country, housing a population of 2,000. Today nearly a score of private firms run more than 100 prisons with about 62,000 beds. That's still less than five percent of the total market, but the industry is expanding fast, with the number of private prison beds expected to grow to 360,000 during the next decade.

The exhilaration among leaders and observers of the private prison sector was cheerfully summed up by a recent headline in *USA Today*: "Everybody's Doin' the Jailhouse Stock". An equally upbeat mood imbued a conference on private prisons held in December 1996 at the Four Seasons Resort in Dallas. The brochure for the conference, organized by the World Research Group, a New York-based investment firm, called the corporate takeover of correctional facilities the "newest trend in the area of privatizing previously government-run programs... While arrests and convictions are steadily on the rise, profits are to be made—profits from crime. Get in on the ground floor of this booming industry now!"

A hundred years ago private prisons were a familiar feature of American life, with disastrous consequences. Prisoners were farmed out as slave labor. They were routinely beaten and abused, fed slop and kept in horribly overcrowded cells. Conditions were so wretched that by the end of the nineteenth century private prisons were outlawed in most states.

During the past decade, private prisons have made a comeback. Already 28 states have passed legislation making it legal for private contractors to run correctional facilities and many more states are expected to follow suit.

The reasons for the rapid expansion include the post-1980s free market ideological fervor, large budget deficits for the federal and state governments and the discovery and creation of vast new reserves of "raw materials"—prisoners. The rate for most serious crimes has been dropping or stagnant for the past 15 years, but during the same period severe repeat offender provisions and a racist "get tough" policy on drugs have helped push the U.S. prison population up from 300,000 to around 1.5 million during the same period. This has produced a corresponding boom in prison construction and costs, with the federal government's annual expenditures in the area now $17 billion. In California, passage of the infamous "three strikes" bill will result in the construction of an additional 20 prisons during the next few years.

The private prison business is most entrenched at the state level but is expanding into the federal prison system as well. Last year Attorney General Janet Reno announced that five of seven new federal prisons being built will be run by the private sector. Almost all of the prisons run by private firms are low or medium security, but the companies are trying to break into the high security field as well. They have also begun taking charge of management at INS detention centers, boot camps for juvenile offenders and substance abuse programs.

Roughly half of the industry is controlled by the Nashville-based Corrections Corporation of America, which runs 46 penal institutions in 11 states. It took ten years for the company to reach 10,000 beds; it is now growing by that same number every year.

CCA's chief competitor is Wackenhut, which was founded in 1954 by George Wackenhut, a former FBI official. Over the years its board and staff have included such veterans of the U.S. national security state as Frank Carlucci, Bobby Ray Inman and William Casey, as well as Jorge Mas Canosa, leader of the fanatic Cuban American National Foundation. The company also provides security services to private corporations. It has provided strikebreakers at the Pittston mine strike in Kentucky, hired unlicensed investigators to ferret out whistleblowers at Alyeska, the company that controls the Alaskan oil pipeline, and beaten anti-nuclear demonstrators at facilities it guards for the Department of Energy.

Wackenhut has a third of the private prison market with 24 contracts, nine of which were signed during the past two years. In a major coup, the company was chosen to run a 2,200 capacity prison in Hobbs, New Mexico, which will become the largest private prison in the U.S. when it opens late this year.

Esmor, the No. 3 firm in the field, was founded only a few years ago and already operates ten corrections or detention facilities. The company's board includes William Barrett, a director of Frederick's of Hollywood, and company CEO James Slattery, whose previous experience was investing in and managing hotels.

U.S. companies also have been expanding abroad. The big three have facilities in Australia, England and Puerto Rico and are now looking at opportunities in Europe, Canada, Brazil, Mexico and China.

The companies that dominate the private prison business claim that they offer the taxpayers a bargain because they operate far more cheaply than do state firms. As one industry report put it, "CEOs of privatized companies... are leaner and more motivated than their public-sector counterparts."

But even if privatization does save money—and the evidence here is contradictory—there is, in the words of Jenni Gainsborough of the ACLU's National Prison Project, "a basic philosophical problem when you begin turning over administration of prisons to people who have an interest in keeping people locked up."

To be profitable, private prison firms must ensure that prisons are not only built but also filled. Industry experts say a 90 to 95 per cent capacity rate is needed to guarantee the hefty rates of return needed to lure investors. Prudential Securities issued a wildly bullish report on CCA a few years ago but cautioned, "It takes time to bring inmate population levels up to where they cover costs. Low occupancy is a drag on profits." Still, said the report, company earnings would be strong if CCA succeeded in "ramp[ing] up population levels in its new facilities at an acceptable rate".

A 1993 report from the State Department of Corrections in New Mexico found that CCA prisons issued more disciplinary reports—with harsher sanctions imposed, including the loss of time off for good behavior—than did those run by the state. A prisoner at a CCA prison said, "State-run facilities are overcrowded and there's no incentive to keep inmates as long as possible... CCA on the other hand reluctantly awards good time. They give it because they have to but they take it every opportunity they get... Parole packets are constantly getting lost or misfiled. Many of us are stuck here beyond our release dates."

Private prison companies have also begun to push, even if discreetly, for the type of get tough policies needed to ensure their continued growth. All the major firms in the field have hired big time lobbyists. When it was seeking a contract to run a halfway house in New York City, Esmor hired a onetime aide to state Rep. Edolphus Towns to lobby on its behalf. The aide succeeded in winning the contract and also the vote of his former boss, who had been an opponent of the project. In 1995, Wackenhut Chairman Tim Cole testified before the Senate Judiciary Committee to urge support for amendments to the Violent Crime Control Act—which subsequently passed—that authorized the expenditure of $10 billion to construct and repair state prisons.

CCA has been especially adept at expansion via political payoffs. The first prison the company managed was the Silverdale Workhouse in Hamilton County, Tennessee. After Commissioner Bob Long voted to accept CCA's bid for the project, the company awarded Long's pest control firm a lucrative contract. When Long decided the time was right to quit public life, CCA hired him to lobby on its behalf. CCA head Massey has been a major financial supporter of Lamar Alexander, the former Tennessee governor and failed presidential candidate. In one of a number of sweetheart deals, Lamar's wife, Honey Alexander, made more than $130,000 on a $5,000 investment in CCA. Current Tennessee Governor Newt McWherter is another CCA stockholder and is quoted in the company's 1995 annual report as saying that "the federal government would be well served to privatize all of their corrections."

The prison industry has also made generous use of the junket as a public relations technique. Wackenhut recently flew a New York-based reporter from Switzerland—where the company is fishing for business—to Florida for a tour of one of its prisons. The reporter was driven around by limousine, had all her expenses covered and was otherwise treated royally.

In another ominous development, the revolving door between the public and private sector has led to the type of company boards that are typical of those found in the military-industrial complex. CCA co-founders were T. Don Hutto, a ex-corrections commissioner in Virginia, and Tom Beasley, a former chairman of the Tennessee Republican Party. A top company official is Michael Quinlan, once director of the Federal Bureau of Prisons. The board of Wackenhut is graced by a former Marine Corps commander, two retired Air Force generals and a former under secretary of the Air Force, as well as by James Thompson, ex-governor of Illinois, Stuart Gerson, a former assistant U.S. attorney general and Richard Staley, who previously worked with the INS.

Because they are private firms that answer to shareholders, prison companies have been predictably vigorous in seeking ways to cut costs. In 1985, a private firm tried to site a prison on a toxic waste dump in Pennsylvania, which it had bought at the bargain rate of $1. Fortunately, that plan was rejected.

Many states pay private contractors a per diem rate, as low as $31 per prisoner in Texas. A federal investigation traced a 1994 riot at an Esmor immigration detention center to the company's having skimped on food, building repairs and guard salaries. At an Esmor-run halfway house in Manhattan, inspectors turned up leaky plumbing, exposed electrical wires, vermin and inadequate food.

To ratchet up profit margins, companies have cut corners on drug rehabilitation, counseling and literacy programs. In 1995, Wackenhut was investigated for diverting $700,000 intended for drug treatment programs at a Texas prison. In Florida the U.S. Corrections Corporation was found to be in violation of a provision in its state contract that requires prisoners to be placed in meaningful work or educational assignments. The company had assigned 235 prisoners as dorm orderlies when no more than 48 were needed and enroll-ment in education programs was well below what the contract called for. Such incidents led a prisoner at a CCA facility in Tennessee to conclude, "There is something inherently sinister about making money from the incarceration of prisoners, and in putting CCA's bottom-line [money] before society's bottom line [rehabilitation]."

The companies try to cut costs by offering less training and pay to staff. Almost all workers at state prisons get union-scale pay but salaries for private prison guards range from about $7 to $10 per hour. Of course the companies are anti-union. When workers attempted to organize at Tennessee's South Central prison, CCA sent officials down from Nashville to quash the effort.

Poor pay and work conditions have led to huge turnover rates at private prisons. A report by the Florida auditor's office found that turnover at the Gadsden Correctional Facility for Women, run by the U.S. Corrections Corporation, was 200 percent, ten times the rate at state prisons. Minutes from an administrative meeting at a CCA prison in Tennessee have the "chief" recorded as saying, "We all know that we have lots of new staff and are constantly in the train-ing mode... Many employees [are] totally lost and have never worked in corrections."

Private companies also try to nickel and dime prisoners in the effort to boost revenue. A prisoner at a Florida prison run by CCA has sued the company for charging a $2.50 fee per phone call and 50 cents per minute thereafter. The lawsuit also charges that it can take a prisoner more than a month to see a doctor.

A number of prisoners complain about exorbitant prices. "Can-teen prices are outrageous," wrote a prisoner at the Gadsden facility in Florida. "[We] pay more for a pack of cigarettes than in the free world." Neither do private firms provide prisoners with soap, tooth-paste, toothbrushes or writing paper. One female prisoner at a CCA prison in New Mexico said: "The state gives five free postage paid envelopes per month to prisoners, nothing at CCA. State provides new coats, jeans, shirts, underwear and replaces them as needed. CCA rarely buys new clothing and inmates are often issued tattered and stained clothing. Same goes for linens. Also ration toilet paper and paper towels. If you run out, too bad—3 rolls every two weeks."

General conditions at private prisons appear in some respects to be somewhat better than those found at state institutions, a fact possibly linked to the negative business impact that a prison disturbance can cause private firms. For example, the share price of stock in Esmor plunged from $20 to $7 after a 1994 revolt at the company's detention center for immigrants in Elizabeth, New Jersey.

Nevertheless a number of serious problems at prisons run by private interests still exist. Back in the mid-1980s, a visiting group of professional guards from England toured the CCA's 360-bed state prison in Chattanooga, Tennessee, and reported that prisoners were "cruelly treated" and "problem" prisoners had been gagged with sticky tape. The warden regaled his guests with graphic descriptions of strip shows performed by female prisoners for male guards.

Investigators at a CCA jail in New Mexico found that guards had inflicted injuries on prisoners ranging from cuts and scrapes to broken bones. Riots have erupted at various private facilities. In one of the worst, guards at CCA's West Tennessee Detention Center fired pepper gas canisters into two dormitories to quell a riot after prisoners shipped from North Carolina revolted over being sent far from their families.

In addition to the companies that directly manage America's prisons, many other firms are getting a piece of the private prison action. American Express has invested millions of dollars in private prison construction in Oklahoma and General Electric has helped finance construction in Tennessee. Goldman Sachs & Co., Merrill Lynch, Smith Barney, among other Wall Street firms, have made huge sums by underwriting prison construction with the sale of tax-exempt bonds, this now a thriving $2.3 billion industry.

Weapons manufacturers see both public and private prisons as a new outlet for "defense" technology, such as electronic bracelets and stun guns. Private transport companies have lucrative contracts to move prisoners within and across state lines; health care companies supply jails with doctors and nurses; food service firms provide prisoners with meals. High-tech firms are also moving into the field; the Que-Tel Corp hopes for vigorous sales of its new system whereby prisoners are bar-coded and guards carry scanners to monitor their movements. Phone companies such as AT&T chase after the enormously lucrative prison business.

About three-quarters of new admissions to American jails and prisons are now African-American and Hispanic men. This trend, combined with an increasingly privatized and profitable prison system run largely by Whites, makes for what Jerome Miller, a former youth corrections officer in Pennsylvania and Massachusetts, calls the emerging Gulag State.

Miller predicts that the Gulag State will be in place within 15 years. He expects three to five million people to be behind bars, including an absolute majority of African-American men. It's comparable, he says, to the post-Civil War period, when authorities came to view the prison system as a cheaper, more efficient substitute for slavery. Of the state's current approach to crime and law enforcement, Miller says, "The race card has changed the whole playing field. Because the prison system doesn't affect a significant percentage of young White men we'll increasingly see prisoners treated as commodities. For now the situation is a bit more benign than it was back in the nineteenth century, but I'm not sure it will stay that way for long."

PRISON INDUSTRY PROFITEERS SENTENCED

Dan Pens, May-July 1996

Former Texas state parole board Chairman, James Granberry, plead guilty in April of 1994 to charges that he committed perjury during an investigation of independent "parole consultants."

After Granberry resigned from the Board of Pardons and Parole in May 1991, he set himself up as a freelance parole consultant. Granberry—as well as other former Texas parole board members—made a practice of marketing their influence as former parole board members, collecting "consulting fees" from prisoners desperate for freedom. This practice has since been outlawed by the state, but only after public furor focused attention on the issue when paroled murderer, Kenneth McDuff, abducted and killed a pregnant convenience store clerk. When McDuff was arrested he had a business card in his wallet from the parole consultant (another former parole board member) who assisted in his successful parole bid.

Granberry was charged with perjury, accused of lying to a federal magistrate about the extent of the consulting business he ran. Federal prosecutors said Granberry served as a consultant for prisoners and their families on 22 cases and was still receiving fees when he testified in 1992 that he had handled only six or eight cases and was no longer in that business.

In entering the guilty plea before U. S. District Judge Walter Smith, Granberry also admitted that while he was still a member of the parole board he helped a Dallas car dealer's son win a parole in exchange for a reduced lease payment on two automobiles.

In August of 1994 Granberry was sentenced to serve six months in a halfway house. Pam Lynchner, a spokesperson for the Houston "victims' rights" reform group Justice for All, said the sentence was "absolutely appalling. The court not only let him walk without any prison time, they are going to allow him not to pay any monetary fine."

Granberry had cooperated with federal prosecutors in exchange for a lenient sentence. He testified before a grand jury that while he was a "consultant" he was routinely given confidential information from prisoner files by then active parole board member, Frank Eickenburg. Eickenburg was indicted by the grand jury for his complicity in those cases.

Two other disgraceful tales of prison-profiteer corruption come from Texas and Kentucky respectively. In the first, a private prison developer—Patrick Harold Graham, using the alias Harold Robert—was arrested in January '96 and charged with plotting to help a convicted murderer escape from prison for a $750,000 fee.

Graham also extended the offer to the convict's girlfriend. But the girlfriend went to authorities, who videotaped Graham, 45, as he allegedly accepted a $150,000 down payment in a restaurant parking lot. She handed Graham the money and told him she was making the payment with stolen funds. He was arrested after taking the money and was charged with money laundering and theft.

Graham was head of N-Group Securities, Inc., which played a key role in developing rent-a-cell jails for several job-starved Texas towns in the late 1980s. Graham and others were defendants in civil lawsuits resulting in a $34 million federal judgment against them for civil conspiracy and violation of state and federal securities laws as part of a fraudulent scheme to finance six private prisons in small Texas municipalities.

The convict Graham was charged with helping to escape was not named in court, but sources identified him as Dana McIntosh, a former computer company executive from Dallas serving a 75-year sentence for fatally stabbing his wife. Graham allegedly told McIntosh that he could secure him a job as a prison trusty, which would allow him to work on jobs outside the prison walls. Once outside, McIntosh would be whisked to Louisiana, where a plane, provided and piloted by Graham, would meet him and take McIntosh and his girlfriend to another country. Graham indicated he had done extensive research on which countries they could safely flee to and assured McIntosh and his girlfriend that new identities, and the documents to support them, would be prepared. Graham apparently used his close ties to James W. "Andy" Collins, former head of the state prison system, to lend credence to his ability to make the plan work. Collins announced his resignation in fall of '95 after Texas Governor George W. Bush ordered an investigation into Collins' business dealings with James Brunson, a former officer with N-Group, and with former Houston Mayor Fred Hofheinz, both of whom were defendants in the federal lawsuits over fraudulent prison development schemes (as well as for Collins' involvement in the VitaPro debacle).

"I have not been shown any evidence to lead me to believe that Mr. Collins is involved in the incident," said Allan Polunsky, chairman of the Texas Board of Criminal Justice. "Of course we are conducting an investigation to ensure there was no complicity by any employee of the department."

One source close to the investigation, though, said that Collins had issued Graham an identification badge normally reserved for criminal justice board members and other high ranking officials. The badge would have allowed Graham unlimited access anywhere in any Texas prison.

Before the escape plot was uncovered, McIntosh had been scheduled for a reclassification hearing, something rarely done in the case of a murderer serving a 75-year sentence. As for the unusual circumstances of the reclassification review, Polunsky said, "That situation is also being reviewed. We don't know for sure how he got [scheduled] back [for a reclassification hearing], but we are going to find out. I have placed the highest priority on this."

If Graham is convicted and sentenced to a prison term, perhaps it would be a fitting punishment to require him to serve his time in one of the substandard rent-a-cell jails that N-Group Securities participated in financing.

The second story is that of Clifford Todd. In 1993 Todd, 68, was chairman of the Kentucky-based U.S. Corrections Corporation, a private prison firm. In March of 1996 he was sentenced by a federal judge to a 15-month prison term.

Todd plead guilty to mail fraud in 1995 for his part in a bribery and extortion scheme. Also convicted in the scheme was Richard Frey, the former Jefferson County, Kentucky corrections chief. Frey was convicted in November, 1995, of extorting $198,000 in bribes from Todd, in exchange for the corporation winning and keeping a lucrative county jail contract.

In addition to the 15-month prison sentence, Todd was fined $40,000, and in an ironic twist, U.S. District Judge John Heyburn ordered Todd to pay for the cost of his incarceration.

According to a 1995 report by the University of Florida, U.S. Corrections Corporation operates four private facilities, all in Kentucky, with a total population of 2,198 prisoners. They are the third largest private prison corporation, with a 6.42 percent market share. In comparison, the two largest prison corporations—Corrections Corporation of America and Wackenhut Corrections Corporation—control 30.48 percent and 25.82 percent of the U.S. market share in private prison beds.

It's difficult to find such immoral behavior by men who sell and trade caged human beings surprising. But it is too bad that their relatively small crimes are the only ones punished, while their greater crime of destroying prisoners' lives is simply furthered and expanded by others who continue to profit from the lucrative business of imprisonment.

Part VI
CRIMES OF THE KEEPERS

Racism, Corruption and Brutality

Acts of racism, brutality, corruption and other criminal misbehaviors are an integral aspect of any prison system. It should be understood that a system in which some people must justify to themselves the caging of others will produce discrimination: how else can a guard make sense of the fact some people of his own class are imprisoned while others are not, in a nation where only a fraction of those who commit crimes are imprisoned? The system will produce violence: as prisoners are dehumanized the methods used to keep them in line become less and less important. The mindset is that they deserve anything that happens to them.

Prison guard brutality highlights more than any other issue the nature in which prisons are fundamentally flawed. There may never be a prison without violence, and what further mayhem will that violence engender? Prisons are a recipe for a progressively scarier and scarier society; the material in this chapter gives us a glimpse why, and a look at the increasing desensitization to prisoner abuse by the outside world that lies ahead.

MYSTERIOUS NEW SYNDROME DISCOVERED!

Dan Pens, July 1996

The Santa Clara County, California, Board of Supervisors decided to commission a report. They assembled a team of independent corrections specialists to study every aspect of the county jail's operation. The county supervisors wanted to find out why jail detainees seemed to mysteriously die after "tussling" with guards.

The experts conducted their investigation and released a groundbreaking report. The most startling conclusion highlighted in the report is that jail detainees and arrested suspects who "inexplicably die" while in police custody may be victims of "Sudden In-Custody Death Syndrome." (We are not making this up!)

The report not only identified the syndrome, but urged that jail guards and medical staff be trained to recognize the "risk factors" of the syndrome. According to the report, prisoners at risk include those who: have just engaged in a violent struggle, sometimes while resisting arrest; who do not respond to pepper spray or pain-compliance holds; have been handcuffed while lying in a prone position, especially face down; who are drunk or drugged; over 50 years old or overweight; and those who exhibit a period of silence.

"We are increasingly concerned about this issue," said John Hagar, an attorney who specializes in jail issues and a member of the team that wrote the report. "In-Custody Death Syndrome is slowly being recognized as a problem with specific risk factors to be watched for."

Of course, this "syndrome" is one which has long been recognized and understood by prisoners, who usually refer to it as "Sudden Torture and Fatal Beating Syndrome." Risk factors identified by prisoners over the years include: guards who smile and say "It's time you learned a lesson, boy," while swinging batons at your head;

guards taking a number and standing in line outside of a mop closet in which you are hog-tied, naked on the floor; guards who use racial epithets, and who may also have blood stains and bits of teeth and bone embedded in their jack-boots; and guards who exhibit periods of intense, violent rage.

Perhaps a bilateral commission composed of experts from both the corrections community and those who have experienced some "corrections" first-hand could further study this mysterious syndrome and develop solutions that would allow prisoners to be tortured without actually dying in the process.

TOTAL POWER CORRUPTS

Guard Racism and Brutality

Dan Pens and Paul Wright, January 1995 - December 1996

Racist Assaults

Ronald Lawrenz was a probationary prison guard at the Charlotte Correctional Institution (CCI) in Florida. On January 18, 1993, Lawrenz was at the home of another guard having a barbecue with four other CCI guards. The ostensible purpose of the gathering was to "celebrate" Martin Luther King day. Lawrenz and another guard were wearing T-shirts which prominently displayed a swastika and the words "White Power."

After drinking, one of the guards fired an AK-47 into the air. Police arrived and investigated the shooting during which the guards confessed to wearing the White power T-shirts to "commemorate" MLK day. After the local media reported the incident, the prison warden fired Lawrenz. Two of the other guards were given reprimands which were dismissed on administrative appeal, and the other two guards resigned.

A different aspect of guard racism—and one obviously more important to the mainstream newsmedia—was reported in Florida by the *Palm Beach Post*. The *Post* featured several lengthy articles in December of 1995 about the racist actions of guards at Florida's Martin Correctional Institution (MCI). The headline? "Racial Tension Growing at MCI: A Probe Details Racist Mail and Slurs Directed at Black Officers."

Oh, so that's it! Guards acting like racists towards other guards. Well, now, that's not nice!

The series of articles detailed a long-standing tradition of Black guards at MCI being harassed, threatened, humiliated and intimidated by their White co-workers.

Seven MCI guards filed discrimination complaints with the Equal Opportunities Commission, which conducted an investigation and released a 200-page report. The report detailed incidents such as: racist mail placed in Black guards' employee mailboxes; a Black doll hanging from a noose in the prison's control booth; dead animals placed in the parked vehicles of Black guards; and retaliation against guards who had reported incidents of racism.

Wayne Bythwood, a Black guard who had worked as a recreation supervisor since the prison opened in 1985, was one of the seven who filed official complaints. Two days after the filing White guards waited until he left work for the day and ransacked his office. Locks were cut from tool and supply cabinets and his office was torn up.

"They're treating me just like an inmate," Bythwood said. "It's nothing but retaliation."

The implication of Bythwood's statement—and of the overall tone of the *Post*'s coverage of racism at MCI—is of course that it's okay to "treat inmates" with racial hatred. It's only a problem, and it's only news, when guards get the same treatment.

In September of 1993, Charles Coates, a prisoner in the Greensville Correctional Center at Jarran, Virginia, was handcuffed and shackled when a prison guard lifted him up and slammed him to the floor face first. Coates says he blacked out and when he awoke another guard was kneeling on his back while the first guard kicked him in the face, neck and ribs.

Douglas Brown, another Greensville prisoner who was also hand-cuffed and shackled at the time, said that when he saw the guards beating Coates he cursed at them. He was then also beaten while handcuffed, knocked to the floor and sustained head injuries requiring five stitches. Brown suffered neck injuries and required eleven stitches to close a laceration above one eye. Brown said the beatings were racially motivated. He and Coates are White and the officers, who are Black, used racial slurs while beating them. Prisoners at the Greensville prison have reported that incidents of Black guards ver-bally abusing White prisoners with racial slurs are common events.

Coates and Brown said they had been beaten on numerous other occasions. In October of 1993 Brown had one of his front teeth knocked out when a guard with a pair of handcuffs wrapped around his knuckles punched him in the face.

Partly as a result of the September, 1993, incident, attention was focused on a pattern of guard brutality at the Greensville prison, which opened in 1990. State investigators turned over evidence of 32 beating incidents at Greensville, dating back to January '93, to the Greensville county prosecutor's office. Some of the incidents involve instances where guards have employed "goon squads" of prisoners to inflict beatings on other prisoners.

In October '94, Greensville guards Alphonso Smith, Larry Bynum, and Sgt. Benjamin Williams were indicted in connection with the September 1993 beatings of Coates and Brown. Another guard, Dennis Price, was charged with one count of malicious wounding. The charge stemmed from an incident where he threw scalding water on a prisoner, resulting in third-degree burns on the prisoner's face, chest and stomach. The four guards were suspended without pay. Price later pleaded no contest and received a sentence of six months in jail.

Retaliation

On June 3, 1994, Washington State Reformatory (WSR) guard Roger Wallace, 28, was arrested at the Monroe, Washington, prison on charges of soliciting a prisoner, Samuel McNeal, to assault Gerald "J.D." Enquist, another prisoner. On June 9, 1994, Wallace was charged in Snohomish County Superior Court with solicitation to commit second degree assault.

The Affidavit of Probable Cause filed by Deputy Prosecutor James Townsend stated in part:

> On 6/3/94, Mr. McNeal agreed to wear a wire and record a conversation with the defendant during the defendant's work shift at the Washington State Reformatory. The recording was authorized by Judge Kathryn Trumbull. During the recorded conversation the defendant indicated the other guard wanted Mr. Enquist to be killed but that he did not think homicide would be such a good idea. The defendant finally indicated he wanted Mr. Enquist to suffer a broken bone or bones. The defendant indicated he would pay a sum of $200 in exchange for Mr. Enquist's suffering a broken arm... Department of Corrections officials have confirmed long term disputes have existed between Mr. Enquist and the other guard.

According to Townsend's affidavit, the offer was first made in

May, 1994, when Wallace approached WSR prisoner Samuel "J-Bonee" McNeal and offered him $200 to break the arm of Gerald "J. D." Enquist. McNeal immediately reported this offer to prison officials who called in the Snohomish County Sheriffs Department on May 25, 1994.

The plot apparently arose out of a desire by Wallace to retaliate against Enquist for the numerous grievances and complaints that Enquist, a prison law library clerk, had filed or assisted other prisoners in filing against Wallace's girlfriend, Cheryl Swanberg. The numerous complaints prisoners made against Swanberg, also a guard at WSR, include her: making false claims that prisoners were informants; smoking in no smoking areas; losing control of herself and screaming at prisoners; and interfering with prisoners' access to the law library and legal interpreters. For years the DOC refused to act on complaints regarding Swanberg's unprofessional and troublesome behavior.

When Wallace was arrested at WSR he was dressed in orange jail coveralls. WSR Superintendent Ken Ducharme said: "I didn't want our [DOC] uniform to go to jail. It would have been problematic for him [Wallace] to go to a cell like that."

Swanberg bailed Wallace out of the Snohomish County jail the same day he was arrested. Unconfirmed reports state that Swanberg was also arrested by county Sheriff's officers at Wallace's court arraignment. Both Swanberg and Wallace were placed on paid administrative leave while DOC officials and the Sheriff's office investigate further. McNeal was moved to the McNeil Island prison.

In an interview at the time Wallace said that he was the real victim in the alleged plot, and that Enquist and McNeal set him up "and they did a damn good job of it." (So good in fact that Wallace is recorded making the solicitation to commit the assault!) In the same interview, Wallace claimed that Enquist enjoys "special privileges" at the Reformatory, and is "untouchable" by staff, as he alleged Enquist was an informant. Ducharme was quoted denying that Enquist was an informant or that he had any special privileges. What Enquist does have, according to Ducharme, is brains. "He's a very bright guy. You'd better follow your policies and rules or he'll call attention to it." Deputy Prosecutor Townsend dismissed Wallace's accusations about Enquist as irrelevant: "That's still no reason to try and break someone's arm."

Wallace's claims of innocence didn't prevent him from pleading guilty to the charge of second degree assault. On November 2, 1994, he was sentenced in Snohomish County Superior Court by judge James Allendorfer to one year in jail, with all but 30 days suspended. Both the prosecution and defense had requested that the entire sentence be suspended. He was also required to pay $625 in attorney fees for his public defender. In exchange for not being charged with any felony, Swanberg had agreed to testify against him. So much for honor among thieves. It is not known whether either will continue their careers as prison guards in Washington.

On October 7, 1994, 15 of about 300 prisoners in the recreation yard of the Terrell Prison Unit in Livingston, Texas, attacked prison staff. One guard suffered a broken nose. Prison guards beat several prisoners in retaliation for the attack. On October 9, 1994, Michael McCoy died in a hospital after being found in his cell unconscious with head injuries. He was serving a six year sentence for burglary and unauthorized use of a motor vehicle.

On October 12, 1994, prison guards Alex Torres and Joel Lambright were charged with murder in McCoy's death and released on $50,000 bail. They were charged with manslaughter for beating and kicking McCoy to death. Both were relatively new guards, hired in January and February, 1994, respectively. Andy Collins, then-Texas prison boss, stated that the murder charges against the guards show the TDCJ "will not tolerate unnecessary force" against prisoners.

On May 23, 1995, Joel Lambright was sentenced to a 2 to 10 year sentence. Initially charged with murder, Lambright was convicted of manslaughter after the jury heard testimony that he and guard Alex Torres had entered McCoy's cell after the October '94 disturbance and beat and kicked him into semi-consciousness. According to prisoners who are familiar with the case, the reason for the attack was that McCoy spat on Torres' wife (a kitchen worker) during the disturbance. In retaliation, McCoy was beaten to death. McCoy died of brain injuries the next day in a hospital (the prosecution argued that McCoy probably would have survived had he received prompt medical attention). With the conviction Lambright made state history: he was the first guard ever convicted of murdering a prisoner in Texas. Lambright's law enforcement career came full circle: from prison guard to prisoner.

He was sentenced to serve a two to ten year sentence. After serving just three months, however, Lambright was granted probation. District Court Judge Joe Ned Dean granted a motion from Lambright's attorney to place his client on "shock probation."

Defense attorney Travis Kitchens, who represents Lambright, said the purpose of shock probation is "to give a person who has never been in prison before a taste of prison in the hope that it persuades them not to get in trouble again." It is not clear how Lambright, a former prison guard, would fit the profile "never been in prison before." And considering that he was convicted of beating a prisoner to death, Lambright presumably is quite familiar with the taste of prison.

Lambright, 21, son of a former Corrigan, Texas, police chief, was released from prison and permitted to return to his Corrigan home. Latham Boone, lead prosecutor in Lambright's case, told reporters that he had no objection to the motion for Lambright's prison sentence to be converted to probation. In response to the judge's ruling, Boone said, "I think the judge had the community's best interests in mind and also the interest of rehabilitating Lambright."

The other guard charged along with Lambright, Alex Torres, 31, entered into a plea agreement and his murder charge was reduced to manslaughter. He was sentenced to eight years in prison. It is likely he will also be granted probation. And you wonder why prisoners call it the "Just-Us" system?!

Sheer Brutality

On September 12, 1995, a guard at the Lee Arrendale Correctional Institution in Alto, Georgia, told 22-year-old prisoner, Samuel Rivers, to clean his cell. Rivers had shredded newspapers and "carpeted" his cell with them. When Rivers refused to clean up the cell, five guards were summoned to take him to the hole. When they attempted to cuff him, he bolted. After a short chase, the guards threw Rivers to the floor and choked him with a baton across the neck until he lost consciousness.

The guards dragged his limp, handcuffed body to the infirmary. A prison doctor was unable to detect a pulse. An autopsy at the Georgia Bureau of Investigation state crime laboratory showed that Rivers died of asphyxiation.

"This is outrageous. This man was not sentenced to death," said attorney Robert Cullen of Georgia Legal Services, which represents prisoners in lawsuits challenging prison conditions. "It's not the place of the Department of Corrections to impose a death sentence for those not sentenced to death."

One of the guards was suspended without pay. The others reportedly still work at the prison. None of the guards were identified.

Analdo Ortega was being held in the Hudson County, NJ, jail in March of 1989, awaiting trial on burglary charges. According to court testimony, Ortega's request for a blanket triggered the anger of some of his captors. Shortly thereafter he was beaten to death.

Four jail guards were indicted on charges of federal civil rights violations. They had originally faced state charges, but those were dismissed.

William Fink, 35, a former sergeant, pleaded guilty March 4, 1996, to a single charge: committing a civil rights violation that resulted in death. He could be sentenced to as much as life imprisonment.

Thomas Murphy, 36, admitted that he failed to report the beating. He could get up to three years in prison.

Raymond Murray, 58, who was deputy warden in charge of the night shift when the beating occurred, and David Dumers, 42, a guard, both face trial.

Another guard, Richard Maroldi, pleaded guilty in 1992 to state charges of falsifying reports about the beating.

The three-count federal indictment charges Murray with conspiracy, cruel and unusual punishment by law officers, and depriving Ortega of the right to be kept from harm while in custody. Dumers will be tried only on the first two counts.

On the night of the beating, Murray told Fink to send guards to the fourth floor of the jail. Dumers and Murphy were also told to go there to "handle a problem," according to the indictment.

They ordered Ortega out of his cell, and took him to an elevator, where the beating began. When the elevator reached the ground floor, Dumers and Murphy put Ortega in a holding cage where Fink and Dumers continued the beating as Murray looked on, the indictment said.

Two days later Ortega died as a result of injuries sustained in the beating.

The Corcoran Debacle

On the morning of May 15, 1995, five prisoners at California's Calipatria State Prison stormed a facility program office and stabbed a sergeant. Other guards rushed to help and a wild brawl ensued. Eight guards were injured in the melee. The seemingly "senseless" attack was apparently conducted in retaliation by members of the East Side Crips for the beating by guards of one of their members earlier that same day.

About six weeks later a busload of 36 Calipatria prisoners was transferred to Corcoran State Prison, home to Southern California's second control unit Security Housing Unit (SHU) for men. About 30 Corcoran guards were on hand to greet the bus.

One by one the 36 shackled Calipatria prisoners were grabbed, some by their testicles, and choked, punched and thrown off the bus. One prisoner's ribs were broken, a window was shattered with the head of another. Guards banged one prisoner's face off a concrete wall and stuffed a towel down another's throat.

Guards "escorted" the prisoners inside to private quarters for more beatings. The guards then laid out 24 of the prisoners on their stomachs, jerked their heads back by their chins and forcibly sheared off their tightly braided hair.

The *Sacramento Bee* obtained copies of grievances filed by some of the Calipatria prisoners. One said: "When I stepped off the bus [and in plain view of at least two Lieutenants] four COs [Correctional Officers] grabbed me and snatched my head back by my hair, then kicked my feet from under me, causing me to be slammed to the ground. They then picked me up to uncuff me and re-cuff me behind my back."

He said he was ordered to squat with his head against a cement wall. "One of my shower shoes was kicked away and the other one was halfway on. It was about 2:30 p.m. and the temperature was in the high 90s or low 100s. The ground was like a frying pan." When he complained, he said, he was told to shut up and the guards joked about his burning feet. The prisoner suffered third-degree burns on one foot and first-degree burns on the other. He said it was four days before he was allowed to see a doctor.

The month following the beatings, Millard Murphy, a California attorney and director of the Davis branch of the Prison Law Office, filed a citizens' complaint. In that complaint he wrote: "As it appears so many inmates were attacked, it is evident that these allegations will not disappear."

Corcoran was already the subject of a Department of Justice probe into the high number of prisoners fatally shot by guards, which seems to have also made it more difficult for the Calipatria 36 "welcome wagon" incident to evade scrutiny. A formal investigation into the incident ensued. Early in 1996 it was reported that seven Corcoran guards were placed on paid administrative leave pending the conclusion of an internal investigation.

In March 1996, eight Corcoran staff were fired as a result of the investigation for their actions relating to beatings of the Calipatria 36. Among those fired were Associate Warden Bruce Farris Jr. and Capt. Lee Fouch, both of whom are named in a wrongful death suit involving the 1994 shooting death of prisoner Preston Tate.

In addition to Farris and Fouch, others fired in March were: Lt. Richard Garcia, Sgt. John Misko, Sgt. Reginald Parra, Lt. Ellis McCant, Lt. Harold McEnroe and Sgt. Robert Dean. Another guard, Eric Rose, "chose to take early retirement."

All eight of the fired Corcoran personnel filed administrative appeals. In May, Administrative Law Judge Jose Alvarez modified the disciplinary actions of five of the guards. One lieutenant had his termination changed to a 60-day suspension, and a lieutenant and three sergeants were demoted to correctional officers. The termination of Fouch and Farris was not overturned, and information about the appeal of Lt. Ellis McCant was not publicized.

Department of Corrections spokesperson Tip Kendel said the discipline against the five was modified after a lengthy review process. Kendel said he did not know what factors led to the easing of the penalties.

The suspension is estimated to cost Lt. McEnroe about $9,000 in salary. The demotions will cost Garcia an estimated $1,000 a month in salary and the three former sergeants about $500 a month each, according to Kendel.

Farris told a captain and lieutenant at a briefing on the day the Calipatria bus was to arrive that the 36 prisoners had participated in the prison office stabbings, were "assaultive and violent," that they fought with guards when leaving Calipatria. He added that the prisoners had threatened to "take over" Corcoran upon their arrival, according to his termination notice. A Calipatria lieutenant who spoke by phone with Farris that morning said that Farris was told that the wild allegations about the busload of prisoners were unfounded rumors. Farris didn't dispel the wild rumors, however, when briefing his subordinates.

The former associate warden was also cited in the termination notice for "validating" the brutality against the Calipatria 36 as proper "disciplinary action"; for failing to investigate the injuries the prisoners reported; and for authorizing more than $1,000 worth of overtime pay for the guards who handled the Calipatria bus.

The investigation and wrongful death suit in the fatal shooting of Preston Tate continues. That suit contends that Corcoran guards deliberately start fights between prisoners from rival ethnic gangs to "provide themselves and/or other guards with an opportunity to use firepower against prisoners."

"I think the prison is rotten to the core," said Catherine Campbell, one of the three Fresno attorneys handling the wrongful death suit for Tate's family. "It is one filthy pig-sty prison. Everywhere we look, we find nothing but massive brutality."

But Warden George Smith (who escaped discipline for formally authorizing the hair shearing of 24 of the arriving Calipatria prisoners) says that prison officials "do not tolerate our staff abusing inmates—we never have and we never will."

"We are not," Smith added, "a bunch of knuckle-dragging thugs."

"PROFESSIONAL CONDUCT" AT THE PURDY PRISON FOR WOMEN

Vicki McElroy, October 1993

Being incarcerated here at the Washington Corrections Center for Women (WCCW) in Purdy for the past few years, I have had the opportunity to observe the behavior of those designated by the state to make sure that we stay incarcerated, that is: the guards. Or more appropriately termed, Satan's Minions, as I so fondly refer to them.

As you may or may not know, we here at WCCW recently won a cross-gender pat search case against a policy the DOC pathetically tried to enact.[1] They even went so far as to say that the male guards employed here could conduct these intrusive body searches in a "professional" manner. Were I a person of a lesser sense of humor, I probably would have been outraged at such a blatant and obvious disregard for our well-being.

I looked up the definition of "professional" in my ever-handy *Websters'*, and interestingly enough, the definition did not seem to fit the behavior of the last four male correctional officers that mysteriously ceased working here in the past two months.

The DOC obviously has a different definition of "professionalism" than any of us incarcerated here, unless we're talking about sex offenders. And of course, the DOC has kept a tight reign on this information being allowed out to the public.

I wonder if "professional" covers the guard that was fired after he was discovered taking "liberties" with an unconscious hospitalized female prisoner, while he was assigned to "guard" her? I think my favorite is the one that resigned to avoid the investigation that was being done on him for sending female prisoners money and packages. I wonder why he was doing that?

As far back as 1983, when a female prisoner incarcerated here won over a million dollars from the state for a suit she filed after becoming pregnant by one of the guards, this "professional" behavior has been hidden by the state. And still they had the audacity to insult and assault us by trying to give their male employees a license to sexually and mentally abuse us even further. Let's not forget the male guard still employed here that was grieved for commenting "I can't wait," in regards to the possibility of the cross-gender pat searches being conducted at Purdy. This did absolutely nothing for the confidence I had in the "professionalism" being practiced here. Thankfully, Governor Lowry saw the insanity of such a violation and prevented the state appealing the ban on cross-gender pat searches to the U.S. Supreme Court.

Also, if the state is so confident that their male guards could indeed act in a "professional" manner, what is their point in telling us recently that our name tags now have to be worn up on our shoulders to draw the guards' attention away from the breast area? Are they afraid that one of their "professional" male employees might suddenly become filled with uncontrollable desire and display his "professional" behavior in front of everyone, thus making it impossible to sweep the incident under the rug, as is the case with the other past and ongoing incidents? Furthermore, why are we no longer allowed to wear short summer tops that reveal our belly buttons or midriff? Don't women on the streets have belly buttons? Will our elusive rehabilitation somehow be thwarted by our belly buttons showing? Or is it that the female prisoners' belly button is too alluring to be displayed in the company of so many "professionals"?

Maybe one day the DOC will see how ludicrous its reasoning is. However, since a good majority of the DOC leadership are of the male species, I doubt this is likely.

1 *Jordan v. Gardner*, 986 F.2d 1521 (9th Cir. 1993)

THE "HONORABLE MEN" DEFENSE

Mumia Abu-Jamal, December 1996

"The noble Brutus hath told you Caesar was ambitious:
If it were so, it was a grievous fault;
And grievously hath Caesar answer'd it. Here, under leave of Brutus and the rest,—
for Brutus is an honorable man.
So are they all, all honorable men."
    —William Shakespeare, *Julius Caesar*; Act III; Scene II.

For jailhouse lawyers and other prison litigators, the "honorable men" defense arises far too frequently in prison litigation.

More often than not, it arises, not on the motion of the party defending against the suit, but *sua sponte*, by the court itself, as a statement of affirmation of the government's representatives.

Say a plaintiff charges a state officer with violating a "constitutional guarantee" claimed within the articles or amendments of the U.S. Constitution, and after a hearing or trial, the claim is found to be true. In such an instance, should a court describe the violators as "honorable men"?

If a court does so, does it protect the Constitution, or the state official who has violated it?

Is it a court's duty to defend the state's interests, or to defend the constitution from violation?

These are not rhetorical questions.

This very thing happened in *Jamal v. Price*, where the plaintiff argued that the government, through its prison officials, illegally and unconstitutionally opened, read and copied his legal correspondence, lied about it, and did it repeatedly thereafter.

Further, the suit charged the state punished this writer for writing *Live from Death Row*, thus punishing one for the practice of his alleged First Amendment "constitutional rights" to freedom of the press, and free speech.

The court, in a remarkable display of judicial solicitude, described the state prison officials as "conscientious and scrupulous persons" and goes to some lengths to disassociate this government from some seen as repressive:

> This is the United States of America; it is not Germany in the 1930's and '40's. Persons do not come before our criminal justice apparatus only to disappear *im nacht und nebel*, as into the night and fog. This is not the Soviet Union; people are not swallowed up in some vast gulag to reappear, or not to do so, randomly. In this country convicted criminals are sentenced to prison, or, as in this case, to death; but they are not stripped of all their rights; and they do not disappear."[1]

From whence springs this discourse?

Why refer to Nazi Germany or Stalinist Soviet Union, in a case where an African-American prisoner charges the contemporary state with violating his alleged First Amendment "rights" of free speech?

(Interestingly, the Court chose to refer to the 1930's rather than the more contemporary, White supremacist repression visited upon the Black majority under the *apartheid* regime in South Africa for the better part of this century!)

In logic, the principle of *extremis probatis, praesumuntur media* (extremes being proven, intermediate things are presumed) is sometimes utilized by creating a contrast that really isn't contrastable.

The writer, being neither Jew German, nor Russian dissident, cannot cite to those experiences as touchstones for the present, and any reference to them can only serve to mislead readers from the repressive realities of the American present.

Indeed, who among us can honestly deny the naked state repression visited upon Black people in this nation, in her prisons, in her suburban state *bantustans* (laughably called "correctional" institutions)? Who can honestly argue against the proposition that the much-ballyhoed "War on Drugs" is but a thinly-disguised War on the Black Poor?

Moreover, the references to Nazi Germany and the Soviet Union don't acquit the U.S., for in both instances, the forms of "law" were met. *The Nazi holocaust was a legal holocaust*; as was much of Soviet repression—statutes were passed, and genocide was "legalized"!

The German-Soviet references were but oblique judicial responses to the horrific truths chronicled in *Live from Death Row*, and therefore amounted to a judicial book review!

How else can one interpret it?

Not content to decide constitutional "rights," the court launches into a defense of the *status quo*, of the reigning sociopolitical order, as "not Germany," nor "the Soviet Union."

Of course not. It is the United States, circa 1990s—and therein lies the rub.

The United States—the prisonhouse of nations, where, at latest count, over 1.6 million men and women were encaged; where the state bombs and maims its alleged "citizens" with criminal impunity (witness the MOVE massacre of May 13, 1985); where men and women are encaged for their social, political and spiritual beliefs (ex., the MOVE 9, Geronimo Ji Jaga [née Pratt], Leonard Peltier, Dr. Mutulu Shakur, Ray Luc Levasseur, Sundiata Acoli, Zolo Agona Azania, Marilyn Buck, Sheik Omar Ali Abdul Rahman, *et al.*[2]).

This United States which waged naked genocide against the indigenous peoples of the "Americas," and called it "Manifest Destiny"; which wiped out more millions than its cousin, Germany.

It was in this United States that the writer was punished for writing, despite the claims of the First Amendment.

Prison officials, although found to have lied on the witness stand, are nonetheless presumably "honorable men," even as the court found:

> [T]he decisions to deny plaintiff media interviews were first made immediately after plaintiff's decision to publish his book was communicated to defendants [DOC counsel] Horwitz and [prison warden] Price. These decisions continued, with a variety of purported justifications, for several months. These purported reasons are demonstrably false.[3]

It was precisely these "purported reasons" that were claimed by prison officials on the stand!

But, alas—"So are they all, all honorable men."

Inherent within the system is the bias of the *status quo,* the preservation of the existing order, and whatever uncovers the horrific dungeons, as did *Live from Death Row*, is seen as disfavored.

In American prisons, men are tortured, women are raped, captives are poisoned, and injustice is ubiquitous. Here, families, psyches and souls are ripped asunder, all administered by "honorable men."

To write about such legal evils *ist verboten*.

1 *Jamal v. Price*, SL., OP., p. 3.
2 For information on many of these cases, see: *Can't Jail the Spirit: Political Prisoners in the U.S.*, Editorial El Coquí, Publishers (Chicago, IL: October 1992). Geromino Ji Jaga was released in June, 1997.
3 *Jamal v. Price*, SL. OP., p. 56.

Part VII
PERMANENT LOCKDOWN

Control Unit Prisons
and the Proliferation of the Isolation Model

Control units are prisons inside prisons, stark and grim modern dungeons where prisoners spend 22-24 hours a day in their cells. Sometimes as small as 70 square feet, the cells are the size of an average bathroom. Exercise is taken in mesh-ceilinged outdoor cages, or in internal cells no larger than the prisoners' own, with only a chin-up bar to mark a difference. Educational and psychological programs are severely curtailed—if they exist at all.

The stated purpose of control units is to concentrate "incorrigibles"—the so-called "monsters" and "predators" that attack both staff and other prisoners—in a small number of facilities which are designed to handle them more effectively. In reality, control units are often used against activist prisoners who have made themselves unpopular with staff as a result of attempts to try to check the brutal excesses that frequently occur in prisons. Control units are also dumping grounds for the mentally ill, terribly exacerbating these prisoners' original problems, sometimes fatally so.

But even for those for whom the units are supposedly intended—the uncontrollably violent—the extreme isolation and lack of positive outlets make them more violent and self-destructive. Traumatic and scarring for the prisoner on a personal level, control units also pose a danger for society at large. Dr. Stuart Grassian, a faculty member at the Harvard Medical School who has studied the effects of solitary confinement on prisoners for well over a decade, has remarked that the use of control units is "kind of like kicking and beating a dog and keeping it in a cage until it gets crazy and vicious and wild as it can possibly get and then one day you take it out into the middle of the streets of San Francisco or Boston and you open the cage and you run away..." "That's no favor to the community," Grassian concluded. And it's no favor to the person prison officials treat worse than a dog.

Control units are the most extreme manifestation of a national prison system that has abandoned rehabilitation as a goal and is only interested in techniques of more effective, and preferably more expensive, warehousing.

A 1997 survey by the National Campaign to Stop Control Unit Prisons found that 40 states, the federal prison system, and the District of Columbia have at least one control unit—many have units for both men and women. The amazingly high cost of control units makes their entrenchment in the penal system a definite goal for the prison-industrial complex.

THE PELICAN BAY FACTOR

Abdul Olugbala Shakur, May 1995

Prior to 1987, the California Department of Corrections (CDC) had a policy which segregated alleged members of rival prison gangs and groups while assigned to the Security Housing Unit (SHU) exercise yard. This policy was designed to minimize prison violence, and based on the available statistics, this was an effective policy. But 1987 marked a change in this policy when New Folsom State Prison partially integrated the SHU exercise yard. This partial integration resulted in a significant increase in prison violence.

It wasn't until 1988 that the integration became complete. Corcoran State Prison forced all rival groups together on the same exercise yard, and this resulted in a dramatic and rapid increase in prison violence. Corcoran was averaging 2-4 assaults a day.

At that time, most of us didn't understand what was happening, but those of us who have been very active in the prisoners' rights movement knew something was not right about this change of policy, especially considering that the old policy had always proven to be effective and logical. The answer was simple: to intentionally increase prison violence among alleged members of rival prison groups.

We then realized that the CDC was using us as a means to develop the propaganda (and statistics) to justify the construction (and over $200 million price tag) of Pelican Bay State Prison. Take note, the CDC justification for Pelican Bay is rooted in two primary criteria: to isolate the so-called worst of the worst who have proven too violent to be held within other prisons, and to minimize prison violence.

The CDC reported an increase in prison violence to the media on a number of occasions between 1987 and 1990. But the CDC neglected to tell the public that it was their policy (both in practice and intent) which was responsible for the rapid increase in prison violence.

There are two other factors that must be considered. In 1987 the CDC implemented the "shoot to kill" policy and in 1988 they changed their weapon/ammunition to a new bullet that was designed to blow up in a prisoner's body—a guaranteed kill!

These changes at New Folsom and Corcoran were not only a prelude to Pelican Bay, but were specifically designed to justify and add credence to the CDC campaign to build a control unit prison. If there's any doubt in your mind to the allegations, ask yourself: "Why did the CDC integrate the rival prison gangs and groups, knowing that violence would surely result?" They were not being pressured by local/state politicians, a court order or the public to integrate the exercise yards. So what was the CDC's motivation?

The CDC knew without a doubt that by integrating the SHU exercise yards all hell would break loose. So why would the CDC implement a "shoot to kill" policy at the same time the forced integration policy was being implemented, and then introduce a new weapon that was designed to facilitate the "kill" portion of the shoot to kill policy?

Based on official reports, in a five year period the CDC murdered 27 prisoners, and at least seven were murdered on the integrated SHU yards at Corcoran State Prison, and five on the SHU yard at New Folsom. Compare this to the rest of the country, where during this same five-year period there were a total of seven prisoners murdered by prison guards in all states combined (excepting, of course, state-sanctioned executions of death row prisoners).

Pelican Bay State Prison, home of "The Worst of the Worst," was born out of the blood of murdered prisoners as a direct result of CDC policy changes which were intended to raise the level of violence and bloodshed. Pelican Bay cost more than its $200 million price tag. It cost the lives of at least a dozen prisoners who were murdered by the CDC in order to promote their political agenda.

CAMPAIGN OF REPRESSION

Mumia Abu-Jamal, September 1993

The most repressive regime in America just got more repressive. In November 1992, the Pennsylvania Department of Corrections implemented revised administrative directives 801/802, which affects all prisoners in administrative and disciplinary segregation. With planned restrictions barring all but personal and legal mail and a ban on all books (save a Bible or Koran), it is a broad-based attack on the mind.

Most insidious are the provisions governing legal material. They suggest the other regulations are mere smokescreens designed to divert attention from the state's principle objective: the stripping of any power from jailhouse lawyers. (Remember, this governs *all* prisoners in the hole, whether for disciplinary or administrative reasons.)

There is solid support, from scholars and statistical analysis, for the notion that jailhouse lawyers are the targets of the new rules. In 1991, one of the most exhaustive studies to date on the targets of the prison disciplinary system were released. The report, titled *The Myth of Humane Imprisonment*, found there is a statistical hierarchy of who receives the harshest disciplinary sanctions from prison officials. Authored by criminologists Mark S. Hamm, Dr. Corey Weinstein, Therese Coupez and Francis Freidman. The study found that jailhouse lawyers were by a wide margin the largest single group in disciplinary units. Blacks, the mentally handicapped, gang members, political prisoners, homosexuals and AIDS patients, were also groups with disproportionate numbers in disciplinary units.[1]

In accounts supporting the statistical data, the authors wrote, "...respondents observed that guards and administrators had a standard practice of singling out jailhouse lawyers for discipline in retaliation for challenging the status quo."

While the data supports the widely held notion that Blacks are often targets of severe sanctions, that jailhouse lawyers are the *most* sanctioned is striking. Jailhouse lawyers—men and women self-trained in law and legal procedure—are among the most studious (in law, at least) in the prison, these new rulings all the more malicious and repressive.

The evidence suggests, and the new regulations clearly supports the notion, that prison administrators don't want studious, well-read prisoners. Rather, they prefer prisoners who are obedient, quiet and dumb. Why else would a prison expressly forbid a person from expanding their learning through correspondence courses or educational programs?

It would seem that any institution daring to use the term "corrections" would *require* all of its charges to participate in educational programs, for how else is one "corrected"? Yet disciplinary prisoners are forbidden from the one resource designed to moderate behavior and enhance self-esteem: education. For them, many of whom are illiterate, books are deemed "contraband" and educational courses are proscribed.

In that one regard, more than any other, lies the solution to the often bewildering conundrum labeled as "corrections." The state raises its narrow institutional interests—that of "control" by limiting people's access to information—over an interest that is intensely human: the right for all beings to grow in wisdom, insight and knowledge, for their own sakes as well as for their unique contribution to the fund of human knowledge.

This intentional degradation of the soul by the state, which allows a being to degenerate or vegetate yet forbids one from mental expansion, is the most sure indictment available of a system that creates, rather than corrects, the most fundamental evil in existence: that of ignorance.

1 "The Myth of Humane Imprisonment" is anthologized in Eli Rosenblatt, ed., *Criminal Injustice: Confronting the Prison Crisis*, South End Press (Boston, MA: 1996).

REPORT
FROM THE HOLE

Adrian Lomax, November 1993

Adrian Lomax is a Wisconsin prisoner and journalist. His story below is typical of the prison administrators' behavior towards prisoners who write realistically and intelligently about prison conditions. Adrian's misfortunes came about after he wrote about an abusive guard at a prison in Wisconsin for The Edge, *a local weekly newspaper. The infraction report Adrian received stated in part: "Inmate Lomax was placed into TLU [disciplinary segregation unit] under DOC 303.11 (4b) due to a newspaper article which appeared in* The Madison Edge *(11.18.92.) that encourages disrespect for captain Patricia Garro. The article encourages inmates to defy the captain's authority and ability to control a particular situation. Because this same article can easily be communicated to other inmates it has the potential for encouraging disrespect and defiance of all staff authority. Possible violations of DOC 303.16 Threats, 303.271 Lying About Staff." We reprint these two letters from Adrian because we've seen so many like them. The "seg units" are the disciplinary segregation units in Wisconsin's maximum security prisons.-eds.*

The fun never ends. I'm in segregation. Guess they didn't like my last column in *The Edge*. They could just keep me in TLU for 21 days and release me without ever giving me a Conduct Report (CR) (I do not have a CR at this point). They've done that shit to me before, numerous times. Or they could ram through a bogus CR and sentence me to long-term segregation. That lying about staff charge carries 360 days.

Of course, there are big First Amendment issues here. I've already filed a lawsuit and asked for a Temporary Restraining Order (TRO) requiring my immediate release from segregation.

The library will send over no law books. They will only send over photocopies of cases (loaners) on an exact cite basis. They will only send two cases at once and won't send more until you return the previous two. There is a 48 hour turnaround so the bottom line is that I can see four cases a week. There is a satellite library in the seg unit but it doesn't have much. And get this: one must wear handcuffs and a waist chain while using the seg library. You can hardly even pull a book off the shelf, much less read it. And if you do get a book off the shelf, don't drop it on the floor because it's staying there. But here's the best part: they only let us have pens for two hours a day, pass 'em out at seven p.m. and pick 'em up at nine. Refuse to give a pen back? Riot gear and mace, of course. We can have pencils all the time but good luck trying to get a guard to sharpen one for you. So guys over here perfect the art of sharpening pencils with their thumbnails.

I'm sure the prison officials love the beauty of locking me up in seg for writing an article, then denying me the use of a pen.

Adrian was infracted, found guilty of the above listed charged, and sentenced to 368 days solitary confinement.

*****

Nine Months Later

The guard stood in the middle of the seg unit, counting 26 of the 40 cells had the 3" x 12" plexiglass windows in the cell doors covered with paper from the inside. The 5:00 p.m. count approached, and the guard knew that if the prisoners kept their windows covered so that they couldn't be seen, the lieutenant would order the guards to suit up in riot gear to forcibly enter each of the 26 cells to remove the window covering.

The turnkey walked back to the control booth, shaking his head. Five hours and 26 "cell extractions" later, the second shift guards were tired and mad. They put in a lot of work that day.

The whole ordeal could have been averted had the sergeant not decided to cancel use of the segregation law library that evening, apparently for no reason other than to avoid the work involved in escorting prisoners to and from the small room containing law books. In protest, 26 of the seg unit's prisoners decided to "make 'em suit up."

From November to June 1993, I was confined in the disciplinary segregation unit at Wisconsin's Racine Correctional Institution. During that period the prisoners there engaged in numerous collective protest actions in response to mistreatment by the guards. The convicts' weapon was their own solidarity combined with the laziness of prison guards. Turnkeys don't mind suiting up on one prisoner, but when they have to perform 15 or 20 cell extractions during one shift, they think twice the next time they consider doing something likely to cause the prisoners to revolt.

The convicts' tactics involved mass flooding of cells, refusal to return meal trays, the throwing meal trays off the tier, and the trusty covering up of cell windows. On two occasions the full complement of prisoners in the outside recreation cages refused to come inside.

The guards frequently sprayed prisoners with mace and other chemical irritants during cell extractions. In those cases prisoners would try to yank the gas masks off the faces of as many guards as possible when guards entered the cell, exposing them to the chemical agents.

After each cell extraction, guards put the prisoner in a shower stall, allowing him to wash off the chemical agents. The guards take this opportunity to remove all the prisoner's property from the cell and clean up the chemicals. The prisoner is then returned to his cell on "strip cell" status, with no property, no clothing, sheets, towels, or blankets. Under Wisconsin law, strip cell status may last no more than three days, but in practice it often lasts longer because it's difficult to get the guards to return one's property. On some occasions, guards' refusal to return prisoners' property after three days has set off a new round of protests.

At one point prisoners began refusing to stick their hands out to be cuffed while they were in the shower stalls following a cell extraction. This brought about a forcible extraction from the shower stalls. Guards responded by refusing to remove handcuffs and leg irons while the prisoners were in the showers. Turnkeys would cut prisoners' clothes off with scissors, put them in the shower stalls in restraints, and remove the restraints only after the prisoners were returned to their cells.

Guards who act like macho tough guys are common in segregation units. They are continually disparaging prisoners, confident that, since they work in seg, no prisoner will ever be able to lay their hands on them. At Racine, there was one Lieutenant Molnar who was the archetype of that character. Walking around with his chest stuck out, scowling and shouting insults at convicts, he appeared to believe he was John Wayne.

Shortly before I was transferred from Racine, a prisoner named Ervie Gray refused to come in from the recreation cage. The "macho" guard got five others suited up in riot gear to "extract" Gray. When the goon squad came out of the building, Gray climbed the chain link fence, braving the razor wire, and climbed to the ceiling of the seg building.

After being sprayed with chemical agents, Gray eventually decided to come down. When he started climbing down the fence, however, Gray didn't climb down the side that would have left him inside the rec cage. Instead, Gray climbed down the side of the fence that put him in the common area, along with Molnar and the other guards.

Upon seeing Gray climbing down the outside of the fence, the tough guy guard immediately ran into one of the rec cages and pulled the door shut behind him! Even with five guards standing by in riot gear, he wanted to take no chances on Gray getting hold of him.

I'm now confined in the seg unit of the Green Bay Correctional Institution. There isn't the same kind of solidarity among the prisoners here, so collective protests aren't the order of the day. But that's subject to change.

THE SCANDAL OF PRISON "MANAGEMENT"

Jill Brotman, August 1994

Throughout the American Friends Service Committee's decades of prison work it has encouraged reconciliation and nonviolent alternatives to conflict. But Massachusetts Governor William Weld has declared that a stay in prison should "replicate a tour of the circles of hell." Current prison management is supposed to be part of the war on crime. But it is not a war on crime—it is a war on prisoners.

A fundamental principle of American judicial practice is that people are sent to prison *as* punishment, not *for* punishment. However, the purity of this ideal hardly ever exists in practice. The prisoners most vulnerable to the secondary punishments of confinement are long-term prisoners or lifers. When we talk about how severely we should punish, we always need to distinguish between long-term and short-term punishment. Some may detest the people in our prisons. Nonetheless, when the prisoners are old and ill, when they have served 20 years and can hardly be identified as the same individual who committed the crime, when the prison term is the person's life and the prisoner struggles to imbue that life with meaning, punishing takes on a different character.

Then there is a most grave consideration: the culture of punishment and status degradation will eventually spill over onto the rest of us. In the design and implementation of punishment policy we must be vigilant, because whenever we deliberately inflict pain, we deform and diminish ourselves.

Reporters quote the average citizen as talking about sending people to prison and letting them rot, locking them up and throwing away the key. How much and what quality of poor or brutal treatment would be considered acceptable in our prisons? Since the perception that prisoners are not punished enough has been projected so effectively by people who—like Governor Weld—have, for the most part, never been in a prison, this is a serious question.

Should we starve people? Or should we simply not give them enough food? Prisoners are underfed as a matter of policy in the Massachusetts Departmental Disciplinary Unit (DDU) at Walpole. Should we violate our own laws that place a 30-day cap on total isolation time? At Walpole prisoners may be sentenced by an internal board to the DDU, where there is near-total sensory deprivation, for periods of up to 10 years. Should our prisons be places with no rules and no reasonable expectations, places of misery and chaos, so that good behavior brings no hope of decent treatment in the future? Should we blink at administrative punishment based on false accusation? Should we force old men with prostate cancer to urinate on the floor if it is count time and there is no toilet in the cell? Should wives, mothers, and daughters of prisoners have to hand over their used tampons for inspection?

Under Weld's regime, medical and dental services have been cut back. Psychological services are gone. Vocational and education programs have been dramatically curtailed. Volunteers, severely restricted, are in many cases just giving up. Staff considered too "nice" to the prisoners are fired. Visits are a harrowing experience. Property prisoners purchased at the canteen is being seized. In every realm of prison life, things are being taken away.

There will be a high cost for all of this. A prison run this way is a prison that produces deformed and wounded people. The current war on prisoners is also a war on taxpayers, with the government sinking millions of dollars into more and more prisons, which are turned into factories of vengeance and rage. The inevitable products of prisons are more repeat offenses and more victims of those offenses, and the predictable returns to prison where once again citizens will be paying the rent.

In Massachusetts prison managers lack expertise, education, and training. They operate with a lack of good sense and an abysmal lack of a sense of justice. How else can we explain the permanent lockdown at Walpole? In the wake of the recent escapes from the Old Colony facility, prisoners with "poor" profiles were transferred out of Old Colony to Walpole. Many of these were men who had been living on the honors block for years. They were "good inmates," foolish enough to believe that if they did what they were supposed to do, the Department of Corrections would do what it was supposed to do. These model prisoners are now locked down 23 hours a day in the dreadful Phase III at Walpole. Dramas like this are staged specifically to justify the building of a corrections-industrial complex.

In the prison system a lockdown is the equivalent of a breakdown. Locking a prison down and constantly moving the scandal around the system is the administrator's way of throwing up their hands and saying "there is nothing that can be done with these folks." That is an inadequate response. Massachusetts has a growing prisoner population whose mean age is dropping. We'd better do something besides chaining them to their beds.

FROM USP MARION TO ADX FLORENCE

(AND BACK AGAIN)

The Fire Inside

Ray Luc Levasseur, October 1994

October, 1994, marked the eleventh year of collective punishment at the United States penitentiary, Marion. It marked a decade of lock-down, control unit regimes, and government lies. No doubt the federal Bureau of Prisons will commemorate the event by rolling out its propaganda wagon, and indulging the public with some contrived fantasy about the lockdown's purpose and effectiveness. Silently, they'll rejoice at the well-orchestrated scam they've pulled off.

In a society that criminalizes poverty and makes racism a redeeming social value, the Bureau of Prisons simply plugs its propaganda arm into a mass media whose corporate ownership serves its own corporate interests. There is significant political capital to be had by scapegoating the disenfranchised and deflecting the public's attention away from the real issues which affect their quality of life.

Marion is the most written about prison in the world. One of the battle lines drawn in October, 1983, was for public opinion. The government has been winning this battle hands down. The Bureau of Prisons utilizes a highly effective public relations strategy which revolves around the agitprop slogan "the worst of the worst" to describe Marion prisoners. It is a soundbite which condenses "nigger, spic, White trash, jobless, homeless, useless underclass" into one dehumanizing phrase. Dehumanizing a population with language is a prelude to dehumanizing it with force.

The Bureau of Prison's statement is false, unless the "the worst" refers to rebels, dissenters, revolutionaries, jailhouse lawyers and group members whose beliefs and integrity the BOP wants to crush.

It is false when one examines who is sent to Marion, and why they're here. Certainly there are exceptions, but those exceptions don't warrant the use of collective punishment. Additionally, I've not met a convicted felon whose misdeeds were in any way comparable to the massive killing of civilians perpetrated by the likes of Nixon, Reagan, Bush, *et al.* No one here has been convicted of crimes against humanity in the court of world opinion.

"The worst of the worst" has no meaning outside the realm of propaganda: any prisoner can be sent to Marion at any time, for any reason, without due process of law. In the BOP's parlance, dissent and rebellion are "management problems" to be suppressed. What the BOP feeds the public is designed to secure support for such schemes.

Effective propaganda diverts people from thinking and acting not only on prison issues, but also on the problems that led to the construction of the American Gulag: poverty, racism and injustice stemming from an unbridled capitalism that diminishes the humanity of its victims. Marion is but one more satellite in the ever-expanding concentric circles of oppression and violence that are consuming society. This is good news for prison and related bureaucracies. Instead of being hung out to dry, these parasitic purveyors of misery are relishing their careers, fattening their wallets and passing themselves off as guardians of white bread culture.

In a recent article on Marion, a denizen of the local community was quoted as saying that Marion prisoners should be taken out and shot as part of the deficit reduction plan. This citizen comes from the same pool from which the BOP recruits its guards. Bleak economic realities feed such fascistic sentiments. Marion's guards are the descendants of once proud coal miners and factory workers— many unionized. But when the mines and plants closed they were left floundering on their own. Their response is to join up with the nation and state's biggest growth industry: human chattel.

In 1994 Illinois approved construction of another state control unit prison. Before the ink was dry on the legislation, the economically depressed counties of southern Illinois were unabashedly begging for the prison to be located on their turf. One state legislator stated there was so much unemployment in his county, "it would be a crime" not to locate the prison there. A crime not to build a prison in an area already saturated with them. "Worst of the worst" means nothing to these people. All they want are warm bodies to feed on. They don't much care where they come from. [Tamms, IL, was the lucky winner. A 502-bed Supermax will open there in the summer of 1997. -eds]

One of the most significant reverberations of the Marion lockdown is the subsequent proliferation of control unit prisons throughout the country. Thirty-six states now have control unit prisons. This proliferation is part and parcel of the rapid expansion of the entire prison system. Marion was the flagship, but no longer the exception.

Even a relatively small state like Maine has opened a control unit for 100 prisoners at an initial cost of $16 million. Already the state is seeking to double the size of the prison. Maine's situation somewhat reflects what's happening nation-wide. The state spent money it could not afford to build a control unit prison it doesn't need. Concurrently, the state cut rehab programs at the youth reformatory and slashed programs to Aid to Families with Dependent Children (a parent with 2 children receives $418 a month). By gouging the needs of children, the state insured a steady supply of youthful offenders to fill its control unit and other cells well into the next generation. New York and Florida have come up with their own creative fraud, diverting funds initially allocated for the homeless and social welfare programs into funding prison construction and daily operations.

Propaganda that promotes control units as effective against crime—in and out of prison—perpetrates a cruel hoax on an unsuspecting and too often gullible public. Like most government bureaucracies, the Bureau of Prisons hides the cost overruns from a public who will foot the bill. In real terms, "more bang for the buck" is quickly eroding their false sense of security.

When men and women are locked in small cells 22-23 hours a day, with little human contact, in a violent environment devoid of respect for the human spirit, there is a steep cost not limited to prisoners or dollars. Certainly the prisoners suffer. And much of it not played out in violent prison incidents is internalized in an organic time capsule. Eventually, they carry the years of abuse and neglect right on through their release dates. This is when it's all brought home. A prisoner doesn't separate him/herself from the prison experience anymore than soldiers separate themselves from the wars they live through.

If prisoners never returned to their neighborhoods and communities—or anyone else's—the public might take some perverted comfort in never seeing them again. But this doesn't happen. Even the most extensive prison system in the world can't keep millions of people locked up forever. While some former prisoners salvage their lives and spare others—entirely through their own efforts—many others proceed to engage in both self-destructive behavior and crime aimed at the lives and property of others. Life's agenda is reduced primarily to one more paycheck or one more payback.

Those who become victimized by the alumni of America's prison system need ask themselves the following: Will the billions spent on prison hardware and the salaries of prisoncrats buy back the lost lives of those who were supposedly being protected? It won't. The funds that could have been invested in human services and community development were pissed away into bottomless sinkholes of violence, heartache and the illusion that repression will provide security.

The misnamed "criminal justice" system churns out an appalling casualty rate. There are now almost one million children under the age of 18 who have one or both parents in prison. One in four young Black men is in prison or under police "supervision." More Latinos than ever before are locked up. More women and children. More of everyone whose lives are plagued by poverty and racism. The proliferation of control unit prisons represents one response of wealth and power to the agony of the oppressed.

Early in the lockdown, Marion prisoners put up a stiff resistance. Whether in this prison or elsewhere, the majority have been subjected to police assaults, beatings, gas, clubs, prolonged restraints, drugs, anal probes, stun guns, humiliations, degradations, harassment, psychological rape and other assorted mistreatments. The U.S. calls such treatment torture when it is committed by other governments.

Little of positive value has come of the lockdown other than us maintaining our personal integrity. Earlier in the lockdown the imprisoned had important outside support. Now that most of this support has worn out, a cloud of pessimism, if not cynicism, descends over the entombed.

During the more than 10 year reign of the Marion lockdown, prisoners have attempted to redress their grievances through the federal courts. They got nothing but a judge's spiteful decision that sordid and horrid conditions do not violate prisoners' constitutional rights. The many prisoners who testified about beatings and other rights violations were dismissed as liars. Courts tend to credit prisoners' testimony only when they testify for the government. Congressional subcommittee hearings did little besides enter Marion's devastation into the public record, where it could be filed and forgotten.

This isn't to say that judicial and legislative efforts should be abandoned. There is pending litigation by control unit prisoners in other districts that may produce more positive results. And various state legislatures may respond differently to their constituents' concerns. Yet given the prevailing political climate and the growing entrenchment of the Marion model, little is likely to come from this approach other than a belated civics lesson.

The Bureau of Prisons cannot continuously apply heat to Marion without allowing some steam to escape. They must know that if they do not do so the place will blow up. The BOP's efforts to contain organized resistance and picking off individual efforts is rooted primarily in the control unit regimen: isolation, separation, controlled movement in restraints, limited communication, and the selective use of violence.

But there is more. The answer also ties in the Bureau of Prisons' arbitrary use of control mechanisms that begin with who is sent to Marion, and why they're singled out. The process continues more arbitrarily—in determining who leaves Marion, and when. Clear conduct (no disciplinary infractions) alone will not get a prisoner out of Marion. Some will leave in the minimum 2 1/2 years; some in 5 or 10; some appear branded never to leave. At least some turnover is necessary because the 375 capacity must have room to warehouse new arrivals, including recidivists.

No one can fault a prisoner for wanting to be on that bus out of Marion. However, the emphasis on catching that bus in the 2 1/2 year minimum has evolved into the most viable method for the majority of prisoners to escape Marion's clutches. In turn, this has led to individual prisoners submitting to programming and a general lack of resistance, rather than a more collective effort to end the lockdown. The lack of outside support reinforces the view that each of us is on his own.

As outside support for prisoners wanes, the government continues to beef up its repressive capacity. A new federal control unit has been built in Florence, Colorado, with the purpose of furthering Marion's brutal agenda. The addition of 200 cells to Florence over Marion's capacity underscores the failure of Marion's lockdown to reduce violence and rebellion in the federal prison system and states which tap into it. Florence's 550 permanently locked-down cells await those who will continue to refuse and resist, as well as those caught up in the spiral of crime that prisons produce. Conditions at Florence promise to be considerably worse with more emphasis placed on deeper isolation.

It's not easy to chart a future course from the inside. Doing time in these joints is like walking a mine field. The Florence prison will present new challenges and other control units are cutting their teeth. We know from Attica, Lucasville, and a hundred other rebellions, both organized and spontaneous, that stiff resistance will continue. Some of it will be violent. We also know that as captive slaves we are extremely vulnerable to offensive violence and retribution by the guards. For this reason, some matters are best left to clandestine maneuvers. What's clear to me now and has been since I first did time in '69-'71 is that no matter how much litigation and legislation is filed and defiled, the road to building a prisoners' movement is paved with solidarity. Irrespective of individual differences and group affiliations, we all have a common ground on which to stand together. Solidarity is our greatest weapon, bar none. Additionally, outside support is critical. A necessary lifeline involves family, friends, professionals, and political activists. We urgently need a stronger voice. And everyone—inside and out of prison walls—can help build it.

Ultimately, control units like Marion and Florence must be shut down. But in the meantime, the growth of a political consciousness; adoption and application of the United Nations' Standard Minimum Rules for the Treatment of Prisoners; and the expanded use of outside observers to monitor human rights abuses in the prison system—taken together, can open a new front in the struggle for justice.

Trouble Coming Everyday:
ADX, One Year Later

Ray Luc Levasseur, July 1997

"And so beneath the weight lay I
And suffered to death, but could not die."

—Edna St. Vincent Millay

Society reflects itself in the microcosm of prison. From a class-based, economically driven, racially motivated construct devolves life as a series of Chinese boxes—a set of boxes, decreasing in size so that each box fits inside the next larger one. I am in the smallest box.

I am in the Administrative Maximum (ADX) prison, the Federal government's latest boondoggle to contain prisoners' rebellion and dissent. I am in a "boxcar" cell. Picture a cage where top, bottom, sides and back are concrete walls. The front is sliced by steel bars. Several feet beyond the bars is another wall. In this wall is a solid steel door. The term boxcar is derived from this configuration: a small, enclosed box that doesn't move. I am confined to the boxcar cell 157 hours of each 168 hour week. Eleven hours each week I'm allowed into the barren area adjacent to this cell.

Each morning begins with the noisy rumble of the steel door opening. A guard steps to the bars and slides food through a small slot. Feeding time. The guard steps back and the door slaps shut with a vengeance. The purpose of a boxcar cell is to gouge the prisoners' senses by suppressing human sound, putting blinders about our eyes and forbidding touch. Essential human needs are viewed with suspicion. Within the larger context of a control unit prison, the boxcar cell is designed to inflict physical and emotional isolation that wears down a prisoner's will to resist. When this regimen undermines a prisoner's health or distorts his/her personality, it's considered the cost of doing business.

It seems endless. Each morning I look at the same gray door and hear the same rumbles followed by long silences. It is endless. Subjected to humiliations designed to buckle our knees we are: bent over, arms clamped behind our backs, pawed, prodded, cell-searched, strip-searched, commanded, marched distances of 50 feet, silenced, and hooked to a chain running through 1,500,000 prisoners. All this is enforced by a porcine abomination called the Goon Squad whose idea of combat is to jump on handcuffed and caged prisoners while applying boots, truncheons and blasts of chemical agents to faces that are pushed into unforgiving concrete.

I'm deeply cornered in their prison. My sight is diminished, but I maintain my vision, I see their hand in the use of four point "restraints" to spread-eagle prisoners, something inherently abusive regardless of the excuse. I see forced feedings, cell extractions, mind medications and chemical weapons used to incapacitate. I see a steady stream of petty hassles, harassments, verbal barrages, mind-fuck games, disciplinary reports, medical neglect, and the omnipresent threat of violence. Airborne bags of shit and gobs of spit become the response of the caged.

The minds of some prisoners are collapsing in on them. I don't know what internal strife lies within them, but it isn't mitigated here. One prisoner subjected to four point restraints (chains actually) as shock therapy, had been chewing on his own flesh. Why is a prisoner who mutilates himself kept in ADX? Is he supposed to improve his outlook on life while stripped, chained and tormented by a squad of guards and prison functionaries?

Some prisoners rarely come out of their cells. Others never come out. I don't know why. Meanwhile, psychologists with heads full of psychobabble roam the tiers supposedly sniffing out pockets of mental instability.

ADX was designed the way corporations design schemes to poison the environment while avoiding responsibility for doing so. They cut into sight and sound with ubiquitous walls and boxes. We exercise in something resembling the deep end of a cement lined pool. Every seam and crack is sealed so that not a solitary weed will penetrate this desolation. Smell and taste are reduced to staleness and sameness. Every guard functions as a spy, watching and listening with prying, voyeuristic eyes, cameras, and microphones. ("Intelligence gathering by the staff is critical."[1]) When they're done with us, we become someone else's problem.

Television deserves special mention. Unlike other prisons, every ADX cell is equipped with a small black and white TV, compliments of the BOP pacification program. Hollywood and Madison Avenue images are churned out through a barrage of talk shows, soaps, cartoons, and B-movies to give us some vicarious social interaction. Feeling rebellious, lonely, angry, miserable, alienated, unskilled and uneducated? Turn on the face of Amerika. The administration replaces a broken TV quicker than fixing a toilet.

There are no jobs for those in boxcar cells. Like millions of others, we are punished with unemployment. Education is restricted to inadequate videos on the TV. One such program featured "The Criminal Mind." I was expecting some analysis of U.S. corporate criminals and politicians. Instead, we got a sketch of drug abusers stealing and cavorting in a landscape of dilapidated houses and abandoned factories. A school we had already been through.

Religious services are relegated to TV. Recently, the prison chaplain presented his video analysis of the U.S.'s decline caused by homosexuality, AIDS and women's rights. Lifting this blight would "make America great again," like in the good old days of land theft and chattel slavery. The chaplain said nothing about the scourge of poverty, racism, unemployment or killer cops and their connection to the prison industry. The chaplain said nothing about the ADX visiting room where floor-to-ceiling partitions rub "family values" into our wounds. And "Christianity" rules. There is no Imam for Muslim prisoners.

Every morning, I go through my own ablution. Every morning there is a layer of chalky dust settled about the cell. It comes through the single air vent. It never stops. Each morning I busy myself with a wet rag mopping up all that is not in my lungs...

Who am I? I am one subjected to the collective punishment within the common ground of ADX. I was sent to prison for political offenses and I was placed in a control unit prison because the State maintains my radical political beliefs and associations warrant extreme measures. Recently I was cited with a disciplinary infraction for allegedly making a derogatory comment about an ADX administrator during a media interview. The constitutional expression of my views is considered conduct unbecoming within the master/chattel relationship.

Worst of the worst is where the illusion clashes with the reality. The illusion—that the criminalization of poverty and the isolation and degradation of prisoners provides an effective, humane response to social ills. The reality—that crimes begin at the top with predatory capitalists profiting grotesquely, while the results of their activities mire the rest of us in economic and social rot.

In a 1993 commemoration of the Marion lockdown I wrote that ADX (then under construction and slated to replace Marion) "awaits those who continue to refuse and resist." Sure enough, ADX became the destination for those prisoners held responsible for the recent uprisings throughout the federal system. The best were sent to ADX after running gauntlets of gunshots, beatings, tear gas, and the destruction of their few personal belongings. A baptism into the ranks of resistance.

Other uprising participants were sent to Marion, still locked down since 1983. To the public, the BOP maintained that once ADX became operational, the lockdown would end. They lied. They doubled their control unit capacity by keeping both prisons locked-down.

For years, prisoncrats raved about the deterrent effect of Marion. If is works so well, why hasn't it put itself out of business? Marion/ADX didn't deter the October '95 uprisings, the most widespread and destructive in the federal prison system's history (See: "Federal Prisons Erupt"). They didn't deter USP Atlanta from grabbing headlines with its high level of violence. They have not deterred prisoners transferred to other prisons or released to the streets from picking up new charges. Control unit prisons are not the solution. They are the problem.

Last year, a prisoner released from the isolation and brutality of California's notorious control unit at Pelican Bay killed a cop before he got home and unpacked his bag. Apparently, someone forgot to explain the finer points of deterrence to him. The response of the state representative from the district including Pelican Bay was illuminating. He introduced legislation mandating that released Pelican Bay prisoners be transported directly to their destination, so that when the bodies drop it will be in some other bailiwick, and not stain the Department of Corrections.

Prisoncrats, like politicians, are amazingly adept at shielding themselves from the consequences of their policies.

Let's not kid ourselves about the prevailing attitude among the political and corporate elite and much of the voting public: prisoners are human waste. The more forbidding the penitentiaries, the more like garbage they define us. As downsized laborers, outcasts, and outlaws, there is no room for us at the table. Exterminating us on a mass scale is not presently acceptable, so plan B is in effect: execute small numbers, corrupt some, co-opt others, drive others mad, and imprison millions. As prisoners, the only value we have is if they can turn a political campaign or a dollar on us.

So our bodies become commodities for someone else's gain. Past recidivist rates documented a failed system. Today's recidivist rates read like the Dow Jones Industrial Average—the higher the recidivism, the more various opportunists stand to gain. The traffickers in bodies insure a steady supply by slashing at fundamental programs serving our poorest families. They demand more police, more children's prisons and more youth incarceration. More bodies, younger bodies, with increased shelf-life due to mandatory sentences. They legislate harsher conditions that make us leaner, meaner, and infinitely more recyclable.

ADX guards say they are just doing their job, which they will gladly do for an annual entry level salary of $32,000 ($50K with overtime). A nice benefits package and a bully pulpit to boot. Some do it with benign neglect, others do it with perverse cruelty. In a Faustian contract with the government, they work the cages and in return get to send their kids to college and take Caribbean vacations. Guards, like all enterprising citizens, can buy a piece of the action through tax exempt bonds that underwrite state prison construction. They can do it with the detached air of the post-modern fascist because such purchases do not hold them liable for anything that happens within the prison. No beating, injury, medical neglect or death will cut into their profit. In the burgeoning private prison industry, stock purchases are available through investment companies. Why not? General Motors invested in Nazi Germany.

There's money to be made in fraud. The government is rife with it, but like most frauds there are a few who profit from prisons while many more are victimized. Taxpayers subsidize most prisons, and it is citizens who pay through the nose. By any financial measure, statistic or body count, the prison system is an abysmal failure. Very high cost, very little benefit. There's a parallel with the Vietnam War: the government takes your money and your children while deceiving you into acquiescence. In return we get a divided society, more violence and an abandonment of the War on Poverty. And like those years, it appears the present "silent majority" isn't ready for a serious policy review until their pockets have been more seriously picked and the cycle of violence has driven its stake deeper into middle Amerika's heart.

1 John Vanyur, Associate Warden, ADX, quoted in *Corrections Today*, July 1995.

Normalizing the Abnormal

Daniel Burton-Rose, July 1997

On November 8, 1996, Puerto Rican prisoner of war Oscar López Rivera was transferred from ADX Florence to USP Marion. The transfer took place after López Rivera completed the 36-month "step-program" at ADX in just 23 months. He received no disciplinary infractions while at ADX, was one of its first "graduates." López Rivera was awarded for his reluctant cooperation with the BOP by a transfer back to Marion, the only other federal control unit for men.

After completing the ADX program López Rivera was asked which prison he wished to be transferred to. He answered USP Lewisburg, Pennsylvania. He was told by an associate warden that the transfer had been approved. He didn't find out this wasn't the case until he was already in transit. He was the only one of 13 prisoners in his transfer group to be sent to Marion. Regional BOP officials have refused to speak about the transfer, and Teresa Banks, a spokeswoman for Marion, said she had no information on the reason López Rivera was transferred there.

ADX Florence spokesperson Louis Winn said of López Rivera's stated preference of USP Lewisburg, "The inmate can definitely request to go to a particular institution, but a number of factors are taken into consideration."[1]

One of those factors is of course "security needs." BOP regional spokesperson Carol Holinka said the BOP looks "at safety and security for all involved." López Rivera has a high security rating due to an alleged escape attempt. In that escape attempt, said Alejandro Molina of the Committee to Free Puerto Rican Political Prisoners and Prisoners of War, "a government informant approached [López Rivera] and said 'I have these people on the outside, what do you think?'" López Rivera, not surprisingly, was interested in the proposition. "So it ended up," Molina continued, "—it wasn't a frame-up, but it was instigated by the government, and that was proved in court."

Jan Susler, a Chicago-based human rights activist and attorney for López Rivera and other imprisoned Puerto Rican nationalists, stated: "What [the BOP is] doing with Oscar is vicious and intentional... You can't say there are no political prisoners in the United

States and then single him out and treat him like this. If they really think their program works, then he shouldn't be an exception."

But perhaps the most insidious reason behind López Rivera's transfer was articulated by Winn: "Marion's mission has changed," he stated. "It's actually a less secure facility than ADX, so conceivably he should have more privileges."

Banks echoed the idea, saying that the prison has "revised" its program and that prisoners can now earn their way out in two rather than three years. But Tony Hintz, member of the anti-control unit activist group Committee to End the Marion Lockdown, points out that Marion is in the process of becoming "a control unit that just isn't being called a control unit."

Anti-imperialist political prisoner Bill Dunne did time at Marion from the time of the '83 lockdown until 1992, and was recently transferred back to Marion for "being a bad slave" (i.e., not being subservient enough at the UNICOR factory). In one of Dunne's first letters after returning he wrote: "Marion has changed little since I left in March of '92."

López Rivera told the Denver weekly *Westword* that he certainly doesn't feel that he has any more "privileges" at Marion: "It's worse now [at Marion] than when I was here before," he said. *Westword* wrote: "In the final months of his stay at ADX he was allowed to leave his cell for meals and work or visits to the commissary. In his Marion 'general population' unit, he's locked down 22 hours a day, is allowed only a few hours of recreation a week in 'a small cage with a cement floor,' and never leaves his cell except in handcuffs— even for medical treatment."

López Rivera stated the transfer was "definitely a punitive move." "Basically," he said, "what they're trying to do is to rob the prisoner of his dignity through absolute control and sensory deprivation. Ever since I arrived in the system, I've been labeled a notorious and incorrigible criminal, and that is enough for them to do whatever they feel like doing."

Only a handful of other prisoners have graduated from ADX, and no others have been sent to Marion. (The other political prisoners who have been released from ADX are former Black Liberation Army member Dr. Mutulu Shakur, who was transferred to USP Atlanta in November of 1996, and Ohio 7+ prisoner Tom Manning, who was transferred to USP Leavenworth. Jimmy Barrett was also transfered from ADT and is scheduled to be paroled.)

Susler said, "I think the Bureau of Prisons feels it hasn't done its job; they were supposed to mess these people up more than they've been able to. If they can break Oscar, it would be an example." Since they couldn't break him, the BOP will use him as an example of what prisoners are subjected to when they refuse to renounce political beliefs they find unacceptable.

The relationship between USP Marion and ADX Florence dramatically illustrates the "normalization" of control units, and the not-so-gradual public acceptance of subjecting prisoners to deep isolation. Marion, condemned by Amnesty International and virtually every human rights group which has toured it as "a human rights nightmare," as Susler has noted, is now viewed as a more or less "normal" maximum security prison. One lawyer from the ADX Prison Legal Project, a prisoners' rights group, who regularly visits prisoners at ADX Florence, said of López Rivera's transfer to Marion, "That's no fuckin' incentive to comply with the BOP's programs... What a reward for graduating from ADX, qué no?"

Transfers out of ADX are slowing down as well. When ADX opened prisoners began at different steps, because the BOP needed to get its program functional. It is now fully functional, and, as Ohio-7+ political prisoner Ray Luc Levasseur, currently in ADX Florence, tells us: "We'll never again see the situation that allowed Oscar, Mu[tulu Shakur] and Tom [Manning] to move so quickly through the program."

Prison officials are attempting to make control unit torture the norm and have permanent lockdowns be business as usual in maximum security prisons. They seem to be succeeding.

1 Quotations from Winn, Jan Susler, and López Rivera are taken from Alan Prendergast, "The Circle Game," *Westword* (Denver, CO), Dec. 19-25, 1996.

Part VIII
PRISONER STRUGGLES AND REBELLIONS

The proponents of harsher and crueler treatment for prisoners discuss the subject as if the prisoners themselves were little more than barely domesticated animals to be treated, or mistreated, as the whim of the prisoncrats and their apologists dictates. Reality is far different. From at least the time of Sparticus, prisoners have rebelled against conditions of captivity that became too onerous.

The heavy punishment meted out to prisoners who rebel has changed little over the millennia. Open rebellion typically occurs when a dramatic fall in living conditions occurs, even if the conditions were dismal to begin with. While the prison riot, with its images of the burning prison, heavily armed guards in flak jackets and the occasional hostage taking comes to mind, when we say "prison struggle," there is more to it than that. Other forms of resistance and protest which take place in the prison environment include the work strike, the hunger strike, and more subtle forms of sabotage and failure to cooperate.

As the downward spiral of prison conditions continues, the resistance by prisoners to this treatment has increased. Improvements in prison conditions that have occurred in the past usually came about only because prisoners actively fought for them, in court or otherwise, *not* from the benevolence of prison bureaucrats or an enlightened policy maker. Though prison walls are relatively fluid and prisoners come from the same largely depoliticized environs as everyone else, there is a certain point of sharp decline in the quality of life at which the human spirit balks and refuses to endure any more. Interestingly enough, the point of reference for that sharp decline in the prison environment is not only previous prison conditions, but also the conditions of the prisoners before they were imprisoned, as this is their frame of reference. As the courts and legislatures become increasingly unresponsive to prisoners' basic human needs, action strictly within the constraints of what is legal in prison is less and less effective. It is apparent to many who monitor prison news that the number of prison rebellions is on the rise.

THE LESSONS OF ATTICA

Attica is the most notorious and well-known prison uprising in the U. S. history. The memory of the 41 prisoners and hostages massacred in the storming of the prison and its direct aftermath was seared into the psyche of a generation of Americans. Here is a brief chronology of the events the uprising entailed:

July of 1971—A list of demands by Attica prisoners is presented to New York State Commissioner of Corrections, Russell Oswald.

August 20—Revolutionary California prisoner George Jackson is murdered by guards in an escape attempt.

August 27—Attica prisoners call a hunger strike in honor of George Jackson. Only 13 men eat breakfast. Only seven eat lunch.

September 3—Commissioner Oswald visits Attica. He delivers a tape recording for the prisoners, asking for more time to consider their demands.

September 9—The spark is lit. About 1,500 prisoners from all cell blocks take over both D-yard and D-block. One guard is badly beaten during the takeover; 40 prison employees are taken hostage. The prisoners elect leaders and draw up another list of demands. The injured guard is released and later dies in a hospital; the other hostages are protected by the Attica Brothers and treated relatively well. None are beaten.

September 11—New York Governor Nelson Rockefeller refuses to go to Attica and participate in negotiations with the Attica Brothers. Attica prisoner Flip Crowley makes the famous proclamation: "If we cannot live as people, then we will at least try to die like men."

September 13—Bloody Monday. Rockefeller orders thousands of National Guardsmen, State Police and prison guards to attack the prisoners. The Guard used extremely lethal weapons and took no account of the lives of the hostages, let alone those of the prisoners. During a six to eight minute period, approximately 3,000 rounds of shot are fired into D-yard, killing 29 prisoners and 10 hostages.

Another 89 men are wounded. After the rain of gunfire died down, two prisoners—James Robinson and Kenny Malloy—are summarily executed by three state troopers in another part of the prison. There is speculation that other prisoners—such as revolutionary Sam Melville—were also either specifically marked for death by the storming troops, or murdered by law enforcement officers after the initial storming of the prison. (Directly after the massacre authorities told the press that the 10 hostages had their throats slashed by prisoners. Autopsies later revealed the hostages died of gunshot wounds.) D-yard prisoners were retaliated against in the most brutal manner. They were forced to pass naked through gauntlets of officers armed with billy clubs, gloved fists and boots, and subjected to other acts to degrade them emotionally and torture them physically.

-eds.

Attica: Looking Back 25 Years

Jaan Laaman, October 1996

Attica. The word conjures up images of struggle and resistance like few other names, not only in the U.S. but for countless millions around the planet. Yet as the years go by, many—especially the younger people, even those behind prison walls—are less and less familiar with what happened there.

So on this twenty-fifth anniversary of the uprising and bloody state massacre, let me quote from a statement that some of the Attica survivors wrote in the weeks following the government's deadly reconquest of the prison: "These brothers whose lives were taken by Rockefeller and his agents did not die in vain. Why? Because the uprising in Attica did not start here, nor will it end here."

I was released from Attica, maxing out on a parole violation, in the spring of '71. I personally knew many of the brothers who rose up and counted some of the leaders and spokesmen as close friends.

The period leading up to the rebellion was filled with a mounting prisoner rejection of brutal conditions of confinement. It was a time of growing unity, of serious pulling together across national, religious and age lines. Men were coming together, discussing conditions, underlying causes, and possible solutions. Study groups were set up among the most serious prisoners, and revolutionary insight and ideology guided the way to a clearer understanding of how and why a place like Attica could exist in 1971 in the United States.

The government's old stand-by divide and conquer tactic was working less and less, and as I left friends and comrades that May morning, we realized that either some resolution to the most horrendous conditions had to occur or serious struggle would soon be jumping off.

It was not simply about bad food or brutal treatment. It was more fundamental, about the oppressed, those without power, about refusing to accept injustice any longer. It was tied into the Vietnamese farmers who at that time were resisting U.S. B-52s. Historically it was connected to African slaves plotting and acting against the enslavers, to Native American people resisting settler occupation and atrocities, to the Puerto Rican and other colonized nations' undying thirst for liberty. In its essence, it was an extreme case of poor and working people stuck on the bottom of an unjust system, standing up, refusing to accept it any longer and fighting back. And it continued and continues even after the Attica Brothers' noble and courageous words and their stand in D-Yard during those September days, the 9th-13th of 1971.

Recent prison uprisings, from Lucasville, Ohio (1993), to the multiple federal prison uprisings last fall (1995), are but some more recent examples. On a broader level, the continuing struggles from the IRA guerrillas in Ireland, to the Shining Path/Communist Party in Peru, to the indigenous peasant guerrilla uprisings in Mexico (to name just a few) are all part of this Freedom Struggle.

Attica was a bright light, a searing beacon showing that even the most oppressed in the tightest of conditions can—and will—rise up. It was also a blood-drenched reminder that the American government will fight against People's quests for justice and freedom and is willing to commit unspeakable atrocities to hold onto its power.

The aftermath of Attica saw beatings, torture, retaliatory transfers, legal action; in other words, much of the usual state repression. But it also brought about longer-term changes, including some meaningful ones, like family/conjugal visits throughout the New York state prison system.

History shows us that even reformist halfway decent changes only occur through hard and costly struggle. But nothing remains stationary. The many prison rebellions during the period of the early 1970s—of which Attica is the most well known—resulted in some real improvements as well as a lot of meaningless changes. Recently, and this is true across the country, a lot of the improvements made then have been taken away. The "tough on crime—no frills" mentality of the government is stripping prisoners of more and more, even as huge increases occur in the prison population.

It's as simple as this: if We the People aren't pushing them, they immediately begin pushing us back—all the way back to servitude and slavery, and that's regardless of race or nationality if you are a prisoner.

So, like the Attica survivors said, it didn't begin or end at Attica— but Attica is a good and necessary place to remember the fallen, recognize the enemy, and continue our Freedom Struggle more determined than ever.

Oppressed classes—people and oppressed nations united in battle against the real enemy, using all methods of struggle that are called for—REMEMBER ATTICA! The future is ours to create.

Attica Means Fight Back

Laura Whitehorn, November 1996

I've been thinking a lot about Attica, as we pass the 25th anniversary of the rebellion and the massacre. Remembering how the courage of the men of D-Yard transformed all our sorrow and anger at the assassination of George Jackson into energy, struggle and hope. Remembering the inspiration of seeing unity built, combating the divisions of race and class the state normally feeds on. Remembering how we hoped against hope, argued against unreason that the brutal assault would not come. Remembering the demand of the Brothers, spoken by L.D. Barkley, that "we are men, we are not beasts, and we don't intend to be driven or beaten as such."

Attica was a rebellion against all odds—a message written in blood: human dignity will not allow itself to be crushed. A slogan the Vietnamese used in fighting for their national liberation and independence—"the spirit of the people is greater than the man's technology"—came alive inside the walls of D-Yard. For almost five days a cooperative, peaceful, democratic society existed in D-Yard, while the prisoners held power. The demands were so basic, and the administrations' long-standing refusal to meet them so clearly inhumane, that public support grew quickly throughout New York State. The police guns were held at bay for awhile by the stark morality of the Brothers' stand.

But only for awhile. As ever, when confronted with a just struggle of the oppressed, the government fired back with massive, brutal murder, killing nearly 30 prisoners along with some of the hostage guards the prisoners had protected. And then, after the assault itself, L.D. Barkley and other leaders were murdered in cold blood, while others were tortured with burning cigars and savage beatings. Stripped naked, chained, beaten to the ground and forced to crawl through the mud—the Brothers received the government's response to their demands to be treated as humans.

In the aftermath, as the Attica Brothers fought (successfully) through charges of murder designed to punish them further for the rebellion, Attica inspired thousands of prisoners throughout the country to rise up and demand their human rights. At the same time, a movement of support for the Brothers grew. In that period, we had two main slogans: "Attica is All of Us" and "Attica Means Fight Back." These slogans couldn't quite capture the depth to which Attica shook U.S. society, nor how the inspiration of that struggle for human dignity will always continue to light the path of resistance.

I thought about "Attica Means Fight Back" in October of '95, when Congress refused to adjust the racist, disproportionate sentences for crack as opposed to powder cocaine, and prisoners throughout the federal system fought back. As in New York State in 1971, we recognized that no one on the outside would take up the responsibility to protest the attack on our human rights—we prisoners had to do it ourselves. Unlike New York State in 1971, there was no sympathetic public response to the October federal prison rebellions.

At least two Attica Brothers, now released from prison, remember Attica every day by working to help prisoners and defendants trying to stay free. Akil Al-Jundi and Frank "Big Black" Smith both work in New York on prisoners' cases. Big Black is the one who said "Wake up—because nothing comes to a sleeper but a dream." Those of us inside need to wake up to the need for unity—to fight racism and the other divisions that hurt our ability to stand up together for our dignity. And I think we need to find a way to wake up all those people out there who dream that locking up more and more people will solve the problems of violence and crime—problems that come *not* from the oppressed but from the very nature of this capitalist system. We need to make them understand that what they are locking up and destroying is, in the end, their own humanity, their own souls.

The U.S. should be held accountable for its human rights violations. The massive long-term incarceration of huge numbers of oppressed people is one of these abuses. Holding more than 100 political prisoners—in a country that claims to have no political prisoners—is another. Others are daily reported in the newspapers—from the U.S. Army teaching brutal counterinsurgency techniques to regimes in Latin America, to the CIA facilitating crack deals in L.A. to fund the illegal "contra" forces in Nicaragua. It's not in the past, not 25 years ago, it's happening now. It's in violation of international law. The U.S. government is the real criminal, the international outlaw. We prisoners, who experience these human rights abuses every day, can help expose U.S. crimes to the rest of the population. Attica is all of us. Attica means fight back.

VARIED FORMS OF REBELLION AND RESISTANCE

Nonviolent Protest Suppressed

Adrian Lomax, August 1992

In the middle of May, 1992, the Wisconsin Department of Corrections distributed a new set of property rules to all prisoners. It contained a lot of new restrictions but the most significant is that the total amount of property a prisoner may possess must fit into a footlocker measuring 32" x 16" x 16". Of course, TVs are exempted from the rules since no prison official would ever discourage an prisoner from becoming addicted to television. The rules are aimed directly at jailhouse lawyers and prisoner writ writers because they accumulate all the books and paperwork.

Three years ago the Waupun prison tried to confiscate everyone's legal papers saying they created a fire hazard. That didn't fly, so now this. Their justification? Prisoner possession of property leads to theft and prisoner property is used for gambling.

The new rules went into effect on the 1st of June '92, for people entering the system after that date. Those of us already here have to be in compliance by June 1, 1993, or upon transfer to another prison, whichever happens first.

Needless to say, everyone is pissed. The Wisconsin chapter of CURE staged a demonstration at the state capitol on June 1st to protest the rules. Since then prison officials have rejected all mail sent to me by CURE.

Seven hundred of the 800 prisoners at one of the medium-security prisons went on a one day food strike, boycotting the dining hall on June 1st.

Before that, on May 23, prisoners here at Waupun took over the mess hall and beat up all the guards. We've been locked-down ever since, eating in our cells and allowed out twice a week for showers.

Nonviolent protests by prisoners are not often heard of because prison administrators ruthlessly oppress prisoners who organize such actions. Waupun prisoners have often attempted to organize nonviolent protests such as strikes and sit-downs. In order to be effective, such collective efforts require mass participation. Organizers must inform the prisoner population of the planned event and encourage participation.

It is impossible to conduct such efforts covertly. Prison officials will inevitably become aware of the organizing, and when they do, they immediately lockdown the prison and conduct an investigation. Any prisoners who can be identified as organizers will be sentenced to long terms in segregation and transferred, usually to prisons in the federal system or in other states. Prison officials simply do not tolerate prisoners who organize nonviolent protests. The Supreme Court has ruled that prisoners have no constitutional right to organize collective protests, so prisoners have no protection from such retaliation.

In April, 1988, I was confined at the Oshkosh Correctional Institution. A group of prisoners tried to organize a mass hunger strike to protest the terrible conditions there. There is no rule in Wisconsin prisons against going on a hunger strike. In fact, prison rules specifically state that prisoners may decline to eat any meals they choose. The activists in this case were therefore encouraging prisoners to do something that they're specifically authorized to do. Nonetheless, the organizers were rounded up, transferred to maximum-security prisons (Oshkosh is medium-security) and sentenced to lengthy terms in segregation.

Prisoners planning a violent protest, on the other hand, are able to organize covertly. Because they need only a small group of confederates, they are spared the necessity of organizing the mass of prisoners. The ability to plan covertly enables violent prisoner protesters to at least carry out their plans. Prisoners thinking of organizing a collective, nonviolent protest must always grapple with the grim likelihood that their prison will be locked-down and they will find themselves in the segregation unit of a max prison in another state before the protest ever takes place.

Of course the prisoners who beat up the seven guards on May 23 will be confined in segregation, but they won't be transferred to Marion [USP Marion and Florence, though federal facilities, accept the "incorrigibles" state prison systems wish to send them. -eds.] The fact that prison officials punish violent protesters less harshly than nonviolent protesters is not lost upon prisoners.

Wisconsin has no administrative grievance system. While one exists on paper it is non-existent in practice. The courts are also inaccessible to the vast majority of prisoners, who have neither the money to hire an attorney nor the legal expertise to proceed in court without counsel.

With the extreme, malicious persecution of nonviolent protesters and the lack of an operational grievance system, it is no surprise that prisoners turn to violent protest. Given the near certainty that the human spirit will rise up against the conditions that prisoners in this country are forced to endure, one might suppose that prison officials would prefer that prisoners choose to protest nonviolently. But prison officials adopt policies that encourage, and even ensure, violent protest.

Every act of violent protest by prisoners strengthens the correctional administrators' hand. In the wake of the May 23 incident, DOC officials have called for increased funding, more oppressive security measures and the construction of more maximum-security prisons. [A free-standing, Supermax facility is currently under construction in Wisconsin. -eds.]

When conservative DOC officials do battle with a Democrat-controlled legislature for dollars to fund their severely repressive program, they can possess no stronger bargaining chip than a record of seemingly senseless prisoner violence. Prison officials actually hope that prisoners react violently to their conditions. It is of course, the guards, not the white collar officials who make policy, who will always be the victims of violent prisoner protest.

The proposition that prison officials want prisoners to lash out violently against guards is a radical one, but I am not alone in making it. Since the May 23 incident, AFSCME Local 18—the union that represents Waupun guards—has publicly alleged that Waupun administrators knew in advance that prisoners were planning the attack, and did nothing to prevent it.

As always, prison officials blame prisoners for the problems in Wisconsin prisons. But it is the administrators who hold the power and make policy. Appropriate policies would render violent prison protest non-existent.

RIKERS ISLAND DETAINEES IN STRUGGLE

Dan Pens, September 1995

Rikers Island is the largest penal colony in the world, holding more than 19,000 prisoners on a 410 acre island. More than 130,000 people spend time in Rikers Island each year. Ninety-two percent are Black or Hispanic. Ninety percent have no high school degree. Twenty-six percent of the women and sixteen percent of the men are HIV+. Most of them are New York City pretrial detainees not convicted of any crime. In late 1994—with the number of detainees expected to increase to as high as 25,000 in the following months as Republican mayor Rudolph Guiliani prepared to make good on his campaign promises to "improve the quality of life" in New York City by locking up the homeless, street vendors, panhandlers, etc.—captives at the jail staged a number of strikes to protest such proposals and the conditions under which they were confined.

To make good on campaign promises to balance the city budget Guiliani proposed over $31 million in budget cuts. These two factors came together to make Rikers Island the focus of the most intense struggle in several years. Among the jail programs to be eliminated as part of the budget cuts were the jail's 900-bed drug treatment program, its 23 person grievance-investigation unit and its food industry job training program. Eight hundred and ninety-seven jail guards and 400 civilian workers were slated to be laid off as well. The new staffing cuts came on top of previous staffing cuts and increases in the detainee population, which resulted in most of the jail's 9,800 guards being required to work 16-hour double shifts three days a week. The city paid more than $110 million to the guards in overtime alone.

Starting November 15, 1994, captives in the jail began staging strikes to protest proposals by Mayor Guiliani to cut vocational, drug treatment and counseling programs at the jail. About 2,000 prisoners refused to eat on November 19, according to a jail spokesperson. The prisoners' demands included: better food and medical care; reinstatement of the GED classes; reinstatement of social workers to pre-budget cut levels; and the transfer of abusive guards who harass prisoners. Family members and supporters were protesting outside the jail complex as well.

Because jail food workers were on strike, jail guards had to serve prisoners their food (at least to the prisoners who would still eat). Three guards were suspended after they refused to serve food: one simply refused, one overturned a cart of food, and the third complained that he was incapable of doing the chore due to a back injury. A spokesman for the Correction Officers Benevolent Association was quoted as saying the guards were "livid" at being ordered to perform "prisoners' work," which they claimed "undermined their authority." (There were also occasions where guards acted to undermine their own authority, such as when Commissioner of Correction Anthony Schembri announced that a guard had been arrested smuggling contraband into the jail, in the form of razor blades and a knife blade, presumably to sell to prisoners.)

Robert Gangi, head of the Correctional Association of New York—an independent prison watchdog group—was quoted in the *New York Times* as saying: "Absent a disturbance, the mayor will get all or most of what he wants." He noted that prison reform usually follows a riot. "What's striking in this is that I can't recall when we've had an organized political protest by inmates about budget cuts coming down the pike. That is an unusual level of sophistication."

Gangi's quote displayed a high level of ignorance about the detainees' situation. Their protests were not based on abstract issues like proposed budget cuts, but on very real overcrowding, brutality, dehumanization and a concomitant decline in services and basic living conditions. Detainees reported to local newspapers that they are fed irregularly and—when fed at all—receive only white rice, white bread and water. Prisoners reported being placed in unheated trailers, sent to yard at 4 and 5 a.m. and then having to lay in bed all day because there are no other recreation facilities. One detainee said: "The officers in there are too violent with the inmates. They stabbed one inmate, and no one knows who it was. This was a week ago [Nov. 20, 1994].

And yesterday, four officers beat up an inmate so badly that he's in critical condition... The officers are so violent with them, you know, treating them like if they were animals." The prisoners repeatedly tried to get their message out to the mainstream media, to no avail.

Update, October 1996

Many of the prisoner grievances that led to the prisoner struggles in 1994 were given more credence when New York City agreed to pay $1.6 million to 15 prisoners to settle a civil rights complaint charging Rikers Island guards with beatings and abuse of detainees' civil rights in February of 1996.

City officials, who insisted on anonymity, told *NYT* reporters that 43 guards are believed to have been involved in incidents of beating handcuffed prisoners, often with clubs. But the city was not admitting guilt or liability in offering to settle for $1.6 million, but rather was making a "business decision" to avert future trial expenses and risk huge verdicts in a civil trial.

On October 9, 1996, eleven current or former Rikers Island jail guards were indicted on charges ranging from second-degree assault to falsifying records. The charges were brought by the Bronx District Attorney's office following a two-year investigation.

New York's Department of Investigation Commissioner Howard Wilson said: "Corrections officers have a very difficult job and work under trying circumstances. However, this does not justify the deliberate beating of inmates."

Peter Meringolo, president of the Correction Captains Association, representing nearly 1,000 captains in the NYC Department of Corrections, said investigators should not trust the word of prisoners. Using an impressive number of buzzwords for a rather short statement, he said: "Corrections personnel in the [Rikers Segregation Unit] simply try to do their job under extremely difficult and dangerous conditions. They should be congratulated for their courage and perseverance, and not prosecuted for charges stemming from the frivolous lawsuits of career criminals."

In choosing to settle for $1.6 million rather than face trial, however, the City of New York lends little credence to Meringolo's claim that the lawsuits were "frivolous."

HUNGRY FOR JUSTICE IN L.A.

Dan Pens, December 1996

More than 50 detainees at the Men's Central Jail in Los Angeles participated in a hunger strike, protesting a lack of legal reference materials and law library access, in August, 1996.

The hunger strike appears to have been confined to one section of the jail. Of the 74 men detained in that section, 54 refused to eat the noon meal on Sunday, August 4. Sixty-one refused to eat the evening meal. The following day, according to local newspaper accounts, 58 detainees refused solid food, 35 of whom also rejected liquid sustenance.

Celes King III, a well-known bail bondsman and state chair of the Congress of Racial Equality of California, told reporters that he received several phone calls from jail detainees in the week leading up to the hunger strike complaining about curtailments in access to the jail's law library. King said he thought the detainees called him mainly to get the word out about the law library issue before the protest started in order to help focus attention on that issue.

By virtue of the fact that the law library issue was prominently reported in newspaper accounts, the detainees' strategy worked. Often prisoners or jail detainees stage a protest—attempting to draw attention to an important issue—but because nobody on the outside has been clued in before hand, when the press reports the incident the only information they have to go on is what the authorities tell them.

In this case L.A. jail officials told reporters that the strikers were protesting "reduced access to telephones, quality of food, a recent lock down, and lack of complete reference materials in the law library."

The official statement makes it appear that the detainees were griping about telephones, food, and being locked-down; the law library access is mentioned only in passing, and probably only because that issue was being reported by other sources.

THE STRAW THAT BROKE THE CAMEL'S BACK

The 1993 Lucasville Easter Uprising

John Perotti, December 1993 - February 1996

In 1990 the State Highway Patrol was ordered to investigate all aspects of the notorious Southern Ohio Correctional Facility (SOCF) outside of Lucasville by then Governor Celeste. This was in response to hundreds of letters written to the Correctional Institution Inspection Committee by SOCF prisoners alleging a wide array of mistreatments and brutalities. I myself, in conjunction with a small number of other SOCF prisoners, had prepared a 38-page human rights petition asking Amnesty International to investigate torture and violations of the United Nations Standard Minimum Rules for the Treatment of Prisoners at SOCF. We had over 200 pages of exhibits detailing brutality by guards, as well as many other atrocities and institutional flaws at SOCF. We were infracted for "unauthorized group activity" and possessing "contraband," and the conditions, untreated, worsened.

In 1990 SOCF warden Terry Morris was transferred to another facility and Arthur Tate was appointed SOCF's new warden. Tate began instituting new and harsher rules on a daily basis, locked-down most of the prison, and began a wave of repression previously unmatched. It was all done in the name of "making the prison safe." In reality there were more stabbings, beatings and killings after Tate began his authoritarian reign than before. All of this came to a head on April 11, 1993, Easter Sunday. Over four hundred prisoners took over L-block in response to, among other things, what was going to be a total lockdown to force tuberculosis tests on all prisoners. Many Muslims were religiously opposed to a TB test that involved injection under the skin of a substance containing alcohol, but their concerns and beliefs were ignored. Nine prisoners and one guard died in the rebellion. The prisoners held the prison for eleven days.

The last of the 407 surviving prisoners to leave the prisoner-controlled block were identified as belonging to the Aryan Brotherhood, Muslims and Black Gangster Disciples. Though some of these identifications were inaccurate, all prisoners who had rioted and were thought to be affiliated with these groups were taken to the Mansfield Correctional Institute (MANCI). They were classified as administrative control status and were held two per cell. They were denied sufficient medical care, had their visitors turned away, their recreational periods cut short, their mail and food tampered with, and were harassed in every other way possible.

The prison administrators easily focused the media on various violent acts committed by prisoners during the eleven day siege to distract news services from investigating the conditions that caused 435 prisoners' desperate attempt to take matters into their own hands. Prisoners hung banners out of SOCF windows during the rebellion asking the FBI to investigate the prison, but were ignored. The prison officials and state highway patrol even tried to keep the media out of sight of the prison so they could not see such pleas. All the warning signs of an imminent rebellion were manifest, and prisoners utilized all means available to them before reaching the point of desperation. Many had been writing civil rights groups for years, petitioning the courts for intervention, and had called for the FBI and Justice Department's Civil Rights Division to intervene—all to no avail. A riot was inevitable.

Instead of changes being made to deal with the atrocious conditions that caused the desperate act of rebellion, the actions of the participants in the rebellion were harshly punished and their concerns—as well as the concerns of many other prisoners trapped in the Ohio DORC—blatantly ignored. Such blindness on the part of prison administrators and the public that tacitly gives them their power will only create another situation where prisoners will react with anger and violence to the miserable and incredibly inhumane conditions in which they are forced to live. Will we treat the conditions that lead up to the rebellion, or will we ignore them and risk another situation worse than the last? The lessons of history are not encouraging.

The overcrowding in Ohio prisons, understaffing and the lack of programs and jobs for prisoners it causes, were all factors leading to the rebellion. But the main issue which caused the drastic action was the religious suppression of the Muslims. The Muslims had refused to take TB tests, which contained alcohol, and it was leaked into the prison that there was going to be a lockdown to force this testing. Other forms of racism against Muslims were another factor. The DORC has no cultural and religious awareness for its guards, or inter-personal relations training programs. During my confinement at the SOCF the minister has showed great partiality towards the Catholics, Protestants and Baptists, and open disdain towards Muslims and other faiths. The guards openly disrespect Muslims in particular and Blacks in general. This overt racism and a warden who ruled his way or no way at all created a situation where unrest was a given and rebellion an ever-growing possibility. (Finally responding to these problems, in 1994 the guard's union called for training in cultural and religious awareness, as well as the hiring of more guards.)

Investigations into the uprising conducted by the state legislature, state highway patrol, Scioto County Prosecutor's Office, and OCSEA, the prison guards' union, all more or less stated correctly the causes of the rebellion as described above. But the mass media chose to focus on 46 crimes committed during the rebellion, rather than on the problems which caused the rebellion in the first place.

As long as the criminal injustice system continues to hand out extraordinarily long sentences and the parole board continues to deny paroles to Ohio prisoners, overcrowding along with the problems that accompany it will continue. Most Ohio prisons are accredited by the American Correctional Association (ACA) whose standards are widely referred to by many U.S. district courts. However, ACA standards call for single-celling in all close, maximum and most medium security prisons. The only single cells in Ohio are in administrative (AC) and local control (LC) which, contrary to prisoncrats' assertions, are punitive in nature. The fact that in August of 1996, Ohio DORC Director Reginald Wilkinson became the president of the ACA, will likely do nothing to help matters.

When Lucasville sent 129 prisoners from the Easter Rebellion to the Mansfield Correctional Institution (MANCI) they were all classified as AC and housed two per cell. This is something not even done at Lucasville and is forbidden by the holdings of *Rhodes v. Chapman*, the leading double-celling case from the U.S. Supreme Court which arose from Lucasville. The plaintiff's attorney in *White v. Morris*, the federal suit requiring integrated celling at Lucasville, attempted to obtain a court order seeking single-celling of all Lucasville cells since violence resulted from forced integration. The district court refused to do so but suspended forced integration until February 1, 1994, by which time the state promised to "have its house in order." The prisoners at Lucasville—as of mid-1994—except for a small portion, are still locked-down two to a cell under "security control" status "pending investigation."[1] Criminal indictments were issued against many of the participants in the rebellion.

The 129 prisoners transferred to MANCI are the scapegoats. They were placed in AC, and when asked why were essentially told "you were self-identified as a member of one of the three groups that had control of the guard hostages." The only identification of the prisoners as gang members or affiliates came from the officials in charge of the surrender, not the prisoners themselves. The state claimed that all these prisoners were either Muslims, Black Gangster Disciples or Aryan Brotherhood, which is simply false. Some were simply just in the last group to exit the building after the prisoners surrendered and the Rebellion ended.

The treatment these prisoners received was rife with the same repression and racism that they saw at Lucasville. Their food was issued in small portions, and left to sit until it got cold. Access to the law library was denied. Mail was stolen or censored. Hygiene articles and cell cleaning supplies were often withheld. Recreation was denied and men were housed two to a cell, twenty-four hours a day, seven days a week, with only writing paper, pencil and limited personal reading material. Some were permitted radios.

When some of the Muslims protested being denied pork substitutes by beating on their doors, the "Ninja Turtles," or prison SWAT team, were called in. The block was surrounded by these men with shotguns and teargas canisters and the prisoners involved were physically beaten and then transferred to other prisons. This is the mentality at MANCI. The entire "Unit 5" control unit was filled up with ACs and the mental health unit "Lynx Program" pod had to be moved in order to house security control and detention cell prisoners.

*****

1995

In the two years that followed the 11-day siege at SOCF millions of dollars were spent on reconstruction of the prison and prosecuting of prisoners the state had charged with criminal acts during the siege. Steel encased control booths with electronically controlled double doors were constructed in each cellblock, with an accompanying escape ladder and hatch built in so that guards could escape to the roof should the security of the double doors be breached. The back walls of the cellblock have been encased in steel so the concrete can't be broken out to get to anyone hiding in the back stairwell. TV cameras have been strategically located outside all the doors and in the hallways to monitor prisoners' movements. Prisoners at Lucasville are only permitted out of their cells for meals and one hour recreation per day, one range at a time and under constant escort and surveillance by Disturbance Control Teams of guards, dressed in black T-shirts and fatigues. This presence was intended to instill fear. Prisoners were rushed through the dining hall like cattle, rushed through their meal then marched back, range by range to their cells. Everything was delivered to the cell, there are no outside passes given except for visits, to which prisoners are escorted coming and going. Young vocal prisoners are set up by guards and placed in the hole, then put into more long-term isolation.

There is one 1994 incident that has stuck in my mind. When I was leaving the dining hall one day a prisoner dropped his milk on the floor. Three guards ordered a young Black prisoner—who they knew hadn't dropped the milk—to clean up the split milk. The prisoner who had spilled the milk offered to clean it up but was told not to. The guard claimed he "didn't like the other prisoner and wanted him to clean it up." They then attacked the Black prisoner for his crime of refusing to clean up "spilt milk." The prisoner was wrestled to the floor then taken to the hole.

Myself and eight others were escorted to the hole an hour later. We were placed under "investigation" for merely witnessing the guards' attack. The news media was told that the prisoner refused to clean up spilt milk. They were not told that the prisoner in question wasn't a food service worker, and that it wouldn't normally be expected of him to clean it up. The news media was told that this prisoner attacked the guards while seven other prisoners cheered him on.

This was and is typical propaganda by the guards' union which has been trying their hardest to have the prison locked-down by intentionally feeding lies to the media and legislators. At the time of this incident the prisoners' attitudes were still a mile high due to the takeover the year before.

In the aftermath of the '93 Rebellion forty-eight prisoners were indicted on 198 charges ranging from assault, kidnapping to aggravated murder with death penalty qualifications. Twenty of the prisoners were found guilty of charges with eight pleading guilty. Some even turned state's evidence against the others. After the Attica riot in September of 1971 eight prisoners were either convicted or pled guilty, but all were later pardoned by the governor due to prosecutorial misconduct. Prosecutors in Santa Fe, New Mexico promised to indict more than 100 prisoners after that riot, but only 30 were criminally charged and early trials ended with not guilty verdicts. There were no death penalty convictions and prosecutors began reducing charges and offering plea bargains.

Ohio hired a team of special prosecutors headed by Mark Peipmeir, an assistant Hamilton County prosecutor. The state's strategy has been to bring the lesser charges to trial and obtain convictions based on the testimony of guards and the fabricated testimony of snitches who claimed to be "eyewitness." The prosecutor then used the plea bargain process to convince the convicted to turn state's witness against other prisoners under indictment. Five prisoners were indicted for aggravated murder with the death penalty sought and obtained. Their names are Jason Robb, George Skatzes, Saddique Abdullah Hasan, Keith LaMar, and Namir Abdul Mateen. The state obtained the indictments after a negotiator during the siege agreed to turn state's evidence against his fellow prisoners regarding the death of guard Robert Vallandingham. This prisoner was described by the media as being one of the leaders of the Black Gangster Disciples.

It's up to us to open Lucasville back up. The guards' union wants it locked-down so all cases of prisoner on prisoner assaults are utilized by them to justify their cry to lock down Lucasville. As a result of the continued lockdown violence at the prison has increased. Fights and stabbings occur on a daily basis due to the effects of frustration of being locked in a cell the majority of the time, in a prison hundreds of miles away from major cities which makes it very difficult to visit with friends or family. We need to work together to further our goals of opening Lucasville back up. We need to stand united against the prison administration and the government, and use all legal remedies we have available: informal complaint resolutions, grievances, suits and legal remedies first. We need the families and friends of those imprisoned to speak to the media and legislators to let them know what is done to us in these camps.

Men cannot be treated like animals and continue to accept this treatment. Blame the prisoncrats for initiating the oppressive conditions that caused men to react in desperation. *Do not* blame your fellow prisoners who are paying dearly now for reasonable treatment. They should be looked upon, not with disrespect, but with respect and praise.

REMEMBER ATTICA, REMEMBER SANTA FE, REMEMBER LUCASVILLE ! !

1 The prison started loosening up again in 1995, when regular library periods were started up again. But into 1997 prisoners still have to go to meals and recreation one range at a time, and prisoner movement continues to be tightly controlled. The goon squad members have been taken out of the hallway.

CHALLENGING THE EVIL THAT ILLS THIS SOCIETY

The September 1995 New York State Prison Strike

A. Johnson/Musaa and Ed Kinane, March 1996

Of the main forms of prisoner resistance, the work strike often has the biggest impact (typically prison officials lump riots and work strikes into the same category of "serious disturbances"). By withholding their labor prisoners use their most potent weapon and literally bring the prison to a standstill. These actions, unlike the riots, are rarely reported by the media. On the occasions when they are, it is usually inaccurately. -eds.

Musaa has served 13 years of a 20 year sentence in the New York State penal system. He has earned three degrees with an emphasis on political science and social critique. Until the fall of 1995 Musaa was at Auburn Correctional Facility.

This interview is adapted from our correspondence. Here Musaa discusses the September '95 statewide prison protest against worsening prison conditions. September 13, 1995, was chosen as the date to kick off the two week protest because it was the anniversary of the 1971 Attica Rebellion. That bloody rebellion was also a protest against worsening prison conditions.

In the aftermath of the protest many prisoners, including Musaa, were shipped around the state and placed in special housing units or deprivation cells. Musaa mentions Jean Marie DeMay, formerly of the NYC Legal Aid Society. She lost her job on September 4, 1995, for allegedly urging maximum-security prisoners to strike.

-Ed Kinane, Peace Activist

Kinane: Was the September action unprecedented?

Musaa: Strikes, boycotts, and protests by prisoners over dehumanizing prison conditions certainly aren't anything new. Rather, they are a classical part of prison experience. Our protest differed in that firstly it was an attempt at a political analysis by prisoners in general. Prisoners were directly connecting their current conditions with the overall political climate of society. This is largely facilitated by the media blitz of opportunist politicians using prison as a platform issue of the electoral process.

Secondly, it was the first time in New York that a citizen [i.e., Ms. DeMay] was directly linked with prisoners on a level of engaged activism.

Thirdly, there was a phenomenal diffusion of activism beyond single group leadership. In prison, it's very difficult to go beyond fragmentation to a large scale unified effort. The protest came out of a "collective" of a single idea which took into account the failures of the past. Simply put, that single idea was: without unity, we all lose.

Finally, rather than being haphazard and spontaneous, the protest was systematic. There was considerable planning in terms of duration and scope of activities. For good reasons, such planning has been missing in earlier forms of prison protest.

Kinane: What kind of good reasons?

Musaa: In times past, advance notice to prison officials led to protest leaders being targeted for reprisal and in the planned actions being thwarted. In this case, we felt a need not to be historically fatal. We're painfully aware that past protests that seemed to achieve some gains eventually resulted in those gains being repealed or eroded.

Kinane: Like at Attica?

Musaa: Attica was a classic protest. Prisoners used violence to achieve an objective. Violence is the result of improvisation and haphazard thinking: a foiled goal fermenting into frustrated "reactionaryism." Violence is too volatile to contain.

In contrast, the September protest used nonviolent confrontation reminiscent of civil disobedience. It was like a sit-in. Prisoners refused to come out of their cells. This hit the prison's economic base: the strike deprived them of free or cheap labor.

Kinane: Some think whatever Jean Marie did was wrong.

Musaa: Those who think so have a vested interest in the system. They are the pro-prison capitalists. However, one should recall that civil disobedience is both customary practice and integral to American society. It dates back to when this country was forming its system of democracy. It's the only true right most citizens have.

Recall that even Dr. King was criticized for using civil disobedience in his civil rights protests. Today, however, he's honored by the same system as one of the greatest advocates of civil rights in this country and in this century. Mrs. DeMay engaged in the same sort of activity that is at most "citative," but not criminal.

Her activity may have been technically wrong, but she was right in being more humane. She challenged the existing evil that ills this society. The recent court ruling halting further double bunking correlates with Mrs. DeMay's stance. She deserves commendation, not condemnation.

Kinane: What problems did the protest address?

Musaa: There were four in particular: double bunking, good-time legislation, dehumanizing abuse, and poor medical treatment. I'll take them one by one.

Double-Bunking: This means having two prisoners crowded into a one-person cell. More and more the state is subjecting prisoners to such abuse. This is despite the fact that double-bunking can lead to increased incidence of diseases like TB, and also to increased violence among prisoners. Lab experiments have shown that mice raised under very crowded conditions tend to be violent. The same seems to be true for people forced to live in crowded ghettos and prisons.

And while we're on the subject of mice and men... shouldn't prisoners, if they're going to be treated like beasts, be treated as well as beasts? Monkeys in zoos get far more space than we do!

Good-time Legislation: NYS asked for the death penalty in exchange for "merited good-time allowance." Good-time is an incentive earned by prisoners toward "rehabilitation" as a sign of "penitence." It shortens their time served. Although the death penalty was installed, the opportunity for prisoners to earn good-time was sacrificed to a political platform built to exploit crime as a commodity.

There are people behind bars who should be released from further imprisonment, and there are those who should never have been imprisoned to begin with. There is a racist and discrimina-tory context to the whole thing. This becomes obvious when one sees that according to FBI statistics, most of the U.S. prison pop-ulation is Black or Latino. Virtually all of those come from slums and ghettos. Of the 46 million African-Americans and 28 mil-lion Latinos in the U.S., all but four percent live under these herded conditions.

Most U.S. violence is inter-racial, i.e. Black on Black, White on White, etc. How then can issues such as executions, tougher sentencing or rehabilitative release not be racist? There's not one Black anti-good-time advocate in the New York state legislature.

Dehumanizing Abuse: Prisoners for the most part are need-lessly abused and degraded, and in a manner that in no way helps to make them better people. On the contrary, hostilities are cre-ated and prisoners become embittered. This occurs in both male and female prisons. Note the number of rapes, assaults, impreg-nations, and sexual harassments perpetrated on female prisoners—also other acts of degradation like strip frisks and body searches conducted by male guards.

Medical Treatment: Prisoners are often denied appropriate med-ical treatment for both curable and terminal illnesses. Among pris-oners, much pain and suffering and death occurs due to neglect. There's no medical plan or insurance covering prisoners that guar-antees them more than minimal consideration. Often they are treated by unqualified and callous quacks who are persuaded to keep med-ical expenses low.

I think it was Senator Kennedy who stated on the floor of Con-gress a couple of years ago that "America's medical availability for all its citizens is worse than South Africa's," and that in the U.S. "health is determined by wealth." That's not the first time America has been compared to South Africa. Percentage-wise, more Blacks are imprisoned in the U.S. than in South Africa.

Kinane. What message do you have for readers concerned about the issues you've raised?

Musaa: The New York state prison system needs a strong reality check. This can be accomplished in part by concerned citizens open-ing up the forum on prison conditions and engaging in pointed dis-cussions with both policy makers and prisoners. Since tax dollars fund prisons, citizens should be able to randomly inspect them. On these inspections they should look for operating values inconsistent with good moral thinking and human development.

I speak to activists as much as to common working people: get beyond the sidelines, get involved. You can influence policies affecting prisons—these ultimately affect you. Prisons reflect our social system; their failure perpetuates a continuing and growing dysfunctional cycle. And finally, make Mrs. DeMay the rule rather than the lone exception.

FEDERAL PRISONS ERUPT

Dan Pens, January 1996

At least five federal prisons erupted in violence mere days after the October 18, 1995 vote in the U.S. House of Representatives to overrule a recommendation by the U.S. Sentencing Commission to end the 100 to 1 sentencing disparity between crack and powdered cocaine offenses. The uprisings were widely reported by the corporate media. Most newspaper reports, however, were buried well off the front pages. The reports focused on accounts from "official spokespersons" who universally denied that the rebellions were related to the vote in Congress. Typical of the type of reporting are the following passages: "Faye Pollard, a spokeswoman for the Federal Bureau of Prisons said Sunday the cause of the outbreaks was still being investigated and could not necessarily be attributed to the vote in Congress"; "Officials were unsure whether the attack [against guards at the El Reno, Oklahoma, prison] was related to the other disturbances," (Associated Press); and, "At her weekly Justice Department news conference, Attorney General Janet Reno said she had yet to receive a conclusive report on what triggered the uprisings..." (Reuters).

A review of over thirty news reports turned up only a single quote from a prisoner involved (*USA Today*). The majority of news articles featured only quotes from official BOP spokespersons. A few, however, included quotes from "unofficial" sources. The *Chicago Tribune* quoted the president of a local union that represents prison guards: "The inmates said they were trying to send a message to the U.S. government. They said the [100 to 1 sentencing] law is racially motivated."

WBET radio in Washington DC reported that thirty-eight prisons had some type of disturbance. According to the Prison Activist Resource Center in Berkeley, California, there were confirmed reports of uprisings in sixteen federal prisons: Talledega, AL; Terminal Island, CA; McKean, PA; Lewisburg, PA; Allenwood, PA; Memphis, TN; El Reno, OK; Greenville, IL; Springfield, MO; Leavenworth, KS; Marianna, FL; Atlanta, GA; Raybrook, NY; Fairton, NJ; and Dublin, CA. Two days after the first rebellion in Talladega, the entire federal prison system was placed on lockdown status.

The unified prisoner action at USP Lewisberg, in Pennsylvania, is an example of a story that did not make the mainstream news. On November 1, 1995, several prisoners created a disturbance in the mess hall at USP Lewisburg. They took a case of soda pop and barricaded themselves into one of the dorms. They proceeded to construct a "cannon," from a hollow pipe that was part of a tall floor stand fan, and using a cue ball for a projectile and shaken cans of soft drinks as propellant. When the riot squad stormed the dorm, the prisoners fired the "cannon" at them. The pool ball went through a chicken-wire enforced window of a door. The prisoners then soaped the floor and turned a fire hose on the riot squad.

The riot squad turned off the water and then tear-gassed the entire unit. They proceeded to drag out and beat every prisoner from the unit, despite the fact that only a handful had been involved. Over twenty prisoners were beaten so badly by the riot squad that they required medical attention.

After they had all of the prisoners handcuffed and stripped naked, they had them lie on the floor for eighteen hours. Men were defecating on themselves because if they spoke they were kicked in the head. Almost the entire unit was transferred to other units or prisons.

After this, the warden went to all of the various prisoner leaders and asked them to have a meeting, amongst themselves, to try and calm the situation down. There was talk of a work strike, but many of the (mainly younger) prisoners wanted to start a largescale riot. The prisoner leaders decided to call a work strike, but with only one demand. They demanded that the prisoners who had been beaten by the riot squad receive proper medical attention. It was a compromise, because many of the prisoners were so angry that the threat of a riot was very real.

The men at that meeting then went back to the units and held meetings. One prisoner said that out of 200 prisoners in his unit, over 190 attended the unit meeting. He said that after eleven years in prison, he had never seen such unity.

The warden immediately locked-down the entire prison. Every prisoner leader who was at the meeting (the one the warden asked them to have) was put in the hole and the majority of them were transferred to other prisons. Over 400 men were transferred in all.

The riot squad would walk up and down the units at night with flashlights and pull prisoners out of their cells. The administration was clearly intimidated by the unity of the prisoners and responded with swift and brutal retribution.

The seeds of federal prisoner rebellion were planted in 1986, at the height of the War on Drugs. Congress passed severely repressive mandatory sentencing guidelines which for the first time made a distinction between crack and powdered cocaine. Under the new guidelines people convicted on federal charges for possession of five grams of grams of crack are punished with a mandatory minimum of five years without the possibility of parole, even for first time offenders. By contrast, possession of 500 grams of powdered cocaine—100 times the amount of crack—carries a five year mandatory minimum.

Crack is the only drug that carries a mandatory prison term for possession whether or not the intent is to distribute. Possession of powder cocaine or heroin without intent to sell is a misdemeanor with a maximum one year jail term.

Since 1986 there has been a wealth of statistical evidence gathered to show that the crack laws are targeted, through selective enforcement and prosecution, almost exclusively at poor Blacks and Latinos. Even though studies indicate that the majority of crack users are White, in the federal courts of sixteen states not a single White person was tried for crack offenses between 1987 and 1992. When enforcement officials arrest Blacks for possession of crack, they are served up to federal prosecutors for long mandatory sentences. When enforcement officials arrest Whites for crack, often they are handed over to local state prosecutors and sentenced to probation or short jail terms.

About 13 percent of the people who use drugs on a monthly basis are Black, but Black people account for 35 percent of arrests, 55 percent of convictions, and 74 percent of all prison sentences on drug possession charges. It is apparent that the War on Drugs is in reality a racist war being waged against poor Blacks in accord with the White supremacist vision of the government and to further criminalize poverty. The proliferation of drugs has hardly been stemmed, which many point to as evidence of the war's failure. But the corporate ruling class looks at the boom in prison populations and considers the war a huge success.

There has been organizing and struggle on the other side of this war. A grassroots movement has arisen to call for the reform of the blatantly unjust sentencing disparity in federal drug sentencing guidelines. Leading this movement is the group Families Against Mandatory Minimums (FAMM). FAMM has worked extremely hard to draw attention to the 100/1 sentencing disparity, being instrumental in generating media coverage on the issue, organizing protests, letter writing campaigns, petitions, and lobbying Congress for reform. After years of organized opposition, it appeared that FAMM was on the brink of victory. In May of 1995 the U.S. Sentencing Commission formulated a recommendation to reduce the sentences for crack possession to bring them in line with sentences for powdered cocaine.[1]

This remarkable turnaround by the Sentencing Commission was due almost entirely to FAMM's efforts in collecting statistical data on sentencing disparities and ensuring that the data was widely disseminated. When the commission ruled for the reduction of crack sentences they said: "Federal sentencing data leads to the inescapable conclusion that Blacks comprise the largest percentage of those affected by the penalties associated with crack cocaine." Judge Richard P. Conaboy, chairman of the commission, said, "When we saw those statistics... our theory was that a law—no matter how well intentioned it was—if it's causing such discrepant results, then the law has to be changed and a new method has to be installed."

The Sentencing Commission's recommendation to reduce penalties for crack cocaine offenses was slated to go into effect on November 1, 1995. What is remarkable is that if Congress had not voted at all the recommendations would have automatically gone into effect. On October 18th, 1995, the House voted 332 to 83 against the proposed sentencing reform. It was the first time Congress had voted not to accept any of the over 500 recommendations sent to it since the Sentencing Commission was established.

Jesse Jackson, speaking at the Million Man March on October 16th, spoke against the 100/1 sentencing disparity and urged Congress to ratify the sentencing reforms. Anybody who thought that Jesse was speaking with the voice of the oppressed, however, should note what he said six days later, after the prison rebellions erupted. Speaking to prisoners at Joliet, Illinois State Prison, Jackson used the voice of political opportunism as he urged prisoners not to react with more violence. "There are people on the outside, in Congress and at other levels of government who are working to change the laws," Jackson said, "but they [prisoners] must help us by cooperating and exercising the same kind of discipline and dignity that we saw last Monday at the Million Man March."

On October 30th Bill Clinton signed into law legislation that rejects the Sentencing Commission reforms. "I am not going to let anyone who peddles drugs get the idea that the cost of doing business is going down," Clinton soundbit to the press. Speaking from the other side of his neck, Clinton acknowledged the disparities, saying that "some adjustment is warranted," calling for "further review of the issue" by the Sentencing Commission.

The stroke of Clinton's pen on that legislation effectively snuffed all hope of politically reforming the 100/1 sentencing disparity. Clinton and Attorney General Reno hinted that the only reform they might consider would be a plan that includes increased sentences for powdered cocaine.[2]

Martin Luther King said that "riot is the voice of the unheard." Prisoners have, quoting Jesse, "cooperated and exercised discipline and dignity" for nearly a decade while awaiting fruition of legitimate efforts to work within the system for political or judicial reform of the 100/1 drug laws. When Congress and Clinton chose to keep those reforms from being implemented, federal prisoners across the country spoke with the voice of the unheard. Through effective government and media spin control, the federal prison uprisings were little more than a murmur. But as the director of the ACLU told the *New York Times*, "When people understand the truth about the way these laws are imposed, the fact they've had no deterrent, and the race-based nature of these prosecutions, then I think a sleeping giant is going to roar."

1 To get involved with FAMM, or subscribe to their quarterly magazine, *FAMM-gram*, write: FAMM, 1612 K St NW Suite 1400, Washington, DC 20006 (202) 457-5790.

2 Efforts toward challenging the 100/1 sentencing laws through judicial reform have been equally fruitless. See: *U.S. v. Dumas*, 64 F.3d 1427 (9th Cir. 1995) and *U.S. v. Armstrong*, 48 F.3d 1508 (9th Cir. 1995).

NOTES ON CONTRIBUTORS

Mumia Abu-Jamal is a death row journalist in Pennsylvania. He is the author of two books, *Live From Death Row* (Addison-Wesley, 1995) and *Death Blossoms* (Plough Publishing House, 1996).

Jill Brotman is the former coordinator of the Massachusetts chapter of the American Friends Service Committee. She has worked on the side of prisoners and disenfranchised people for decades.

Daniel Burton-Rose is the editor of *win: a newsletter on activism at the extremes* ($20/12 issues; PO Box 53013, Washington D.C., 20009) and a freelance journalist.

Danny Cahill, a long-time prisoner activist in Ohio, was released from prison in the summer of 1999. He's a founding member of Prisoners' Advocacy Network, and can be contacted at: PAN-OHIO, PO Box 218453, Columbus, OH 43221.

Noelle Hanrahan is director of the Prison Radio Project/Quixote Center and the producer of Mumia Abu-Jamal's radio essays. Hanrahan has been instrumental in grassroots organizing to expose the right wing's racist strategy of mass incarceration.

A. Johnson/Musaa is a prisoner in New York.

Ed Kinane is a peace activist who was arrested while protesting the School of the Americas and is serving time in a federal prison in Montgomery, PA.

Jaan Laaman is a political prisoner who was a defendant in the Ohio-7+ case.

Ray Luc Levasseur is a political prisoner indicted under the federal RICO statute as one of the Ohio-7+. Levasseur is serving a forty-five-year federal sentence from charges stemming from bombing of United States military contractors, General Electric offices, and the South African consulate. After a substantial stay in USP Marion, Levasseur has been in ADX Florence since its opening.

Adrian Lomax is a prisoner in Wisconsin and a prisoners' rights activist and journalist. He is currently working on his first book.

Vicki McElroy is a former Washington state prisoner currently doing time in Missouri.

Philip McLaughlin is a former Washington state prisoner. He is now released and living in Arizona.

Jon O. Newman is the Chief Judge for the U.S. Second Circuit Court of Appeals.

Dan Pens is a Washington state prisoner, freelance journalist, and *Prison Legal News* co-editor.

John Perotti is an Ohio prisoner who has spent most of his years in the notorious Southern Ohio Correctional Facility (SOCF) in Lucasville. He is an activist and a jailhouse lawyer, and in recent years has been very involved helping to organize student prisoners' rights groups on Ohio campuses.

Abdul Olugbala Shakur is a prisoner in California's Pelican Bay State Prison security housing unit.

Ken Silverstein is a Washington D.C.-based journalist. His books include *Washington on $10 Million a Day*, *Washington Babylon*, and a forthcoming book on the arms trade.

O'Neil Stough is a prisoner in Arizona where he frequently contributes to local newspapers.

Laura Whitehorn recently finished a fourteen-year sentence for revolutionary anti-imperialist activities. While incarcerated, she was involved in prisoner struggles and HIV/AIDS awareness work, as well as being a quarterly columnist for *Prison Legal News*. She is currently living in New York.

Willie Wisely is a California prisoner activist and journalist.

Paul Wright is the co-founder (with Ed Mead) and co-editor of *Prison Legal News*. Paul is a Washington state prisoner, jailhouse lawyer, a political activist, and journalist.

Index

About *Prison Legal News*

Prison Legal News (*PLN*), the source for virtually all of the material in this book, is a monthly magazine which has published since 1990. It is the only wholly independent, uncensored, prisoner written, edited and produced publication in the U.S.

PLN is a 501(c)(3) non-profit and is almost entirely reader supported. Freedom of the press, it has been quipped, belongs to those who own one. Buy a piece of freedom. Subscribe to *Prison Legal News* today.

If you would like to support *PLN*'s work, you may do so by sending a tax-deductible contribution to the address below. Those who subscribe at the $50 level and those who donate allow us to subsidize subscriptions for prisoners in lock-down control units and on death row.

A *PLN* subscription (12 issues) is $25 ($15 for prisoners) and $60 for high-income/institutional. A sample copy may be obtained for $1 from:

> Prison Legal News
> 2400 NW 80th Street, PMB 148
> Seattle, WA 98117

PLN is also establishing a presence on the Internet. *PLN*'s goal is to offer the single most comprehensive prison-related site on the World Wide Web. The idea is simple: If you need information about the U.S. Gulag System, there's no better place to begin your search than:

> www.prisonlegalnews.org

The editors of *PLN* thank you for reading this book. We hope your interest does not end here. To continue receiving monthly updates and articles about the U.S. prison system, prisoner struggle, news, and information found nowhere else, subscribe to *Prison Legal News* today.

Dan Pens/Paul Wright
The Editors, *Prison Legal News*